Ayrton Senna

Ayrton Senna

As time goes by

CHRISTOPHER HILTON

Haynes Publishing

First published in April 1999
Reprinted in August 1999

A catalogue record for this book is
available from the British Library

ISBN 1 85960 611 3

Library of Congress catalog card no 98-75399

Haynes North America Inc.,
861 Lawrence Drive, Newbury Park,
California 91320, USA.

Published by Haynes Publishing, Sparkford,
Nr Yeovil, Somerset BA22 7JJ, UK.

Tel: 01963 440635 Fax: 01963 440001
Int.tel: +44 1963 440635 Int.fax: +44 1963 440001

E-mail: sales@haynes-manuals.co.uk
Web site: http://www.haynes.com

Designed and typeset by
G&M, Raunds, Northamptonshire
Printed and bound in Great Britain by J.H. Haynes & Co. Ltd, Sparkford

Contents

This day and age we're living in
Gives cause for apprehension
With speed and new invention
And things like fourth dimension

Yet we get a trifle weary
With Mr. Einstein's theory
So we must get down to earth at times
Relax, relieve the tension

And no matter what the progress
Or what may yet be proved
The simple facts of life are such
They cannot be removed

You must remember this
A kiss is still a kiss, a sigh is just a sigh
The fundamental things apply
As time goes by

And when two lovers woo
They still say 'I love you'
On that you can rely
No matter what the future brings
As time goes by

Moonlight and love songs
Never out of date
Hearts full of passion
Jealousy and hate
Woman needs man
And man must have his mate
That no-one can deny

Well, it's still the same old story
A fight for love and glory
A case of do or die
The world will always welcome lovers
As time goes by
Oh yes, the world will always welcome lovers
As time goes by

Acknowledgements

THANKS IN NO PARTICULAR ORDER TO Max Mosley, President of the FIA; Ron Dennis, Creighton Brown, Peter Stayner, Anna Guerrier and Nancy Edwards of *McLaren International*; Martin Hadwen of *Racing Past Ltd (Motor Racing Archive and Research)* for extraordinary kindness and active assistance of the most valuable kind. Thanks, also, to those who shared memories so willingly or who just plain helped: Sue McAleese, David Hayhoe, Perry McCarthy, the enigmatic Angela of *The Senna Files*, Frank Bradley, Joey Greenan, David Kennedy, Sarah Taylor, Neil Austin, Peter Merrilees, Alex Sinclair, Jacky Noonan (now Breathnach) of the Royal Irish Automobile Club, Debbie and Jackie of Mondello Park; Eddie Jordan, Trevor Foster and Giselle Davies of *Eddie Jordan Racing*; Mike Dixon, Petter Dahl, Andy Ackerley, Dan Partel of *EFDA*, Jeremy Shaw, Chico Serra; *Brands Hatch* for permission to reproduce the programme of Senna's first single-seater race – Maria Ballanca helped; Brian Jones of *The Brian Jones Organisation*; Murray Walker, Martin Brundle, Keke Rosberg, Wagner Gonzalez, Gerald Donaldson; Gordon Murray of *McLaren Cars*; Alberto Nico and Antonella Guidazzoli of *CINECA*; Maurice Hamilton of *The Observer*; Derek Warwick; Jayme Brito of *TV Globo*; Vinicio Dall'ara, Press Officer, Comune di Imola; Owen O'Mahoney, Senna's pilot; Pierluigi Martini; Rory Byrne and Nigel Stepney of Ferrari; Peter Warr, formerly of *Lotus*; Johnny Cecotto; Bernd Abel of *BMW*; Nigel Roebuck, Gordon Kirby of *Autosport*; Matt Bishop and Tom Clarkson of *F1 Racing* – with a special thanks to Bishop for making available an extensive interview he did with Emerson Fittipaldi; Barry Griffin, formerly of *Goodyear*; Ken Tyrrell; John Watson; Michael Andretti and his support team of Marty Hill and Leah Rechen; Mauricio and Stella Gugelmin – for good food, good company and good memories (not forgetting Mauricio's cousin Zeca Melo); Marco Ragazzoni and Alberto Antonini of *Autosprint*; Simon Arron of *Motoring News*; Alex Hawkridge, formerly of *Toleman*, now *Reynard*; Gerard

Ducarouge, formerly of *Lotus*, now *Matra*; Brian Hart of *Brian Hart Limited*, who gave of his expertise, loaned lovely photographs and allowed me to use his contemporary notes from 1984; Mark Wilkin of the *BBC*; Jeremy Lew of *New Line Cinema* in Los Angeles, California, who kindly allowed me to use a page of his script for a Senna film; Stefano Galli of Studio Legale Calzolari-McCracken, London; Nicola Santoro.

Some particular words of gratitude – to Dick Bennetts of *West Surrey Racing*, who ran Senna in 1983 and kept (as he always does with his drivers) a complete record of their season: every lap, full results, circuit maps annotated by the drivers. He was kind enough to let me reproduce some of this original and priceless material. I'm also deeply indebted to Amanda Gadeselli for taking such care over annotating and translating the judge's report on the manslaughter trial after Imola; and to an astonishing man, Martin Zustak, a Czech currently working in Galway. Unbidden, he copied off the Internet – numeral by numeral – the mountain of telemetry regarding the crash, sent that, and graphs, and his conclusions. All of it was invaluable.

Terry Whittaker of *Carlin* made the route to reproducing the words of *As Time Goes By* simplicity itself, and for that particular thanks.

Nine Network Australia kindly provided their interview by Jackie Stewart of Senna in 1990, and thanks to Gary Burns, Network Head of Sport, and Kerrie Thomson, his personal assistant, for finding it, copying it onto video and mailing it. This is reproduced verbatim in Chapter 10, with permission.

Robin Muir, and his wife Olivia, showed amazing and touching care in arranging introductions to people in Sao Paulo who, in turn, opened further doors. They also provided background and invaluable advice. In Sao Paulo, many helped and none refused to help. I am particularly grateful to Carolina Naegeli and Silvania Pellissari of the *TransAmerica Hotel* for getting me organised and helping with translations; Antonio Monteiro; Reginaldo Leme of *TV Globo*; Lula May Reed; Primo Pascoli Melare, Director General of the *Colegio Rio Branco*, and the English teacher, Professor Paulo Torres; Alexandre Sassaki Rosa and Marcos Vinicius Moura e Silva of the *Instituto Ayrton Senna*; Lucio Pascual (Tche); and a boyhood friend, Alfredo Popesco.

Simon Taylor, Chairman of Haymarket Specialist Publications, kindly gave me permission to quote from their titles *Autosport*, *Motoring News*, *Motor Sport* and *F1 Racing*. In Chapter 9 I have leaned heavily on *Autosport*'s weekly coverage in the years – yes, years – leading up to the trial of Frank Williams and others.

Wherever I've quoted (briefly) from motorsport books I've indicated all the relevant credits in the text but thanks to *HarperCollins* for an extract from *Green Races Red* by Eddie Irvine and Maurice Hamilton; *Macmillan* for extracts from *Damon Hill: Grand Prix Year* by Damon Hill, and *Life At The Limit* by Sid Watkins.

Introduction

FIVE YEARS NOW – or a moment ago. It depends who you are and how you feel about these things.

Time allows grief to soften into the bearable, permitting reflection and meditation. Tranquillity opens the path to a proper perspective and then to understanding. That is what this book is about: a full understanding of Ayrton Senna's extraordinary life and elusive personality, from childhood to the mortal wounds he suffered 12.800 seconds into lap seven of the San Marino Grand Prix on 1 May 1994, and the almost spiritual way his memory has grown *since*.

The perspective is shaped by many, many insiders: childhood friends, school teachers, go-karters, a panorama of racing colleagues – friend and foe, little known and household names – and strangers whose lives he touched. They speak about him as never before, and their words are woven into original material never seen before. It embraces a wealth of personal photographs taken by those colleagues, annotated circuit maps, incident sheets and his own corrections to an earlier manuscript about his career. From this the man emerges in all his bewildering contradictions and complexity – but always constructing his life around a core of speed. He did this from infancy and it remained a rigid constant. Here he is as a teenager driving a car on the roads:

"Braking was the last option. It was always avoid, back off. If avoiding wouldn't work he may *consider backing off, if that didn't work and he felt things were going to be really ugly then he* may *consider using the brakes – but I never saw him do it."*

Mauricio Gugelmin, friend

If that had been the whole story it would have been interesting enough, although only a modest variation on the many other racing drivers' tales which are told; but he was not like ordinary human beings. A thousand drivers are fast. Only one of them was Senna.

"He handled stress differently, he handled joy differently, he handled winning differently, qualifying differently – I just haven't worked with anybody quite like that."
Gordon Murray, racing car designer

The speed was something intangible and inexplicable, a gift that seemed to come from eternity. It was so mysterious that during his early days in Formula 1 the opposition claimed the car must be illegal.

"I said: don't lose any time any more checking the bloody car just after we've been making a pole position. If you want to disqualify something, disqualify the bloody driver because he's just too fast."
Gerard Ducarouge, racing car designer

If *that* had been the whole story it would – also – have been interesting enough but Senna was literally driven by an obsession to take pole position for every race, set fastest lap and win. In its wake this brought unsettling incidents, bitter recriminations, near physical violence and public condemnation but:

"Other drivers were involved in other incidents and his view was, if they can do things like that and there is no penalty, and that is the standard, then so be it – but he didn't like the standard. I felt afterwards that he regretted, very much regretted, lowering himself to drive in that way."
Ron Dennis, who ran him at McLaren

Senna had a gorgeous purity of control in a racing car – the most delicate, sensitive touch – and felt that certain aspects of technology were levelling that, enabling anyone without the touch to do it. He strongly objected.

"I have a Christmas card from Senna from December 1992 with a long hand-written plea to eliminate electronic driver aids."
Max Mosley, President of the FIA

The way the world is – running headlong into tomorrow and all of us assaulted daily by a machine gun of information – Ayrton Senna ought properly to have found his resting place in history, five years ago. There was a need for tranquillity after the crash at Imola, which confronted the world with mortality on their television screens and churned a terrible dilemma for those who had to describe it live on air.

"As the whole scenario unfolded it became more and more evident that arguably the greatest driver ever – certainly of our generation – was

dying in our living rooms. That I think is one of the most powerful images ever, ever seen in people's homes."
John Watson, former driver and TV commentator

But somewhere back there, at an undefined moment, he rose again. The words are not chosen carelessly and the second part of the book is about that: the inquiry and trial after his death, with all the complexities, claims and counter-claims laid bare; his precious legacy of improved safety, from which every driver today benefits; and the creation of the Ayrton Senna Instituto to raise money by his name to help deprived, destitute children in Brazil.

"We want to create new outlets, to be a hope factory, because we are trying to mass-produce hope which has a name and a child's face."
Caio d'Araujo, working with the Instituto in Rio

Ayrton Senna was – and is – much more than a symbolic presence bringing at least some hope amid the wretchedness of poverty. He came to embody the dignity of his own vast, troubled country and that hasn't gone away.

"Sometimes when you are abroad you are very ashamed about Brazil. You see on TV that if there is an airport shooting the only person doing it is Brazilian, but when you have the kind of example like Ayrton you learn that it is not always this way. You say: look, I am Brazilian too, I am from the same country as Ayrton Senna."
Antonio Monteiro, school friend

But it is the private Senna, the unreported Senna, the Senna touching the lives of strangers who completes the portrait. A glimpse of that. Quite by chance he was introduced to a British woman and her four-year-old son. Both were too overawed to speak to him but that didn't matter at all.

"He was so good with children and related so well to them because they expected nothing from him whereas adults, he always thought, wanted something. He said children never wanted anything."
Sue McAleese, mother

Part One

TIME GONE BY

(21 March 1960–1 May 1994)

Chapter 1

This day and age we're living in

THE CIRCLE OPENED where the long grass grew and strutting kids went to play, careless of their mortality. It was called Interlagos and it was noisy as hell.

The circle closed a handful of kilometres away, where the grass is manicured so precisely all down a long, gentle incline. It is called Morumbi and is as silent as eternity. There's a metal plaque in the ground with name, dates and a proclamation in Portuguese, *Nada pode me separar do amor de Deus*, Nothing can separate me from the love of God. The plaque bears a number, 0011. All the plaques bear numbers. This is his.

Late 1998: fresh flowers have been left all around – 13 vases, reds and yellows and whites – and dried candle wax lies smeared in the grass from some departed vigil. A small tree stoops towards the plaque as if trying to offer shelter.

A man in uniform points the curious, as they come, towards the plaque. They come in currents and eddies, borne by a need for proximity, or longing, or who knows what? Michael Schumacher came: hired a taxi from the TransAmerica Hotel – where the Formula 1 fraternity stay for the grand prix – to take him discreetly, stood with tears pouring down his face. Japanese tourists come by the coach load, linger for up to five hours and are extremely reluctant to get back on the coach, go out under the low entrance buildings and close their own circle with a final farewell. Others come from who-knows-where, come mute, incredulous to be actually here, lost in the awkwardness of mourning. You can tell. They look nervous, not quite sure how to conduct themselves facing the finality.

The cemetery at Morumbi is a haven within the city of Sao Paulo and Sao Paulo is a terrible immensity of an expanse from which you need a haven. It was into this expanse that Ayrton Senna da Silva was born on 21 March 1960 to Milton Guirado Theodoro da Silva and Neide Joanna Senna da Silva. He had a three-year-old sister, Viviane. A brother, Leonardo, would be born in 1966.

Milton had made a great deal of money through his car component businesses and farming. Senna put it like this when clarifying matters arising in the first book I wrote about him (*The Hard Edge of Genius*/PSL, 1990): *The factory had about 750 people employed and he'd started from nothing. There were about ten farms + a total of 400.000 –* and he wrote it out in full, in brackets *(four hundred thousand) – hectares, with well over 10.000,* and he wrote it out again *(ten thousand), heads of cattle.*

It was here that Senna was nurtured and shaped, and for which he felt a ferocious affection. To outsiders, surveying the poverty and the pollution, that's difficult to understand. It was from here that, as a shy, gangly teenager, he ventured into distant, dangerous worlds and conquered them; from here that he became what he still is, a global presence rather than just a great racing driver. But always he remained a *Paulista*.

Sao Paulo has its history, of course. In 1822, Brazil's independence was declared from here when it was a frontier town. The cultivation of coffee drew immigrants from Portugal, Spain, Germany, Eastern Europe, the Middle East and Japan, and by early this century serious industries were starting up. Sao Paulo had begun to grow towards the terrible immensity of today: 15 million inhabitants (or 17 million, depending on who is talking), plus millions more in the slums, the *favelas*. By the year 2000, for sheer numbers Sao Paulo will be past Shanghai and only behind Mexico City.

There are many themes in this book, the tumult of races and championships among them, but the plight of those in the *favelas*, and what Senna and his family were – and are – trying to do about it, is as important as any of them and more important than most.

Flying in to Sao Paulo, you are over the city for a full 20 minutes before landing. Because of its vastness Sao Paulo does not have the feel of a city at all, but rather somewhere shapeless and unbounded. Imagine a thread of a river with hills on one side, flatland on the other and, as far as your eye can see, anybody could build anything they liked anywhere they wished. So petrol stations are mixed in with row after row of shabby little houses, mixed in with columns of communist-style apartment blocks, mixed in with neon-clad shopping malls straight from Los Angeles, mixed in with luxuriant and tawdry hotels, mixed in with fast food joints, mixed in with the *favelas* – tight, cramped clusters of dwellings made out of whatever came to hand and which seem to slip, or have been arrested in the act of slipping, down the hillsides towards the river. And the river is so polluted its colour no longer resembles water. There are four million vehicles here and, at any one moment, four million people driving them creatively.

It's natural to be loyal to your roots and, if you're not, something is wrong. It may well also be that the worse a place is, the more protective you become of it – and, anyway, there's more to Sao Paulo than choked roads passing like veins through 200 square miles of the architecture of abandon: an easy jauntiness to the ordinary people, a kindness, a way of spreading warmth over strangers. People who have nothing to smile about smile the whole time because they're made like that. There's the weather: a fabled sunny climate. Nor must anyone forget that in Senna's formative years – 1960 to 1975 – the mass migration from the north east of the country was only gathering pace. Sao Paulo was a much less violent, more cosy place then.

These days, there's a New York feeling. *We can take anything here.*

Viviane has said that, as a youngster, Senna moved about so ceaselessly that he was for ever tumbling over and when you looked at him you could see the bruises. Evidently Neide thought all this movement indicated something was wrong and wanted a doctor to have a look at him but, Viviane concludes, it was only normal restless energy seeking an outlet. He would find the outlet very soon. He was a chubby-faced kid carrying a little puppy fat, she said, and always had a toy car in his hand. He'd sit in a real car and pretend to steer it, he'd mimic the sound of engines and brakes – notably what an engine sounded like when revved.

Milton gave him a go-kart propelled by an engine at the age of four and, with much less traffic around then, he could play with it on the street for hours. The street sloped slightly, feeding down to a cobbled square and he'd go down, round and back up, down, round and back up.

Later the family moved to Rua Pedro, a quiet, narrow suburban street in the north of the city. The house was detached and pleasant: the external walls a soft mosaic of tiles, the garden shaded by two tropical trees. More than all that, Rua Pedro sloped – steeply. Senna and friends, among them a near-contemporary called Alfredo Popesco, built buggies and would go roaring down the street from various vantage points. They'd descend through the intersection with Rua Padre Cicero de Revoredo and keep on coasting towards the main road at the bottom.

Senna still had a kart, of course, and although he couldn't race until the age of 13 (well, nearly) he was taking it more and more seriously. Popesco insists that after school Senna practised every afternoon or took the kart to pieces and reassembled it, spending hours on, say, the brakes until they were exactly as he wanted them. Popesco admits he himself lacks that sort of patience. Most other human beings do.

At 10, Senna went to one of the best private schools in Sao Paulo, the *Colegio Rio Branco,* just west of the city centre. It is a tall building with an ornate exterior but plain interior of linoleum corridors which echo with movement and laughter. The classrooms are plain, almost anonymous, and large, with up to 50 pupils per class. Youngsters sit in ranks at plain desks which are more like worktops on tubular frames, and face a teacher on a slightly-raised podium. A vast blackboard covers the wall behind the teacher, and another runs down the right-hand wall. It was here, as it would seem, that the young Senna sat hour on hour not receptive to anything academic. He was thinking of Interlagos.

Interlagos was the kart track next to the grand prix circuit, whose full splendour could be seen through a rusty wire fence. This was not the circuit we know today, with a stabbing left–right at the end of the pit lane straight.

Instead it flowed directly ahead into a mighty, slightly-banked curve which people still speak of in awe.

The kart track was rudimentary, as they invariably are. You reached it down a dual carriageway with, along the way, a *favela* butting onto the rim of the road before you came to a shopping arcade or two (where, today, half a dozen workshops prepare and sell karts and associated products). You reached it through a gateway and along a broad carpark where service vans disgorged karts. The pits were two long, open buildings supported by concrete pillars and covered by corrugated roofs. Here the karts were readied before they accelerated out onto the snake-like circuit which doubled back on itself. Rudimentary, yes: a concrete grandstand over on the far side with six tiers of concrete ledges for seats, tyre-barriers to keep the karts from the curving perimeter wall. The infield was where the long grass grew.

The corners were tight, the way karting corners should be because you can pitch karts hard into them and adore the carousel ride of going round. Evidently when he began he was no good in the wet, but he practised remorselessly until he was.

It was, surely, intoxicating.

It intoxicated him from here, surely, when the circle began opening, to a corner called Tamburello at Imola, Italy, on 1 May 1994, when the circle was closing quickly and finally.

Antonio Monteiro was a *Colegio* pupil at the same time as Senna. He describes it as "a very important school in Sao Paulo and very well known. It is rigorous, old fashioned, you could say severe. It's expensive, but in Brazil for the middle class you only have private schools. The thing I remember about Ayrton was that he only paid attention to car races ... or his kart ... or motor cycles. Only motors! He was very serious, very 'closed' and he divided his time between school and his kart at Interlagos. That track is famous in Sao Paulo because it's very old and we all tried to drive karts there. It's part of my childhood. I drove for two years but at that time Ayrton was among the 'professionals' [the best]. I was not so good.

"I think it's true that Ayrton wasn't very good academically because he simply wasn't interested in classes. He was obsessive about cars instead. He was very, very quiet, he didn't talk in class and I can't remember him with a lot of friends at school. He *was* a quiet guy. I had a motor cycle and, of course, I also liked the karts and so we made a relationship. We weren't close, we weren't proper friends but I visited his home, I think twice. We'd meet at Interlagos and every day in the class."

In 1970, while young Senna was settling into the *Colegio,* another *Paulista* was preparing to make his grand prix debut with the Lotus team. In 1972 he was World Champion and, Senna would say "when I was a young boy racing go-karts in Brazil, Emerson Fittipaldi was in Europe winning. I remember how important Sundays were to me because I was eager to see how Emerson would do."

Senna was pushing himself in the direction of speed, dreaming speed, thinking speed and, whenever he could, living speed.

Monteiro is adamant. "Ayrton was a good guy, nice to talk with about motors and we knew that he was a very good driver. He had fixed ideas, and although it is very strange to say this, I think he was sure he was going to be someone different. He had a mission and he was *so* self-confident that I assume he knew he would be special. When I say self-confident I don't mean in the classroom, because there his behaviour was very *discreet,* but in the races, in the things he knew how to do, in the places where he was good. That's where the self-confidence was. For example, at school I played football but Ayrton, no, because he didn't like it. He wasn't a football fan. I had a motor cycle and he had a motor cycle – well, I'm not sure if the motor cycle I saw him with belonged to him. I rode with him twice very close to Rio Branco."

What was he like on a motor cycle?

[CHUCKLE] "He rode very fast, yes, he was faster than me. It was not too difficult to realise he had a special talent and he was anxious to show that. He was prepared to pay a high price to do that" – take risks – "and I wasn't prepared. For him it was natural."

The Director General of the *Colegio,* Primo Pascoli Melare, taught Senna the Portuguese language and literature. "He was average: not mediocre, not below average but average. He seemed to be a person looking into the air" – daydreaming of overtaking moves in the kart, no doubt – "and very serious."

Senna had come to the opening of the circle, and to the first crossroads of his life. Karting can be a self-contained activity in the sense that going round and round on lonely, private afternoons is an end in itself. The decision to extend this to competition – to racing – alters everything. Racing is a merciless examination of any human being, not least in proving they have the nerve to do it at all. In retrospect he could have done nothing else and would say, all those years later: "Racing – competing – is a part of my life." They put the words on monuments to him. But in the beginning, the gawky, angular kid who was so damned shy, and now so damned lean a gust of wind might have blown him over? He didn't duck the merciless examination, he headed towards it; and never backed off anything ever again up to and including Tamburello, 1 May 1994.

I wonder if he sensed his own strengths? He comes to us as a contradictory kid, shy and yet sure of himself, alone but often with friends. Did he sense the abilities which separated him from other people: the speed and clarity and originality of thought, the iron will-power, the reflexes, the physical balance? He comes to us as quiet, unexceptional, better off than most but so what? Others had money too.

The family are private people who keep themselves to themselves, and so the internal dynamics of it are quite – and perhaps quite rightly – unknown. But one thing is fairly certain. In a traditional place like Brazil, as the first-born son Ayrton would be expected, without question, to take on the burden of the family business – and, in time, that was exactly what he wouldn't be doing. He'd take on his own burden, on another continent in another sphere altogether, instead. What this brought in its wake to the family structure is also quite – and perhaps quite rightly – unknown.

In finding himself, the timid, average kid would have to break with a whole creed. It might, surely did, take more guts than driving karts and cars. And he would do it.

The second grand prix of 1973 was at Interlagos, a celebration of a thing because Emerson Fittipaldi – *from* Sao Paulo – came to it as World Champion. Fittipaldi remembers "a boy is brought to see me by his father, a young Brazilian, and it is Ayrton. Well, it reminded me, *I am World Champion and Ayrton is testing karts.* And after that I always watch Ayrton, follow Ayrton because he was so fast, so serious, so gifted, just brilliant. And he always came to me, talked to me, asked me. And of course I feel him special because we are both Brazilian."

The youngster had a mechanic of Spanish origin, Lucio Pascual, known as Tche. He says: "We worked together for seven years and for me he was like another son." It started almost by chance, shortly before Senna was due to race for the first time in the summer of 1973. Senna was at Interlagos practising, and broke his engine. He wondered what to do and somebody said *you need Tche.* "At this time I had a workshop on the other side of the city," Tche says. "Senna came and asked if I could re-build his engine. I said *it's logical I should do it – that's my job.* My first impression of him was that he was a simple person. He didn't ask much, didn't give orders and was very quiet. But when I saw him I felt something inside myself. When I'd finished the engine Senna arrived in a car and said *thank you so much for what you've done* but I said *it was nothing special. It was my obligation to do it properly."*

Reportedly (in *Ayrton Senna: Trajectoire d'un Enfant Gate* by Lionel Froissart/Glenat, Grenoble) Milton invited Tche to his office and asked him to become his son's mechanic. Milton was surprised to learn that Tche had already been impressed by watching the lad practising.

Senna's first race was on 1 July 1973 – he couldn't race before because you needed to be aged 13. (Well, he *had* been in a race against older boys when he was eight, although details of this are misty. Senna would explain that the grid positions were fixed by drawing lots and he drew 1 – "the first pole of my career" he'd say with an ironical smile – and he led until, with three laps to go, another kart touched him and he spun off.)

Now, on 1 July at Interlagos, he prepared. His father was there, wearing a sleeveless white shirt, the very slightest beginnings of a paunch straining the front. Senna, wearing a polo-necked pullover, what seems to be a tracksuit bottom and trainers, stood beside the kart pulling driving gloves on. He had a bush of long hair and his face was as it would be until adulthood: almost feminine.

In the race he broke the track record – according to Tche – and won. Precious film of it exists. The sky is blue, decorated by a bank of plump white cloud. The long finishing straight is edged by white boundary lines. The man with the chequered flag wears a white shirt, sleeves rolled up. As Senna comes bombing along the straight towards him he waves the flag in great, carving motions. There are virtually no spectators: a tall man some ten metres from the flag – possibly Milton – clapping enthusiastically; a couple of people sitting on a large box, someone seeming to wave limply on the far side of the track from the flag.

This is how it generally begins, a nondescript race on an ordinary afternoon, a small fraternity of spectators, a winner and many losers.

For Senna, the intoxication increased. It would be largely controlled intoxication; even so, he would arrive at Interlagos at 6am on race days in order to have time to make his preparations to his absolute satisfaction. Most teenagers don't think like this, never mind do it.

In 1974 he won the Sao Paulo junior championship and in 1975 was runner-up in the nationals. He'd met Alfredo Popesco through Popesco's younger brother who was already friends with him. The two families lived near each other. Now Popesco was 17, Senna going on 16, but the year's difference meant that Popesco was already going out with girls. "Ayrton used to play ping pong and mess around in the street but he liked the things I was doing." Namely, to "go out and meet girls, not just ping pong! Senna was ceasing to be a child and starting to enjoy the pleasures of the teenage years. He was a normal teenager, although not quite like the others of his age because he was a little bit ahead of them. They played football on the streets but he wanted something different."

Popesco, whose family were decidedly not rich, studied at a school called McKenzie near the *Colegio Rio Branco,* and had started part-time work aged 13. Daily he trekked to McKenzie by bus while Senna travelled in a chauffeur-driven car. One time Senna said *hey Alfredo, would you like a ride home?* Popesco said yes and the trekking was over. Now Popesco was regularly chauffeur-driven to and from school with Senna.

"At the weekends Ayrton used to drive his kart and I loved that. He practised all the time, like on Tuesdays, Thursdays, Fridays and Saturdays and I went with him. We also liked to play around and flirt with girls." Senna had model aircraft and model racing cars which they built together. Milton bought Senna a motor cycle – the one Monteiro saw? – and Popesco loved that too. "Ayrton never worked, because he was so protected by his family. They protected him a lot. But you could see the potential he had, with the model planes, the toy cars and karts."

The friendship was "like a movie where you have a rich guy and a crazy guy and they go around having fun together." Popesco delighted in what Senna could do with a kart, Senna delighted in the social life of the slightly older Popesco.

"When Ayrton started to race outside Sao Paulo we'd travel together. We went to cities like Itu [55 miles north west of Sao Paulo] and Campinas [north west of Itu] as well as other places. There was a race at Natal [far up on the northern coast] and Ayrton won it. We were very happy and Ayrton was becoming a little bit famous. He'd already won several races in Sao Paulo. At Natal, however, we almost didn't see each other. Ayrton was going out with one girl and I was going out with another. Ayrton's girl liked to go out at night and my girl liked to go out during the day – so he slept in while

I had to get up early to take my girl to the beach! When he woke up I'd already got to the beach. Ayrton's girl was more excitable, she was like crazy and mine was more correct – the good girl!

"We had so much fun. This was the time of our lives.

"When we got back to Sao Paulo, Ayrton would stay in his garage showing me his kart until four o'clock in the morning. He'd mount it, dismount, mount it again. He'd have to get to practice at eight o'clock on Saturday mornings but all the time he'd say *Alfredo, Alfredo, we have to go out on Friday to have fun but if I go out on Friday I have to leave the kart fully prepared and everything settled for Saturday morning.* He knew every little piece of the kart and he did everything for himself, studied every little piece of it. Technically, he knew all about it. I loved those times with Ayrton, and Ayrton's kart, and the races. He used to let me drive a little bit but I didn't go to the races for the machinery, I liked Ayrton's company and his friendship.

"When Ayrton wanted something he would persevere until he reached it. I compare it to [chasing] a beautiful woman. When you see a beautiful woman you'd love to be beside her but, if that happens, when you see her every day and get used to her it's not the same thing as it was at the beginning" – when you have attained your goal you stop reaching. "Ayrton had a very, very important characteristic: that didn't happen to him. If he'd worked for a big company he'd have worked and worked and worked to reach the top" – and never stopped reaching.

"I was very good at ping pong. I used to go to a club called Esperia and I practised a lot. I didn't have money to buy a ping pong table. Ayrton did, he bought one and we played each other. I won the first, second, third, fourth time and Ayrton started playing with my cousin, his own cousins, my brother and everybody else. He practised, practised, practised four and five hours a day and then when we played again sometimes I'd win, sometimes he'd win but he kept on practising, practising, practising until one day I didn't win any more. Ayrton won, won, won.

("There is also another story, about ten years later at Angra dos Reis, Ayrton's house." This house was in fact a luxurious complex on the Atlantic. "There was a tennis court and one day a guy from Benetton played Ayrton and won. Ayrton played other people and lost to them: he was losing all the time. He got so upset that he started practising, practising, practising. Before that, hardly anybody had used the tennis court. Soon enough he was good at tennis and after he got good he called Benetton and invited the guy who'd beaten him to come to Brazil for a match – so he could beat him!")

Popesco taught Senna an invaluable lesson in how to negotiate from a position of weakness. It centred on water-skiing. "I had family in Santa Catarina [a State south of Sao Paulo]. I used to go there and learnt the art of water-skiing when I was 13. I didn't have a boat but some friends did and we used that. Then Ayrton got another motor cycle – it was a Suzuki, a 185cc – and he liked to ride around the district. He'd have a little fall here and another fall there and his father decided to sell it.

"I had an idea. Just tell your father *it's fine to sell the motor cycle, that's OK, dad, you can sell it but I want a boat, a good boat.* His father Mr. Milton could give him that because they were rich and they lived near a lake. *You're going to lose the motor cycle anyway,* I told him, *so be intelligent, use it to get a boat!*

"Mr. Milton was very strict. He was strict because he'd worked since he was young, he'd worked hard, he liked punctuality and he didn't like people doing wrong things. Mr. Milton used to argue with Ayrton because he arrived late at night and he did wrong things with his friends – not wrong things, teenager things. Mr. Milton didn't like that. While Mr. Milton was strict, Ayrton's mother, Mrs Neide, was the ideal mother.

"His father bought the boat.

"We'd go to the lake and Ayrton practised, practised, practised and he got very good at water-skiing. He did every style, not just standing up on the skis, and he got good at them all. [Water-skiing includes the slalom, tricks and jumping.] He was *so* determined when he had an objective."

Popesco says that a businessman, Senhor Armando Teixeira, became Senna's manager and taught him many basic philosophies. Among them: *your word is stronger than a contract; surround yourself with people you can trust; you are better off with a friend than someone who can just pay.*

"Ayrton used to follow these and he trusted people, he genuinely trusted people. He appreciated friendship, he had real friends and this is one of his authentic characteristics as well as an important one. Armando also taught him to be a very humble person and I don't say that because I'm giving an interview to someone who is writing about Ayrton, I don't say that because of the interest in him: you can ask any ten people who knew him well and all ten will confirm that he *was* humble, *was* a simple person, *was* friendly, *was* someone you could trust."

In January 1976 Milton took his son to watch qualifying for the Brazilian Grand Prix at Interlagos. There is no record of whether they went on the Friday or Saturday but, given that Senna was at school and Milton worked extremely hard, the Friday seems unlikely. This, then, is what we can assume Senna saw on that very hot Saturday afternoon: James Hunt (McLaren) taking pole from Niki Lauda (Ferrari) – 2m 32.50s against 2m 32.53s. Jean-Pierry Jarier (Shadow) was third, Fittipaldi (Copersucar) fourth and John Watson (Penske) fifth in this session.

It may be that at the age of 16 Senna was still careless of his mortality, and rightly so, but of the 21 men and one woman (Lella Lombardi) he saw, Carlos Pace (Brabham) – seventeenth here – would be killed in an aeroplane crash and Tom Pryce (Shadow) – tenth – killed in the South African Grand Prix the following year. Ronnie Peterson (Lotus) – sixteenth – would be fatally wounded at Monza in the Italian Grand Prix of 1978. Clay Regazzoni (Ferrari) – sixth – would be crippled in a crash at the USA West Grand Prix and Patrick Depailler (Tyrrell) – seventh – killed testing at Hockenheim in 1980.

However Ayrton Senna rationalised it from 24 January 1976 over the next few years, it is impossible that he did not come to comprehend mortality because he had been witness to living people – skimming round that mighty, slightly-banked curve from the start-finish straight to rub itself along the wall from the kart track – who were dying. When, later, people accused him of truly being careless of it, he refuted them with some dignity. (He was once asked about danger and replied: "Only an idiot could fail to realise the dangers. Do you think I am an idiot?" He told me: "Of course I can get hurt or killed, as anybody can, and this feeling or this knowledge is what keeps you together in self-preservation.")

We may surmise, however, that as Milton drove him home from Interlagos, in the south of the immensity, to the district of Tremembe in the north, his thoughts were of cars averaging 190 kilometres an hour. To someone already so attuned to speed it *must* have had the most profound impact.

Aged 16 Senna moved up among the seniors and into 100cc karts. He won the championship of Sao Paulo, was third in the nationals and won a race called Three Hours of Karting at Sao Paulo.

One of Senna's school reports from 1976 captures precisely how average he was academically. His address is given as Rua Pedro, 817 *tel. 298-41-96*. There's a head-and-shoulders portrait of him beside that, severe, eyes locked straight ahead onto the camera. The marks for each subject are set out in columns, recording successive periods of the year and examinations with the totals averaged out at the foot of these columns. Here they are, out of ten:

Portuguese Language, Brazilian Literature	7.30
Physical Education	8.33
History	5.60
Geography	7.70
Morals and Civic Rights	7.83
Maths	5.02
General Physics	5.00
Chemistry	7.63
English	5.12
Art	8.10
Practical handiwork	7.60

That gave an average of 6.83. How fair it is to wring meanings out of such statistics is questionable, especially with a teenager who doesn't seem to have minded either way. No doubt (as an investment) he would have applied his intellect to English but how could he have known, as he sat in a bare classroom off one of the linoleum-floored corridors, that he'd spend 13 years speaking English in a predominantly English-speaking environment?

Through the middle and late 1970s, Senna's comparative fame grew as he won kart races here and there, junior championships and then in 1977 the South American Championship itself. That was in Uruguay.

Tche tells a revealing story about another race, at Interlagos in December 1977. Various local champions were competing. The picture of the start is on page 130. Tche had three of these champions, including Senna and a certain Chico Serra, who would travel to England to race cars, reach Formula 1 and open the way for Senna to do the same – despite their keen rivalry here on the kart track.

Serra was well-known among the karting fraternity and evidently when he was practising wouldn't allow anyone to practise with him. He preferred to do it alone. He had already spent the summer in England in Formula Ford 1600, and been outstanding. Senna was only 17 and accepted that Serra (aged 20) was ahead of him in terms of career. But he had said to him: *one day we'll be in the same race and then you'll know me.* That race was now, because Senna had just moved up to the category Serra was in.

"Chico was an excellent driver," Tche says, "but he would never permit anyone to overtake him." When another driver came up close behind Serra, he lifted his foot off the accelerator and the kart behind would either hit him and go off or, presumably, swerve to miss him and go off. Tche did not feel a conflict of loyalties. He said to Senna *pay attention. He will do this with you. Don't stay right behind him, don't get too near.* There were two points on the circuit where Serra would try the lifting ploy. In the race Senna bided his time, feinted to the right, Serra tried the ploy, Senna took him on the left – and won. Serra said to him *OK, that was good – but not so good!*

Professor Paulo Torres taught Senna English at the *Colegio* from 1976 to 1977 and what he says confirms the impression we already have, but is also revealing. "He was just a quiet, shy person, a little bit introverted. He didn't really look like a person who would be a great champion one day – he didn't like showing off. He was very, very timid, in fact. His English was just average, nothing extraordinary, no. I didn't know that he raced because he didn't make that clear to everybody. I didn't know that he did this or that outside the classroom, and they were large classes. Then he disappeared."

When you were trying to teach him English, he wasn't thinking about English?

"No, perhaps not."

He was thinking about go-karts, wasn't he?

"In all the subjects he was taking I think it happened the same. He really liked the go-karts."

A question to Director Melare. Did you realise he was obsessed with racing?

"Yes, I knew. He was a champion in karts."

He was here for seven formative years. Did he remain the same?

"The fact is that I was not his teacher all the time, but he was always responsible and quiet and shy and timid. He never changed his personality although, of course, he was developing, growing up as a person."

You could reasonably expect that a young, eager, fit Ayrton Senna would, even if he didn't enjoy playing football, at least take pleasure in the

Colegio's gymnasium. (In later years, certainly, he followed the Brazilian national team avidly and one time in Detroit preferred to pay the fine for missing a mandatory Press Conference rather than miss a match on television.) "At that time," Director Melare says, "you got marks for gymnastics, so he did it like every other student." And that was it.

In general, studying was not important to him?

"Not exactly. For example, if it was necessary to get a mark of 5, he'd get a mark of 5." And that was it, too.

What is interesting to me is that he was one of the most intelligent people I have ever met.

"Yes. He was highly intelligent but he wasn't interested in the classroom, he was interested in something else, which was racing."

Then he left the *Colegio* and went to a university in Sao Paulo called FAAP, for which he had to pass an entrance exam. Torres, who also taught there, says, "he started to take a course in economics but he didn't really attend lessons and he left."

In 1978 the karting was getting more serious and he was applying the full range of his intellect to it. The Brazilian championships that year were at Porto Alegre, a town far to the south and there Senna met another ambitious young karter, Mauricio Gugelmin. "My cousin Zeca and I drove go-karts together for 11 years. He taught me to drive. When we got to Porto Alegre, Zeca introduced me to Senna. He had one mechanic and a station wagon, a Chevrolet from his dad with the kart and tyres inside. It was such a mess! I was doing the cadets, the junior title, Zeca was on the 125ccs and Senna was on the 100ccs so we were not competing against each other. That was important.

"We had a transporter where we could hang the karts up on the walls, we had everything made up to work properly and he was driving backwards and forwards in that station wagon. One day he asked if he could leave his go-kart in our transporter so he could have the back seat of his car returned to the normal position. We said *yes, fine*. He won his championship, I finished second in mine and we became friends."

What did you make of him?

Gugelmin offers further confirmation that academia "wasn't a priority. He had to go to school, it was something forced on him. I guarantee you, at the weekends when he was driving, that was the school he wanted.

"The way he used to work, I already learnt things from him. First, never lend him a road car! I did that and he crashed it – no, he didn't crash it, he got a speeding ticket. He came back all apologetic and said *when the ticket comes, send it to me and I'll pay*. I said *don't worry about it,* I never ever charged him and that's one of the reasons why we got on so well – I probably never got the ticket anyway!" Porto Alegre is in Rio Grande do Sul, a different State from where Gugelmin lived.

Gugelmin learned more than that at the kart track. "Senna was just about to race – it was the warm-up lap. With go-karts, you warm up, then you stop, then you go like Formula 1. He spun and had a crash and the chassis seemed to be beyond repair. Zeca and another guy stood on it and squeezed it back square but it was never right. He *still* drove and he *still* left everybody behind. He was sitting there and one wheel was a good two inches off the ground and he *still* left everybody behind …"

This is the intellect in action which the *Colegio Rio Branco* never saw: "He had a guy called Robertinho who used to go round with him," Gugelmin says. "After Senna had been running somewhere for a couple of days, Robertinho would walk to one particular corner. Senna would go slow everywhere on the track and each lap he'd do that corner in a different style. Then he used to stop there, right on the corner on the side of the track, and look at the time differences with Robertinho to establish which style was quickest. Then they'd do the next corner and so on until they had covered all the corners.

"Another thing he used to do – which we learnt to do – was this: he had only one chassis but he had a few engines so he'd get one set of carburettors and one exhaust and go through all the engines to pick out the best one, leave it aside. Then he put in the third best engine and went through all the carburettors and picked out the best, put that aside. Then he'd take the third best set of carburettors, put them in and go through the exhausts, put the best aside. So he selected the best separately and then, with maybe two days to go, he'd put the best package together.

"He'd watch what the others were doing but he'd have his timing point *over there* on the far side of the circuit, not where everybody else had theirs. He'd go fast *over there* and then close the lap off so people wouldn't know the potential that he had."

What did you think of him as a kart driver?

"Raw talent."

And as a man?

"Really smart, a thinking guy. He was pretty wild on a track at that stage. I remember we met at another Brazilian championship and he took a lift in my road car. I was 16 years old, it was my third road car and I still didn't have a licence. It was a standard car on the outside but I'd had all the engine and carburettors done. His dad Milton was with me as well and we were going back to the hotel. It was a short trip, just like a hundred yards, and I accelerated and he heard the engine, even though I was just driving slowly. *What was that? Did you hear that? What do you have here, Mauricio?* He was totally berserk about this road car.

"I've seen him doing things in a road car and I'd think *he will have an accident within the next 30 seconds.* I remember a white car that he had and he'd go and be flat out, but it didn't matter if he was driving a transporter or a supercar, he just had this raw talent. If there was ice ahead, or rain, or whatever, *I'll sort it out,* and he did. Maybe he'd scrape the side of the car but usually not more. It wasn't a big deal

"Braking was the last option. It was always *avoid, back off.* If avoiding wouldn't work he *may* consider backing off, if that didn't work and he felt things were going to be really ugly then he *may* consider using the brakes –

but I never saw him do it. One particular car that he used to drive like this … well, one day he came back home with the speakers [from the radio] and the ignition key. His mother Neide asked *what's that?* And he said *it's all that's left of the car. The rest wasn't worth bringing."*

He had reached another crossroads, this year of 1978. The World Karting Championships were at Le Mans in France and he had never been out of South America before. The importance is many-fold, beginning with measuring himself against the best – with all the risks that involved – and travelling, still a teenager, to another continent to do it. Tche explains that "Ayrton needed to learn more, obtain more experience. Here in Brazil we had no-one who could make competition with him." Perhaps it was as simple as that. "I said to Ayrton *if you want to go, you have to go by yourself.* His father didn't want me to go with him. I said to Ayrton *you go, but I cannot help you there.* It was the Parrilla factory who asked me to go."

This situation needs to be examined, because it contains an implicit friction. Milton da Silva was a self-made man who had created a very successful business. He understood the ethics of work and would one day pass the business on to the next generation of his family. That's the most normal thing in the world. Brazil is a male-orientated society and, in the nature of it, this would tend to disqualify Viviane, the first born. Senna's brother Leonardo was six years younger than him. The succession would therefore fall upon Senna himself. The friction, as it would seem, was that Milton regarded karting as one of the activities his son happened to pursue en route to the responsibility of the family business and his son regarded karting as something else altogether. More than that, karting can swallow a great deal of money and it may well be that Milton saw this with great clarity. No wonder he didn't say to Tche *I'll pay you to fly to France, pay your hotels and food so you can tinker around with a kart my son will be driving!* Conversely Tche, so steeped in the importance of karting, could not understand why anybody else could not grasp that importance. To him, karting *was* life.

Listening to Tche, this clearly was friction and between them stood the quiet, shy, lanky teenager. If Ayrton Senna suffered an agony of conflicting loyalties he never, so far as I am aware, confided them in anyone else. He wasn't like that. Certainly Tche claims that Milton didn't want to spend money on the karting and also claims that one time words between father and son became "so high" that he stepped in between them. According to Tche, father and son fell out over the matter of payment to Tche after those South American Championships in Uruguay. This reportedly resulted in Senna retreating to a farm in the middle of Brazil and staying 45 days. He took a motor cycle and said he'd never do karting at Interlagos again – Tche, as it would seem, tuned the motor cycle's engine!

He did do karts again, of course. Tche describes him as a "terrible, terrible" kart driver, meaning in the sense of a terrible intensity: "He was a very good young man but when he was in the kart he was totally different.

The present contract stipulated between DAP and Mr. Ayrton Senna da Silva is valid for a period from 1st May 1981 upto 1st May 1982 and is intended and agreed mutually for the following items:

1) Mr. A.S.Da Silva will be engaged to drive for DAP in the following competitions:

   a) COPPA DEI CAMPIONI/ JESOLO
   b) WORLD CHAMPIONSHIP
   c) GRAND PRIX OF JAPAN
   d) GRAND PRIX OF HONG KONG

2) All prizes in money of the above named races will be Mr.Da Silva concern.

3) Any expenses for and in transfer of the driver will be charged to DAP and difference in travelling by car from England to Italy instead of airplane will be by DAP reimboursed to Mr. DA Silva.

4) DAP will pay in addition to Mr.Da Silva the price of US$ 2.210.= as flight payment from San Paolo/Brasil to Milano/Italy, both it will take place or not.

5) Any money transfer will be done by DAP through bank to the English bank of which Mr. Da Silva has is own account.

6) The amount for any above named competitions is agreed mutually as follows:

   - COPPA DEI CAMPIONI   ) US$ 900.00 fixed for racing any
   - GRAND PRIX OF JAPAN   )   competition
   - GRAND PRIX OF HONG KONG) US$ 900.00 in case of win in any
                                            competition

   - WORLD CHAMPION   US$ 1.500.= fixed for racing
                                 US$ 1.500.= in case of win

In agreement of what above stated both the parties sign herewith under

The contract Angelo Parrilla drew up near the end of Senna's karting career. (Courtesy of Angelo Parrilla)

To win was everything. He had to win whether he was driving well or driving badly. He was living in another world. He *had* to win. I'd say to him: *Ayrton, drive well, you can get hurt, it's not good for you* – your luck can run out – but Ayrton said *no, no, I know what I am doing.*

"When you gave him the chance to sit in a kart with a good engine he was another man. He was free. He could do what he wanted and show he could be someone. So he was totally crazy unless he was winning, winning, winning. Out of the kart he was timid. All he asked from me was an engine he could race with. And I was a shoulder he could cry on. He never spoke about his family."

Senna's world karting exploits are recounted elsewhere (*The Legend Grows*, PSL, 1995). Contact was made with a leading Italian karting family called Parrilla and Senna flew to Milan, where they were based. Tche was at Sao Paulo airport and as Senna went through he said *go with luck, my son, I will be waiting for you here*. In fact Tche would also fly over to Le Mans – there would be time for that, because Senna was going early to practise on the Parrilla kart at the circuit of Parma.

When Senna landed at Milan, Angelo Parrilla – who'd been warned that Senna only ate Brazilian food – took him to a luscious Italian restaurant and from that moment Senna's love affair with Italy began. Soon enough he began applying his intellect to learning the language. He got to speak it fluently and was still fluent a decade later, despite never having lived in Italy. What would the *Colegio* have made of that, and their average pupil?

Senna liked the Parrilla family and the family liked him, although Angelo was surprised by how he concentrated only on the karting, how alive he came at the kart track. Together they'd make a concerted attempt on the 1978 World Karts Championships at Le Mans (where he was sixth), the 1979 Championships at Estoril (where he was second, and felt robbed by a change to the points scoring system), and the 1980 Championships at Nivelles, Belgium (where he was second, watched by among others an 11-year-old West German called Michael Schumacher).

At Le Mans, Senna seems to have experienced something approaching self-doubt because he was pitting himself against the best in the world. He told Tche *look at him, he's fantastic, and look at him, he's fantastic too*. But after he started practising he said *no, I don't believe they are the best, I don't believe they are better than me*. Tche, incidentally, paid for himself to go to Le Mans.

Tche says that Senna's aim was to win the World Championship and then stop. He never thought about racing cars. However at Le Mans he met Chico Serra, who said *Ayrton, I will make representation to Van Diemen in England, and you can drive a Formula Ford. You'll think differently then.* [Van Diemen, run by Ralph Firmin, were a leading FF1600 manufacturer. Serra had driven for them in 1977, and was friendly with Firmin.] Senna replied *no, I don't want to run in cars. My thing is only karts*.

This explains why he kept on trying for the World Karting Championship until 1980 when, no longer a teenager, he reached the next crossroads – and kept on trying in 1981 and 1982. He yearned to win it, and the fact that he never did gnawed at him for years.

The crossroads he reached in 1980 would be the biggest choice of them all. There were three main directions to take: stay in karting; join the family firm and do as much karting as that would allow; or race cars, which meant going to live in England. Senna went to England.

You can argue that his father regarded it as a way of toughening and maturing the young man before he returned to the bosom of the family businesses, a kind of university of life. In that sense, Milton was willing to finance a season of racing in Formula Ford 1600. The conversations between them remain unrecorded. What we do know is that Senna's father paid 50 per cent of the season's cost (Senna confirmed this to me) and presumably Ralph Firmin made up the other 50 per cent.

Alfredo Popesco suggests what may well have happened. "Ayrton had an older sister and a very young brother so the only one who would be able to take care of Mr. Milton's business affairs was Ayrton. This is the reason Mr. Milton got a little bit upset and didn't easily agree. Mr. Milton had given him the kart not to be a professional, not to be the best, not to earn money, he just gave him the kart to have fun and to do something which young people at that time liked. Mr. Milton couldn't agree with the idea that Ayrton was going to move from Brazil to another country just to drive cars and race them."

Senna's journey to England is clear: it did happen courtesy of Chico Serra. "Senna was good in karts. Very, very good. I asked him to come to England and tried to arrange things for him. The funny thing was, I helped him but I was not really trying to help *him,* I was more helping Ralph. I knew that if Ayrton came to England he would win – and therefore be winning for Ralph. It was my idea that Ayrton should come to England. Maybe he had thought of it, maybe he wasn't thinking of it at that moment – he was very young and still racing go-karts in Brazil – but I am sure he was thinking of going to England some day and being in Formula 1 some day.

"When I suggested it, how did he react? He was very determined, he was a racing driver, he knew that was what he wanted to do and one day he would have to do it – go to England. I was living in England and Ralph and I used to call Ayrton, and, because *Ayrton* is a very difficult name to pronounce for English people, Ralph used to call him The Quick Man.

"I'd told Ralph about him and I said he never drove a racing car, he was just doing go-karts but normally when you have a good go-kart driver, for sure he's going to be good in a car. You talk about speed. It was natural to him. I mean ... he was the best. Natural talent he had, and more than anyone else.

"I'd said to Ralph *look, I have a friend in Brazil, the guy's very, very good in go-karts and if he comes he's going to win the Formula Ford for you* and so on. And Ralph used to call him The Quick Man – you know, *when's The Quick Man coming?* Then one day I rang Ralph and said *now The Quick Man is coming.*

"Senna flew over, I met him and then I took him to Norwich – to Snetterton, actually [where Van Diemen are]. We went out for dinner. The funny thing was at the dinner Ralph was really giving a good deal for him. I don't remember the money or anything like that but Ralph was saying *ah, I'll let you have so much testing and you don't have to pay all the money, only a little bit,* and everything Ralph gave to him he asked for more! For example, Ralph said *I'll give you 30 test days* and Senna said *no, no, I want 50 test days* – this kind of thing. Everything Ralph gave to him, more! Then Ayrton went to the toilet and Ralph said to me *who in the hell does he think he is?* A few years later, when Ayrton was in Formula 1, I reminded Ralph. I said *you remember that dinner we had and what you said to me: 'who does he think he is?' Well, he knew he was Ayrton Senna ...*"

So a deal was struck and Senna would spend the 1981 season driving Formula Ford 1600s. He came to England with a bride, Liliane Vasconcelos de Souza. A degree of mystery surrounds the circumstances of the marriage – in the next chapter, Mauricio Gugelmin will be giving his rationale for it.

Tche says Gugelmin told Senna that to live in England without a wife is the worst thing that can happen to you, and Serra also said to him that if he intended to stay in England he must have a wife. Tche recounts how one day Senna said *I'm going to get married.* Tche said *I've never seen you with a girl. You're making a joke, aren't you?* Senna said *no* and repeated *I'm getting married.* Evidently the two families knew each other, and consequently Senna had known Liliane since childhood.

The ceremony was in Senna's house.

She was young, blonde, pretty without being a supermodel but the mystery still holds her. I'm told that when the circle closed at Imola in 1994 some news reporters in Sao Paulo tracked her down but she gave them short shrift; that when Senna was lying in state in Sao Paulo she filed through among the other thousands, unannounced, just a face in the crowd; that she remarried and may have remarried again. Of her brief months in England, wed to this shy young man, we know almost nothing. She came as a stranger and went away as a stranger, which she still is today.

Senna was certainly homesick and so, possibly, was she. There's a revealing passage in Emerson Fittipaldi's 1973 book *Flying on the Ground* (with Elizabeth Hayward/William Kimber). Fittipaldi was then living in Switzerland and, wrote Ms. Hayward: "The Swiss will be horrified to know this, but it seems very important to Emerson's well-being that he is surrounded as much as possible by the life he knows and loves – Brazilian life. Magazines and newspapers from Brazil are crammed into a shelf. The television set is rarely turned on." And: "'When our friends come over from Brazil,' explains Emerson, 'we get them to bring us food, things we can't get here.'"

This sort of thing constituted the background.

The racing occupied the whole of the foreground.

Ayrton da Silva, as he was, made his debut at Brands Hatch on 1 March in the opening round of a championship called P&O Ferries after the company sponsoring it. (He would also contest the RAC and Townsend-Thoresen Championships.) Writing in the programme, journalist Jeremy Shaw said: "In the best traditions of the formula, one would be hard-pressed for a likely winner of the BARC Formula Ford 1600 Championship race. Again, any of a dozen or more have the capabilities and the machinery with which to win, even though a good proportion of them are 'foreigners'.

"Mexican Alfonso Toledano has the honour of starting 'Number 1' with his works-entered Van Diemen RF81, although he will be given a hard time by his equally talented 'team-mate' Enrique Mansilla, while Brazilian Ayerton [sic] da Silva will be making his British debut having shone in last year's World Karting Championship."

Shaw was a journalist who also worked "at Brands towards the end of the

EVENT THREE   12 LAPS (14.44 miles)

BARC Formula Ford 1600 Championship Race

This is the first round of the 1981 BARC Formula Ford 1600 Championship for single seater racing cars using near standard 1600cc Ford Cortina engines. Racing tyres used by these cars are identical.

No.	Entrant and Driver	Town	Car
1	Van Diemen International Racing Services Ltd (Dvr: Alfonso Toledano)	Mexico	Van Diemen RF81 Minister
2	Rushbrook Racing (Dvr: Dave Coyne)	Sunbury	Van Diemen RF81 Scholar
3	Van Diemen International Racing Services Ltd (Dvr: Enrique Mansilla)	Argentina	Van Diemen RF81 Auriga
4	Team Royale (Dvr: Rick Morris)	Hertford	Royale RP29 Nelson
5	E. L. Gibbs Ltd — Building Contractors (Dvr: Robert Gibbs)	Sittingbourne	Van Diemen RF81 Minister
6	Van Diemen International Racing Services Ltd (Dvr: Ayerton de Silva)	Brazil	Van Diemen RF81
7	Steve Lincoln	Bristol	Van Diemen RF81 Nelson
8	Brands Hatch Racing (Dvr: David Hunt)	London	Van Diemen RF81 Minister
9	Christopher Marsh	Bath	PRS Nelson
10	David Jones	Borough Green	Sark 2 Scholar
11	Tim Jones	East Grinstead	Ray 80F Auriga
12	Image Racehire '81 — Tel: Chichester 527011/2 (Dvr: Mark Smythe)	Chichester	Image 681 Auriga
14	Mick Cook Racing with Atlas Marketing (Dvr: Roy Steele)	Marlow	Van Diemen RF81 Minister
15	Doug Wood	Beckenham	Van Diemen RF80 Dart
16	Thierry Baillieux	Belgium	Van Diemen RF81 Minister
17	James Boswell	Basildon	Crosslé 32F Minister
18	Jubilee Racing (Dvr: TBA)	Basildon	Van Diemen RF81 Minister
19	Andy Blyth	Workingham	Crosslé 30F Scholar
20	Pine City Racing (Dvr: John Pratt)	Bournemouth	Van Diemen RF81 Scholar
22	Ray Kite	London	Hawke DL11 Auriga
23	Paul Weavers	London	Van Diemen RF80 Minister
24	Melvin Denton-Thompson	Lymington	Van Diemen RF80 Minister
25	Ilias Efessios	Athens	Van Diemen RF81 Auriga
26	Andrew Shilstone	St Leonards	Van Diemen RF80 Auriga
27	Image Racehire '81 — Tel: Chichester 527011/2 (Dvr: Peter Williamson)	Chalfont St Giles	Image 681 Auriga
28	Hope Computer (Dvr: Jesper Villumsen)	Denmark	PRS RH02 Minister
29	Mouldcraft Ltd (Architectural Aluminium) (Dvr: Colin Child)	New Ash Green	Sparton FF80 Auriga
30	Dave Ryan	Ashford	Van Diemen RF81 Auriga

LAP RECORD:		secs	mph	date
Formula Ford 1600 Racing Cars				
Roberto Moreno (1599cc Van Diemen RF80 Minister)		49.4	87.71	2.11.80
Race Record: Roberto Moreno (1599cc Van Diemen RF80 Minister)			86.23	2.11.80

10

The Brands Hatch programme on 1 March 1981 – Senna's first race. (Courtesy of Brands Hatch)

INFORMATION SHEET NO.15		BARC CAR RACES		TIME OF ISSUE: 3.15 p.m.		
EVENT THREE		P & O FERRIES FORD 1600 CHAMPIONSHIP RACE			12 LAPS	
BRANDS HATCH		START: 2.41 p.m.		1 MARCH 1981		
					Time	Best
Pos'n	No.	Entrant and Driver	Car		M S	Laps:
1st	3	Van Diemen International Racing Services Ltd Dvr: Enrique Mansilla	Van Diemen RF81 Auriga		10.18.1 84.12 mph	50.7
2nd	4	Team Royale Dvr: Rick Morris	Royale RP29 Nelson		10.19.5	50.5
3rd	2	Rushbrook Racing Dvr: Dave Coyne	Van Diemen RF81 Scholar		10.20.4	50.7
4th	1	Van Diemen International Racing Services Ltd Dvr: Alfonso Toledano	Van Diemen RF81 Minister		10.24.6	50.2
5th	6	Van Diemen International Racing Services Ltd Dvr: Ayrton de Silva)	Van Diemen RF81 Ford		10.26.1	50.8
6th	5	E.L. Gibbs Limited Building Contractors Dvr: Robert Gibbs	Van Diemen RF81 Minister		10.30.8	51.3

The result. (Courtesy of Brands Hatch)

week putting the programmes together, doing the press releases and so on."

Where did you get the information from? The programme notes are very detailed.

"Well, yes, I'm afraid I'm rather a sad character: I go after the details, I love it."

You'd found out who Senna was and it's unlikely you would have heard of him as a karter.

"True, but I'd heard of him as soon as he started testing the Van Diemen, simply because Ralph Firmin had come up with this guy and I'd been round racing a few years then. I knew Ralph and the people at Van Diemen and whenever they said there was someone special coming up I'd pay attention. Ralph always seemed to find these stars from Brazil, even then. Senna was far from the first. So I'd think *well, who's the latest one?*"

Shaw wasn't at Brands Hatch for Senna's debut in the opening round of the P&O, where he finished fifth [see above], but was at Thruxton a week later for the first race of the Townsend-Thoresen Championship. "You could tell right then the guy was a bit special and he probably hadn't tested at Thruxton so it was entirely new to him."

And those 1600 cars were difficult to control …

"… but karting's all about control so that wasn't a problem to him. Even from the start you could see his mind set was of a champion. He was *so* focused. He had his wife in tow, very quiet, good looking and seemed a very nice person. She was quite content to stay in the background, it appeared to me, and I don't think she approved of the English weather too much. Whatever he was planning to do, she was going to go along with it."

Senna finished third and, a week later, returned to Brands Hatch for the second round of the Townsend-Thoresen. Now Shaw wrote in the programme: "After their almost dominant performances last year, it comes as no surprise to see Ralph Firmin's Van Diemen cars making up the bulk of the field, and we can expect the works-entered cars of Enrique Mansilla, Alfonso Toledano and Ayrton da Silva to be the pace-setters. Mansilla, an Argentine, won the opening BARC Championship round here on March 1, capitalising on his experience gained last year, while his Mexican team-mate Toledano set fastest lap in spectacular style. What about young da Silva, though? In his very first Formula Ford race – on March 1 – the former karting star finished a magnificent fifth and must be a man to watch this season."

The emphasis was still on Mansilla and Toledano, with Senna as newcomer and outsider. He would alter this at a few seconds after 4.45 that same afternoon, when the 20 little cars crossed the line to complete the Final of the 1600 event.

At this third race, Senna encountered a driver called Andy Ackerley. "As a kid I was more interested in motor bikes and when I went to college to be a school teacher I actually did a couple of motor bike races, but by then I was really more interested in cars," says Ackerley. Not having the funds to contest national championships, and in any case racing "purely for fun", he opted to be a big fish in a small pool, concentrating on events at Brands Hatch.

It was a long day, with the 1600 runners divided into two groups. Each group had its own practice session in the morning and its own Heat in the early afternoon. The top ten finishers from the Heats went forward to the Final at 4.30.

Ackerley was in the same practice group as Rick Morris. They went out at 9.30 and had just 15 minutes. Rain fell and the track was wet. "In this practice I learnt a lot from Rick about the wet line. Rick had a particularly different line round Paddock Bend – a lot of people use it now – which was 'dragging' round in the middle. He also had an unusual line round Druids: round the outside. I had my own ideas of various lines so we were both learning from each other in terms of these wet lines and I knew Ayrton Senna didn't know that at all." Morris favoured a wide line round Druids and Clearways, Ackerley preferred the inside.

The practice finished with Ackerley on 59.0 seconds, Morris on 59.2, Toledano fifth on 1m 00.2s.

The rain had slackened when the second group went out at 9.55 for their 15 minutes. Officially the conditions were described as "overcast, track wet." Senna had the latest Van Diemen and exploited it so that this practice finished with him on 1m 00.0s, Mansilla 1m 00.5. Reportedly *(Autosport)* the Heat "served to underline the promise of young da Silva, who withstood both a concerted attack from Enrique Mansilla and a very hard downpour to win."

In Heat One – of ten laps – Morris won from Ackerley, Toledano third; in Heat Two Senna won from Toledano and Lincoln. The times governed the grid for the Final, so Morris (10m 00.5s) took pole from Ackerley (10m 02.3s), Senna third (10m 06.1s). The front row of the grid comprised three cars and Senna was on it.

"I remember Rick Morris won the first heat, I was second, and Senna won the second Heat," Ackerley says. "Rick's and mine was the fastest Heat so the front row of the grid was Morris, Ayrton, then me on the outside. Behind us were Alfonso Toledano and Enrique Mansilla. At this stage I had not spoken to Senna at all. I knew nothing about him except what we all did, that he was a works driver. I remember Brian Jones [the Brands Hatch PA commentator] saying *this chap's got some weird lines round Brands Hatch*. Senna seemed to be learning as he was going, you know. It was just pure car control, really, that was enabling him to find his way round."

At the green light Senna led "in atrocious conditions" *(Autosport)* with Ackerley after him. They approached Paddock, the adverse-camber right-hander at the end of the start-finish straight which fell sharply away into a long descent before rising towards the horseshoe of Druids. Ackerley was poised to strike – by going round the *outside* as the two cars moved into Paddock. "When I overtook him there it caught him completely by surprise, but I knew, from following Rick earlier on – and it's stayed with me ever since – that actually that was a quicker way round in the wet. I'd only just learnt it even though I'd raced a few times round Brands." Senna had raced there only once before of course and, as Ackerley has already said, didn't know all about the lines for the wet.

"It was a good move, and it well and truly beat him." Now the two little cars are through Paddock, down the descent and coming up towards Druids.

As with Paddock, there were two distinct schools of thought about Druids in the wet, inside or outside. Ackerley explores that. "Well, Druids is almost banked and all the water drains to the inside, so when it rains you actually get more grip on the outside. However, I was trying to close down any attempt by Senna to re-pass – so I'd go inside."

All these geometrical niceties mattered nothing. Senna counter-attacked on the way into Druids and Ackerley "pulled over to block him. I tried to close the door and he proved an uncompromising foe: *I don't back off*. That's where I learned the lesson that you don't close an uncompromising foe off on a straight – because he just kept his nosecone there, 'caught' me and off I went. The car was slightly damaged, a minor bend or two, but retired on the spot. Senna stayed on the track and just kept racing."

Despite a setting sun which glinted and glowered through the clouds towards the end of the race, so that at moments the runners risked being blinded, Senna won his first victory in a racing car comfortably enough. He finished in 15m 07.2s, Toledano in 15m 16.6s.

"I always remember him coming round on the victory lap and him looking at me and me looking at him," Ackerley says. "For the victory lap the first three finishers got on a car with a gantry, a Ford Capri or something, and stood on the back waving to the crowd. I was standing by the side of Druids – by the side of the car, in fact. Senna sort of looked at me and I sort of looked at him. I gave him The Look and he gave me a shrug of the shoulders. I thought *well, shall I take it further?* and I never bothered to.

"Subsequently I felt he respected the fact, or was relieved by the fact, that

I hadn't gone up and given him a mouthful. After that, when I'd see him – even in Formula 1, because I was working at Brands as sales and marketing manager – he'd always come and say hello. We'd nod, recognising each other from Formula Ford days."

Jones confirms Acklerly's assertion about the lines. "It is absolutely true that Senna was taking strange lines. My memory for races is incredibly bad – it's one of the disappointments of my life – yet I remember specifically he won this race in spite of himself because, having talked my way through so many races, I knew this guy was quick despite being all over the place. Yes, he was all over the place and that's what I was saying during the commentary, particularly through Clearways, and yet he was clearly the quality of the field. My commentary position had an unobstructed view across to it.

"Now at that stage there was no question that we saw any greatness in it or anything else, and it would be foolish to suggest otherwise – he was a kid that we knew hardly anything about but he immediately attracted attention. It wasn't long before it began to unfold. But I have a picture in my mind of him going through what they now call McLaren, which links the two legs of the grand prix circuit when you're on the club circuit."

There's a big corner there and you can experiment.

"You can and in fact that is what he was doing. He was already working at it and he was trying some pretty extreme things but it didn't seem to slow him down, that was the extraordinary thing."

To clarify this, you need a lap of the club circuit. From the start-finish line the cars accelerated into Paddock Hill Bend, went down the dip and up the incline to Druids, descended from that to a left-hander, ran along behind the paddock and then, instead of twisting left on the grand prix circuit, turned onto the McLaren link and right at the end of it onto Clearways, the curving sweep back to the start-finish line. The point about the McLaren link was that both the entry and exit were broad enough to allow a driver room for experiment.

This third race of Senna's career had been on 15 March. That same day, in distant Long Beach, 24 cars took part in the USA-West Grand Prix, first round of the 1981 World Championship. Two of them – Elio de Angelis and Alain Prost – would become team-mates; one of them – Keke Rosberg – would give Senna a rough ride round Brands Hatch; another – Watson – would be rendered damn near speechless by what Senna could make a Formula 1 car do. (And, incidentally, the restaurant at Brands Hatch left Senna himself speechless one of these 1981 days. Brazilian cuisine does not evidently make much use of chilis and in the circuit restaurant Senna spied chili con carne. He wondered if it was good, *oh yes* someone said, and it was *very* spicy.)

Ackerley had one other encounter with Senna on the track, on 12 July at Brands Hatch. By then Senna had contested a further nine 1600 races, finishing respectively second, second, second, first, first, first, second, first and first.

"I think I might have been on the second row of the grid, he'd had a problem with his car in practice and only qualified about eighth or ninth. So he started behind me, on the third row," Ackerley says.

At the green …

"D'you know … I tell you this … he just came past me like … like I've never seen anyone so quick in my life. He was *leading* by Druids and I'd never seen anything like that before. It was amazing. He was past me before we got to Paddock. I was on the inside and to be honest you sometimes move over a little bit [towards mid-track] because the racing line into Paddock Bend is a bit wider." Senna saw this gap to the inside and went through it like a missile. "I just thought *Jesus Christ,* then I thought *yeah, that guy is just …*

"I-had-never-been-subjected-to-that-kind-of-thing-before! OK, Senna had a works car, a works engine and all that sort of thing – and I don't know whether he jumped the start: he might have done – *but* as far as I was concerned, even if he had, to get to the lead by Druids was … astonishing. I thought *this is a chap on a mission.*

"Whereas in his first race I'd thought *this is a guy I could have beaten,* after what he did at the start, no way. I'd won a lot of races, I've won a couple of championships and when you are driving as best you can you think *I am unbeatable.* Then, when someone comes along and is quicker, you think *well, hang on, I do not know how to do that.* Everything is going right for you, everything is perfect and you've got no excuses. You know, deep down inside – because a lot of race drivers are not very honest with themselves – that you will never be that good. I might be as good as the other guys, and the other guys might be good, but not as good as *that* guy. It's what I saw up the hill to Druids. He just made mincemeat of the whole lot of us in that start."

Senna, however, did not win this race. He spun when a radiator pipe came adrift, possibly as a consequence of a jostling match with Mansilla shortly after the start. The race had been a raw and ragged thing. *Autosport* were moved to hoist a headline FORMULA FORD MADNESS and in an editorial wrote that the race produced "some of the most aggressive driving seen in the formula for some time. Most of the action came from Van Diemen's highly volatile works trio". *Autosport* conceded that they had shown ability but each used "questionable tactics" and "this behaviour, if it is allowed to continue unchecked, will land someone in hospital sooner or later."

Early in August Senna won the sixth round of the RAC Championship at Snetterton. It rained during that race and a lean, almost spare-looking man with long hair noted how, while the others floundered when the rain came, Senna effortlessly increased his lead. The man was Dennis Rushen, half the force behind a Formula 2000 team. Formula 2000 was the next step upwards from Formula Ford 1600. After the race Rushen hastened to introduce himself and said impulsively *if you come back we'll give you next season for £10,000.*

It was the next crossroads and an absolutely crucial one. It may well be that if Rushen had not made this offer Senna would have been lost to motor racing altogether.

He duly won both the championships he contested (the Townsend-Thoresen and the RAC). In the final Townsend-Thoresen round, at Brands Hatch on 29 September, he finished second but one contemporary report said his "antics virtually defied belief." He was on the third row and in slippery conditions made a monumental start, "chopping" past several cars then spinning. He didn't hit anything and nothing hit him so he resumed sixteenth and began overtaking half a dozen cars a lap. Then he spun again. Then he began overtaking half a dozen a lap and came second.

Traditionally at Brands Hatch the winners were taken up onto a platform adjoining the control tower for the victory celebrations and a word or two with Brian Jones. The race winner, Morris, plus Senna and Toledano (third) made their way up there and the folklore insists that when Jones said *we're all looking forward to seeing you next year* Senna murmured into the microphone *I'm not coming back.* So what did happen?

"I'm not sure it was as blunt as that," Jones says, "but he made it clear there was a big question mark over whether he was coming back, that he was uncertain about what his future was going to be. It was quite a shock, because we wanted to see this guy press on into Formula 3. Quite what the reasons were for his idea that he might give it all up were less clear to us. One of the problems of the commentator is that when you interview people they are full of adrenalin. They haven't slowed down, they haven't got back to normal so you tend to get monosyllabic answers, which is a bit frustrating because you want to know, you want to find out, you want to discover. And because they haven't settled down they're not very communicative.

"Nor was I able to fully appreciate his situation at the time, because I imagine he was in a state of mental turmoil. He was married and it was all going wrong. I can, however, confirm that he did say there was considerable doubt about whether he was coming back. He had been runner-up in the World Karting Championship on two occasions so he was an acknowledged star there, and he had taken Formula Ford 1600 by storm. Clearly we wanted to see him back, so it was both a surprise and a major disappointment when he said what he said but it wasn't absolutely cast in stone."

In *Motoring News* Senna was quoted as saying: "Next year I will most probably drive my road car! I'm near to giving up racing. In racing, talent is not important. A bad driver with money can get a good team, but a good driver with only a little money can only get a bad team. Next year I will do some kart races just for fun. I need to do some racing for sure, I really want to but I don't want to become so involved that my racing becomes business instead of pleasure. Before I came to England I used to do a few races in Europe in karts but I could still live in Brazil. This is what I want to do again."

These sentiments are echoed by Mike Dixon, a freelance photographer from 1967 to around 1991 who also "did a bit of writing as well for *Autosport*." He specialised in Snetterton, covering 95 per cent of the meetings there. "Senna came into my orbit in 1981, and he was certainly the best thing I'd seen since Emerson Fittipaldi had been in it in the 1960s.

Towards the end of 1981 – it would probably have been a few weeks before the Formula Ford Festival – I'd got agreement from *Autosport* to try and put a little piece together about the foreign drivers, because basically they were all living in Norfolk at the time. I went out of my way to interview all three of them." They were, of course, the volatile trio of Senna, Toledano and Mansilla. Dixon took them to one side in the paddock at Snetterton and took a picture of them [reproduced on page 143].

"Senna was living in a house which I assume Ralph Firmin had found for him. It gained notoriety after that because I think Mauricio Gugelmin went and lived in it and various other people lived in it later on. It was at Eaton, in the suburbs of Norwich. I met up with him there one evening.

"It was a conventional detached house on a normal housing estate, not the sort of rat hole that a lot of them used to live in! When I interviewed Roberto Moreno the year before [for a similar article about Moreno, Luiz Shaffer, and Raul Boesel] he was living shacked up with two or three other drivers literally in a room – and most of them lived like that. But Senna at least had a decent place in a very nice residential area.

"I interviewed him in the kitchen because his parents were both there. I was introduced to them and have to say his parents seemed less than impressed that here was someone who I think they saw as positively encouraging their son to stay in motor racing. It was clear from Ayrton that their purpose was very much the opposite: get him back to Brazil and into the family business.

"Interestingly enough, if you look at the head and shoulders photograph of the three of them in the paddock, there is Senna, in a plain set of overalls with, apart from a Brazilian logo on one shoulder, not a single shred of advertising on him. Toledano was obviously sponsored by Marlboro, various other things are on his overalls, and there's Mansilla absolutely covered in little sponsorship patches. Senna's family basically funded him that year, did it themselves without any sponsorship whatsoever.

"From what I remember of the interview, it was very much a matter of his parents finally caving in to let him come and play motor racing. It wasn't something they wanted but I think they thought *well, he'll get over it, he'll get it out of his system and that'll be the end of it*. Of course that wasn't the case at all. There was Senna on the one hand saying *well, look, you know* – he didn't tell me at the time but I know now that he owed quite a considerable sum to Firmin – but there was him saying *look, you know, I'm rather cheesed off with all this. I'm under great parental pressure to go back to Brazil, I don't like the thought of having to go round and drum up the sponsorship to stay – drivers ought to get drives on their merit rather than effectively have to buy it – and there's no opportunity for drivers to get through just on talent etc etc*. It was a very low ebb.

"I thought afterwards, when he came back in 1982 to do Formula Ford 2000 and subsequently when he moved on from there, that he tried to set me up in that interview – but I've thought about that over the years since then and I judge he wasn't that sort of guy. I feel, however you think about Senna, that underneath everything he was a very honest, God-fearing sort of guy. I don't think he took advantage of me to try and plead his case.

"The mood he was in that day, he was genuinely cheesed off with life. He didn't know which way to turn. He was under great pressure from the family to go back to Brazil and it was *clear* he was under that pressure. It was also clear he wanted to carry on in motor racing, but having demonstrated his talent he didn't want the hassle of begging and scraping to try and get funds.

"His wife was there, a very quiet girl, very, very pleasant. He was very much in charge, no doubt about that. It was literally *Liliane do this* or *Liliane do that* and Liliane jumped and Liliane did it. He made great fun out of the fact that she served me a piece of cake and he described it as *A Liliane Cake*. She was good looking. I must admit she didn't spend a great deal of time with us – she cleared off and joined the parents – but, yes, not an unattractive girl.

"From memory, and I am really dredging back, she wasn't particularly tall and slim or anything like that. She smiled sweetly. I think the thing that struck me most was that she knew her place, she wouldn't speak unless she was spoken to and very much it was him who was calling the shots. Very, very much so. That was what the piece of cake had been about: she felt it her duty to do that, but after it she sort of vanished. She really would only speak if he encouraged her to and her English seemed limited. She knew enough to be able to say *hello* and *thank you* but that was about it. She must have found it uncomfortable living there on her own while he was away at the circuit. His parents seemed very wealthy, almost autocratic, almost aristocratic people and you felt an atmosphere in the place with them there.

"Ayrton's English? I didn't find him that difficult. It's not that I had a lot of experience in talking to these guys, but obviously I'd talked to those three the year before and I'd chatted to Ayrton when I set this thing up in the paddock. I could follow what he said OK.

"After that, I rather got a tiny feeling he traded on it. Sometimes he wanted to be seen *not* to converse in English terribly well when it suited him. He took a lot of people in with that but when he felt he could relax and talk to somebody then it dropped. Don't forget 1981 was the first year he had been over here and yet, as I say, I found no difficulty in talking to him at all. In my interview the quotes are what he said. If he said a sentence, the sentence was taken down as he said it.

"Looking at the photograph now, you realise quite how slim he was – very slight of build, tall but gangly. His driving? Well, he was amazing. The car control was amazing. He was so tidy compared to everyone else, he always seemed to be in control whereas usually in Formula Ford there's a lot of scrapping.

"Considering the current standard of driving in Formula Ford and comparing the way that Senna drove is like comparing night and day. OK, the cars were different but they were still difficult and even then he was a master. I'd never seen anyone position a car like Fittipaldi until Senna came along, and he was born with this. It was so interesting to watch him compared to the others who were probably getting through it on bravery alone. Senna had the skill. There was no *aggravation* in the way he made the car behave. He knew what it would do and he knew how to exploit it. You sometimes felt other people got there by default. I watched Senna through the esses at Snetterton – what they now call the Bombhole [see map on page 55] – and I remember taking pictures of him in, I think, practice. He had the car in exactly the same place every time. That used to show in his lap times as well."

The *Autosport* feature was headed LATIN LESSONS. In it Dixon conjured this delightful paragraph: "Having driven karts of one form or another for 17 of his 21 years, Ayrton constantly refers to the 'sensation' of such driving. From the age of eight to 13 this involved illicit closed road practising, the next three years legally racing in 125cc and the past five in [the] 100cc International [class]."

Dixon added: "Ayrton and wife Liliane have not taken to the English way of life when compared to the style they enjoyed in Brazil." Senna had savoured Formula Ford 1600 but "there is not the fight of karting, in every respect – in braking, cornering, and acceleration the karts give me more sensation."

He felt that coming to England had been the right decision because it enabled him to decide what he wanted, and that was to go back to Brazil and race karts for pleasure. He would have no more of what he described as the "mental pressures" of winning to impress sponsors, and if he was heading to a race meeting and decided he didn't want to take part he'd turn round and go home.

There was talk of a Formula 2 drive for a Swiss team called Maurer, who'd been in touch by telephone, but Senna nursed doubts about any such move. He had been back to Brazil for a month and was due to return for the Formula Ford Festival. In his absence an Irishman, Tommy Byrne, had tested his Van Diemen in preparation for the Festival and made it go fast. That alone made Senna a favourite to win.

He did not return.

This, then, was the next crossroads. He'd had his 'university of life' season in England indulging his hunger for racing and now it was time to return to Brazil and the family businesses. The problem was that the hunger had increased and the crossroads offered the most stark choice: if he came back to England to continue his driving it would almost certainly become his life.

In *The Hard Edge of Genius* I quoted a friend as saying "his father wanted him to stop racing and help in the factory so Ayrton went there not to disappoint his father. But his father felt he was really unhappy so he decided to give Ayrton another push. *'Would you like to go and try in England? OK. I will help you, but you do just one year and then you finish. That will be fine for you.' Ayrton agreed, he came to England. But from that time he couldn't stop."*

Senna drew a pencil line through the whole paragraph and then he wrote: "He [Milton] simply made me free to decide what I wanted to do and after I decided we agreed together (father, myself and the family) that this was simply GO [he underscored this twice] and not look back anymore just look ahead. That happened after my first season after I got back to Brazil and had tried my best to help him in his business from October '81 to February '82. It was in that February that I made up my mind and together we decided to go for it. For sure without my father's help, life would have been a lot more difficult but we also agreed as a matter of principle that the day I could be in a position [to do it] I would pay back all the investment. That happened when I got to Formula 1."

In a television interview he once said: "I was already very strong in my mind that I wanted to try properly, try very hard, and that meant I had to learn to live in a different country away from my own people – and if that was not such a good side of my new lifestyle it was fulfilling slowly a personal goal, a personal desire. We had a very successful year [in 1981] and I won two championships but my father had some difficulties and it required me to return to Brazil to try to help him out with a few things. So I decided then to try not to race and see the difference [GESTURING WITH HANDS, SLOW SMILE]. I tried racing professionally, then I tried really not to race and do some normal business. I realised then how strong the desire was that I had to be a racing driver."

The name Ayrton leant itself to a certain measure of confusion to the English tongues trying to get round it. Should it be pronounced *Airtun*, with which his new team might be reasonably comfortable, or should it be the Portuguese rendering, *Ireton*? When Senna decided to take up Dennis Rushen's rash offer, Rushen and the boys decided to keep their tongues unencumbered from these vowels and consonants.

They nicknamed him Harry.

Then and now

The Colegio Rio Branco has a laboratory named after Senna. His niece Giovanna opened this in 1997 (Viviane had a prior commitment). The laboratory has a plaque over the door with the metal outline of a red and white racing car on it. An oil painting in a gold frame shows Senna with that wry, benevolent smile. Primary pupils do practical work, art and science here. It's a light, airy room with goldfish in tanks, and shapes made of glued stones. This lab is much more about the future than the past.

Tche is a small, urgent man who speaks in bursts. He stands in his office while outside in the workshop karts are being prepared. There's a large photograph of Senna on one office wall. During the interview Tche impulsively ripped open his overalls to reveal a tee-shirt bearing the legend I miss you, Ayrton *in Japanese. "I wear these tee-shirts every day," Tche explains, "because I miss him every day."*

Andy Ackerley formed his own corporate hospitality business in 1983. "We do a lot of dealer training projects – we train them about products on new cars and how they work." Yes, he watched the race at Imola, "and, well, desperately tragic. Murray was very good about that sort of thing, not dwelling on what was happening out there. I've had this photograph stuck up here [see page 140] on the wall, and I thought the message 'so what happened to you?' suddenly became more poignant." Ackerley is 49 and still racing an MG in single-make championships. Why? "I just can't stop it! I love racing."

Mauricio and Stella Gugelmin are nicely settled into the American way of life in Miami and are building a spacious house there. Gugelmin is driving for PacWest in the CART Championship series and, when I'm due to interview him, has to go to Sebring, the circuit in central Florida, for a seat fitting for the 1999 season. Which is how I came to hire a car and discover that road signs in the United States are a state of mind rather than a reality; and how I came to devour a lively meal in a Mexican restaurant at Sebring while, opposite, Gugelmin – square and fit and open – talked with touching candour and no fear, as a born gentleman would; and how, next day, I saw this sign in a petrol station:

In God we trust. Everyone else pays cash.

Senna would have understood – perfectly.

Chapter 2

No matter
what the progress

HEARD THE ONE about the Englishman, the Irishman and the Brazilian? No?
Well, the Englishman was distinctly aquatic: he sold eels for a living, and if
he couldn't walk on water he could certainly drive on it; the Irishman had
kissed the Blarney stone all right; and the Brazilian you have already met.

The joke? The eel-man, Frank Bradley, truly beat Senna, and the Blarney
Stone-man, Joey Greenan, truly led Senna. We are in the land of the
wonderfully improbable: 1982 was the year of that, and maybe the last year
of innocence.

Dennis Rushen, of course, had backed his gut-feeling and made Senna an
offer for Formula Ford 2000 in 1982: £10,000 for the season, a sum which
all are agreed, even building in inflation and the distortion of the mad
money in sport now, represented a genuine bargain. Senna knew a bargain
when he saw one and here he was back in England for 1982. But who was
Rushen?

"I started in motorsport in 1968, at Lotus, but just missed knowing Jim
Clark. I began as a boy in the stores, worked my way through the buying
department and got involved with the design department. I did know
Graham Hill, Jochen Rindt, Emerson Fittipaldi. I've seen all the great ones
since then. How do I evaluate Ayrton? I would say that he wanted it more
than anybody else, he could be more focused. He was certainly the
quickest …"

Across the span of some careers you can, with hindsight, isolate certain
crossroads with great clarity; with other careers you sense only a great,
gathering strength. In Senna's you find both. His strength had begun to
gather in 1981 and that intensified in 1982: out of 28 races with Rushen
Green he won 22.

"He had a very human side with us in '82," Rushen says, "but he only
showed that to his friends. Most journalists, for example, said *ah, he's
arrogant, he's this, that and the other* but they didn't realise two things.

Firstly he was very shy. Secondly they'd ask what he considered dumb questions and ask them at the wrong time – and *that* came across as arrogance. But to his friends he was just a normal guy who'd mess around, play about. He'd do really funny things, pull practical jokes. Then again, if you caught him at the wrong time – when he was stressed up – it was quite hard to get through to him because he was so focused on what he was doing."

A serious young man then, still slender, now single, and continuing to apply his enormous intellect and memory to the act of driving a racing car.

Mauricio Gugelmin had watched from afar as Senna drove in England in 1981. "I used to follow how he was doing. We got in touch and then at the end of 1981 he decided to go into his father's business. They were not getting on well when his father wanted him to stop racing and come back to Brazil. Before he did, I said *can you find me a place with Van Diemen?* He got me a place there. I went and, late in February, I got a call from him. He said *recently I have decided to race again. I'll be there tomorrow. Can I stay with you?* I said *yes*. It was at Eaton. We used to pay £160 a month rent."

Senna returned without Liliane, although he never discussed this with Gugelmin, who says, "his marriage happened before he went to England. When you are Brazilian, the culture, the way you live in Brazil is a little bit more spoilt than it is in England. You don't leave your home to live on your own, you normally stay with your family until you get married." So, Gugelmin surmises, "he was going away to England and that was going to be tough and it was better to have a woman you loved with you – which was the case. England is a very different place from Brazil, he was really involved with his racing and she was sitting at home in a cold country without much to do, which was bad. Then they started having disagreements and, in the end, when he came back to Brazil he decided to leave her there until it got sorted out. But really I don't know why, I never asked about it, we never discussed it, I'm just assuming what happened. And of course when he came back in 1982 he had friends he'd made in England so he knew he could do it on his own. I never met her, I never spoke with her – well, I spoke with her on the phone sometimes, because occasionally she used to call when I was in the house, but that only lasted a couple of months and then it was over."

There were two championships, the domestic British Formula Ford 2000 Championship and its European sister, the EFDA (European Formula Drivers' Association). This had been formed by an American, Dan Partel. "We were founded in 1979, based in Germany and very active in the development of Formula Ford 1600 on the Continent. It had gotten to the point where we were racing against the Dutch and the Austrians. I said *why don't we resurrect the European Championship for 1600?* We needed some kind of a governing body to organise it and I said I'd take a shot at this. By 1982, their racing was Formula 2000."

Senna won the opening British round at Brands Hatch on 7 March by 9.8 seconds from a Norfolk driver, Calvin Fish, who would be his main opponent throughout the season. Three weeks later he prepared for the second round, at Oulton Park. By then a Swedish mechanic, Petter Dahl, had joined him to look after every aspect of the car except the engine. Dahl is pragmatic. "We had a working relationship, but we didn't socialise. I don't think he did with many people. He chose the friends he wanted to socialise with and that's the way it was."

Dahl, who did Formula Ford in America in 1981, had been asked over by Ralph Firmin. "I actually missed the first race. As I understood it, Van Diemen didn't want a works team in 2000 so the car was entered and supported by Rushen Green – but actually belonged to Van Diemen and I was with Van Diemen. We had works engines from Nelson so we didn't touch them. My job was to prepare the car, transport the car, look after setting it up and do anything which needed doing.

"I hadn't met Senna before but I had heard of him because I followed 1600. My first impression was that it was difficult to get close to him. You didn't make good friends with him *just like that*, but he was very fair and he never complained of anything. I mean, the car just went on and on and it didn't break down – well, two times it did, once it was engine, once he had a puncture, and he went off on a couple of occasions, but that was it over the whole season."

Senna took pole and won at Silverstone and Donington Park, then took pole at Snetterton and led – then suddenly slowed.

Peter Merrilees remembers that. Merrilees worked for Ralph Firmin when he first started in the 1970s. "In 1981 I had my own business preparing cars but the recession was on, I got fed up and thought I'd go back racing. I spoke to Ralph and did a deal to work for him in 1982. I hadn't seen Senna and didn't see him until 1982 when he was running the 2-litre. What did I make of him? It was obvious to anyone who'd been around that he was going to be World Champion and the only question was how long he would take to get there. In 1982 he was just an outstanding talent.

"At Snetterton he was in the lead, slowed down and Calvin Fish caught him. Fish passed him then, all of a sudden, Senna got going again, passed Fish and won the race. I went afterwards to see what had caused Senna's delay, and everyone was looking round the car. A stone had damaged the front brakes and he'd had no front brakes at all, so he'd altered the brake balance to the rear, got the hang of driving the car like that for three or four laps, then reeled in Fish and beat him. That's astonishing, isn't it? You have to be superhuman to do that."

Gugelmin remembers this race. "I was there – and it was ridiculous! He had no front brakes, only rears. He soon realised that there were only two braking points on the circuit and he thought *ah, I don't need brakes*. He was leading and somebody went off on the first lap. When Senna came round on the second lap there were some stones on the circuit. A stone cut the front brake line. Next corner he tried to brake, thought *damn, I'm going to have to park this thing*. Well, he slowed down and lost first place to Calvin Fish, then he lost second place to Russell Spence.

"They were going away from him until he began to maintain the distance because he was learning to drive the car without brakes. Then he caught them up a little bit, then he worked out how to get Russell Spence back – which he did – then he worked out how to get Calvin Fish – which he did. Then he opened up a decent gap and kept that to the finish. I knew something was wrong because he had dropped back, knew it must have been some kind of a problem.

"Then he came in really slowly on the lap after the finish, jumped out of the car and his eyes were shining as if they were saying *you're not going to believe this*. He said *I had no brakes*. I said *bullshit! You're full of bullshit!* I went around the car and put my hand on the front brakes. They were cold. I put my hand on the brake disc. It was ice cold. I looked at the front and saw the cut, then I looked at him and said *yeah, but you had rear brakes!* To suddenly find yourself in a situation like that during a race, and think about it – *think about it* – and solve it is remarkable."

A man well-versed in the folklore of motor racing, Trevor Foster – now in Formula 1 as race director at Jordan – says he will always remember Dennis Rushen telling him about it: "They said *what happened?* Senna replied *well, it gave me a moment for a few laps but then* – because in those days they had little adjustable anti-roll bars – *I realised that if I put the rear roll bar Full Soft and I kept pitching the car into the corners go-kart style it was OK*. He'd done most of the race without any front brakes at all. Can you imagine the amount of travel on the pedal? Imagine suddenly going from having a nice, hard brake pedal to it literally being half way down – and all he did was soften the roll bar off."

And beat his team-mate Kenny Andrews by 12.6 seconds.

Senna took pole and won at Silverstone, then went to the first round of the EFDA series at Zolder on 18 April. It's worth pausing briefly here to recapture the atmosphere of 2000 and EFDA. Partel describes it as a "hallmark" that young drivers were treated firmly but fairly. "I'm an American, my whole approach to sports is quite different from the Europeans'. I grew up playing American football and the whole thing is developing young professionals." Partel had, yes, firm but fair views about that. If he told all the drivers to report for a photograph, for instance, any that didn't were out of the race. "My idea was to build a training programme towards Formula 1."

At Zolder the engine failed. Senna took pole and won at Donington (EFDA), won at Mallory Park and they went back to Zolder again for the third EFDA round.

Petter Dahl remembers that Senna was "very professional, as he always would be throughout his career. He never left anything behind, everything had to be tip top.

"He was very concerned about, say, tyres and he was very good at picking tyres, choosing the right ones all the time. He could have a set and, for example, he'd want one of the rears changed because it was no good. He could feel this in a couple of laps and I'd never worked with anybody like that before. I'd set the car up to his instructions: you always had a basic set-up and then you made small changes as he decided, wings, anything to gain speed.

"He knew what he was doing. He had the most tremendous control over everything. He could keep an eye on five things at one time when he was driving. In qualifying he'd do five, six laps and say that's it, nobody can beat me because I know where all their limits are and they can't go quicker. He would be right, yep, right!

"Also his memory in the race was astonishing: those days they didn't have any data-logging but in a 15-lap race he could tell you in order which one was the quickest lap, then the second, then the third and so on. You'd look at the time sheets and, yep, he was right!"

It was only his second season of motor racing, and yet there are Formula 1 drivers who can't do what he was doing.

"Yes, there are. I mean, everyone knew he was going to reach grand prix racing one day. We did the Euroseries, the races were supporting events for the grands prix and there was always people from Formula 1 coming around and having a look, especially from McLaren, and Peter Warr of Lotus.

"I remember all Senna's Euroseries races particularly, although at Zolder he went off. He had three goals for every race, and they were to take pole position, set fastest lap and win. At Zolder he had pole position, he was leading the race by miles and he was chasing for the fastest lap. Our race was after the grand prix so there were a lot of marbles" – slippery rubber globules burnished off the Formula 1 car tyres. "There was just one line to go: the racing line really was the racing line, no room for mistakes. Senna got out onto the marbles and went off. He blamed himself very much. Very much. He was very upset that he had made this mistake, no tears, just angry."

Dan Partel says: "Ayrton skated off when he was well in the lead – gone, out of sight even – and I think he got bored and lost concentration."

This was the weekend when Gilles Villeneuve was killed at Zolder in a Ferrari, near the end of second qualifying for the Belgian Grand Prix. When Roland Ratzenberger died at Imola in 1994, many people tried to account for Senna's devastated reaction by pointing out that it was the first time he'd been at a race meeting where someone had died. They forgot Zolder so long before.

Whether Senna was physically present at the circuit when Villeneuve crashed is unclear, although Dahl is pretty sure he was. "I didn't see the impact but I saw what happened next with my own eyes, not the hit but things flying in the air. I don't know whether Ayrton saw that because I was working with the car behind the pits in the paddock area."

By now, Partel was getting to know Senna. "I was hard on Ayrton. He came to me as a shy kid with all of this hype already started in England from his Formula Ford 1600 programme and he was tipped as a Formula 1 prospect right at that point. But I felt that it wasn't good for any of them to get their egos pumped up like that. I wouldn't concede to him that he was a star. He was just like everybody else and we developed a very special relationship. That carried all the way through his career."

By now, too, Gugelmin was getting to know him well. "We used to do a lot of things in everyday life together apart from going to the races – go to the supermarket, run the house. He had his sponsors, I had mine and if we found ways of raising money in Brazil we used to share that information. But mainly, day and night, we used to watch Formula 1, talk about different circuits, how you do this and how you do that – he helped me a lot. I was learning the circuits, he'd been there one year and he knew them. And we drove almost every day as works Van Diemen drivers. Hard work? Racing was never hard work. We were the lucky guys. What had once been a hobby we were now getting paid to do. Racing only gets hard work when you reach Formula 1 and there's so much money involved.

"I always had the feeling that he wanted Formula 1. When he first went to England, a lot of people in Brazil thought he would get tired, or something would happen. Then they thought *he's on his own and it's so easy to go home*. That happens to a lot of us but that just didn't happen with Senna."

After Zolder, Senna won a celebrity race for Sunbeam cars at Oulton Park (it was on the same card as Round 8 of the 2000 series), and this takes an oddly significant place in his career. He was proving he could drive anything consummately. He suffered a puncture in the 2000, then won at Brands Hatch, won at Mallory Park, won at Brands Hatch again.

Eddie Jordan invited him to try a Formula 3 car at Silverstone. "I could see straight away that he was the business. He certainly looked the business to me. I've had lots of drivers who weren't, but he really did look absolutely *it*. I tried desperately to sign him but he went to Dickie Bennetts because Bennetts had more experience. As a team, Jordan were just coming but at least we had the *nous* and the foresight to go and do it – put him in the car."

That day at Silverstone Senna covered 38 laps in the Jordan Ralt and, on the South circuit, recorded a time of 54.03 seconds. As *Autosport* noted, this compared very favourably with the fastest lap set in the Formula 3 race there on Whit Monday, 54.04. Senna said he "enjoyed it very much and it was better to drive than I thought it would be. Things have not changed, though, I still want to concentrate on Ford 2000 and perhaps try a few more Formula 3 cars to see how I go."

After the test he went to Hockenheim for Round 4 of the EFDA.

Dan Partel remembers that. "This is a funny (peculiar) story. I had given the drivers a warning the day before at the drivers' meeting that *for Christ's sake don't screw up in the first chicane. If one goes, nine of you will go.* Now why did I say nine? I don't know. Anyway Cor Euser [a Dutchman] took the lead but went skating off through the sky blue yonder at the first chicane, obviously braking too late. Then *nine* of them got collected in the accident, including Ayrton." The car was damaged too badly for him to be able to compete in the restart, which Argentinian Victor Rosso won.

It was surely the last year of innocence, when the racing was serious – especially for Senna – but a lot of what surrounded it was rather less so. See the photographs of Senna cracking up with laughter at Hockenheim (page 146).

Yes, and when the race had finished Partel was "called to the victory podium over the tannoy three or four times. There was this argument going on and on in Spanish. The German organisers didn't have the Argentine national anthem and were going to play the British one instead" – Rosso had won in a British car *and* the organisers did have God Save The Queen. But ... "it was the time of the war in the Falklands. I said *you gotta German beer drinking song?* And they said *yes* and I said *put that on!* Victor Rosso got his trophy and the crowd roared."

Bradley was third. "Ayrton made a muck-up at the start [cooking the clutch] and I nearly led him. Cor Euser used a low gear at the start, went off like a bat out of hell, Ayrton stayed with him and Euser took them all out at the first chicane. I was the first to arrive as the accident was happening so I was the first to be able to dive away and see where the accident was going." Hence Bradley's car survived and he found himself on the podium in the re-started race.

Days of laughter: Bradley tells a tale about Hockenheim. "I got to know Ayrton reasonably well because I used to fly to Europe and back, I was more of a professional driver [or rather a driver with a profession] because I'd come back to work all the time whereas the others just tested and tested. I'd often be on the plane with Ayrton and the silliest thing happened coming back from Germany ..."

Bradley, Senna and a Very Important Person in the sport sat side-by-side, with a chap reading *Autosport* seated next to VIP. So VIP asked if he knew anything about motor racing and the chap said "a little bit." It was Ari Vatanen, famous in rallying, but when he revealed who he was VIP asked: "Oh, you're good then, are you?"

Bradley and Senna, who were both perfectly aware of who Vatanen was, were almost choking on the laughter they were trying to suppress.

Bradley captures the atmosphere. When he wasn't flying, he'd take a caravan to the European races "because I liked a bit of comfort while I was there – I'd sleep in the thing quite often – and I'd make a spaghetti for fun. We'd all have this spaghetti, and Ayrton liked my spaghetti so he used to be coming in my caravan. It was a good atmosphere. As soon as the flag dropped it was war. 'Til the flag dropped it was something which I don't think happens in motor racing now: there was fun and personalities. You're not allowed to be a personality now, because either you're so professional you haven't got time to be or you're such a wally it's not worth being a personality!"

Petter Dahl recalls an incident that happened after Senna had won at Oulton Park and journeyed to the Zandvoort circuit in Holland for Round 5 of the EFDA.

"Actually, it was a big mistake from me. It was at the Dutch Grand Prix meeting. A bracket for the seat was cracked and before going to Zandvoort, where the qualifying must have been on the Friday, I had a quick look at the car at Snetterton. I had to weld a bracket onto the car's frame and the clutch pipe ran into a piece of tube where I was welding – what's the name of this material? It's really a sort of plastic. Then I took a ferry and rushed to Zandvoort.

"Ayrton went out for the first qualifying and when he put his foot on the clutch it was like putting his foot against a wall! The clutch was stuck, and that was because this piece of tubing – which was the clutch pipe to the master cylinder – had melted from the heat from when I was welding.

"Because of that, we missed first qualifying *and* of course he was a little bit angry *and* he had never been to Zandvoort before so he didn't know the track at all. For second qualifying the tubing was replaced and he went out there and decided to follow a guy who knew the circuit – to get the lines – and then within six, seven laps he was on pole. After second qualifying it was OK between us. We never spoke about it again.

"After the second qualifying he was very happy with the result and then on Saturday he went on to win the race – and he used to win by between 15 and 20 seconds. It was ridiculous, it wasn't like going to a motor race."

A sort of exhibition?

"Yes."

Zandvoort was on the Saturday. The following day Senna was at Snetterton for Round 13 of the British Championship and Frank Bradley was waiting for him. To appreciate the full context you need the background.

"I am 53 now so I was 37 in 1982," Bradley says. "I didn't start racing until I was 25 because the business – jellied eels – has always been first. My father came out of the Army, made a barrow, filled it with eels, put it outside a pub and sold them, made another barrow, filled that with eels, put mother on it and sold more eels – then he learnt how to cook them and built the business up.

"I left school and learnt engineering, which I didn't want to do, then went and worked in a fruit market for three years, couldn't earn any money so in the end my father said *look I'm going to go to Scotland with eels, you'd better come and work in the business*. I don't like killing things so I didn't really want to do it but in the end I said OK. About the third eel I did, I put the knife across my finger and cut myself so I thought *right, from now on it's the eels or me*.

"My father was really against me motor racing, so much so that he didn't know I was racing for the first three years. I love racing and I am not a stupid person, I realised that I was never going to be a World Champion. I was a competitive driver and I was enjoying myself. I became the old man of Formula 2000."

Bradley adorned and adored Formula Ford 2000 for years (and ended up running it). "The cars were reasonably quick, 0–60mph in probably three and a half seconds. The fastest we went would be Hockenheim, about 135mph.

"No, no, they weren't difficult. The 1600s were sods but no, the 2-litres were lovely cars to drive although because 1982 was the first year with wings and slicks most people took a while to get the best out of them. Most people couldn't believe how far you could push the car, because it was such a lovely car. And the Van Diemen was brilliant. This is again where Ayrton was so special – he climbed in and immediately bang, he'd got it, he was quick."

Anyway …

"I have always been a realist: you can only race if you've got money. All my life I've seen racing drivers who believe God is going to give them money to go motor racing. I didn't."

Instead, Bradley secured major sponsorship from a company called Tredaire, manufacturers of carpet underlays. "It meant I could go racing every weekend and actually earn a lot of money. Tredaire sponsored me for 12 years. In 1982 I had some money for another car and I was going to give it to Ayrton – then this crazy thing inside me said *no give it to a British boy* and I did, I gave it to Rob Cooper. It wasn't a regret, because Rob was a nice fellow, but it was the one time I made a bad business decision. If I'd gone with Ayrton it would have got me an awful lot of coverage – wouldn't have got me any more friendship with Ayrton, because we were friends anyway – but it would have got me a lot more credibility. Ayrton was outstanding because usually everybody won races but nobody else won them all."

Bradley suggests that Fish had an engine advantage. "Ayrton knew there was something wrong because Calvin just wasn't as quick as him. What Ayrton could never understand was how Calvin was so quick down the straight and we all had basically the same cars. It had to be something: Calvin could always catch up on the straight and none of the rest of us could. Gradually it got so that Calvin was pushing him all the time, although Ayrton was such a good driver that even in the circumstances he could still do something about it.

"Anyway, I didn't take a lot of notice of the Formula Ford 1600 people because you tend to have tunnel vision on your own formula. I used to look at the up-and-comings but only when they came to 2000. Some make it that far, some don't.

"When Ayrton started, he did things *right*. If it wasn't right, he wouldn't do it. He went to Dennis Rushen and he knew Dennis was going to do a good job. He always pleaded poverty – well Ralph [Firmin] did! When I got the Tredair money he said why don't you give it to Ayrton? We didn't really know what sort of strength of money Ayrton had. I think this was where his astuteness came through: he didn't want to spend more money than he had to! Therefore, if pleading poverty meant he got a better deal, he got a better deal – although if, at the end of the day, he had to spend money he spent it.

"So when Ayrton came in saying *right you promised the deal,* [the £10,000 for the season] *we'll go for the deal* they all thought how could they justify the money? This is why Ralph wanted Tredair money put into him – because it would have helped."

But now it's 4 July 1982, the 2000 race was the fourth on the card and rain is falling by the second race. Fasten your seat belts for Bradley's Great

Ride. Some 19 drivers assembled on the grid for the 20 laps.

Bradley says, "I've always been good in the wet and I fancied my chances against most people in the wet – wouldn't be too far behind Ayrton sometimes. I knew Snetterton reasonably well and if it stopped raining it didn't take too long for it to dry out. I said to one of my mechanics *I think we can win this on slicks*. He said *you're mad*. I said *no, no, it's going to dry*.

"I wasn't looking at the situation in the same way as some of these other *boys*. If they didn't do well it was a set-back; if I didn't, *sod this race, I haven't done well, I'll have a good race next week*. That was the difference. I had the arrogance of being able to come back home and sell fish and go racing the following week, earn some more money racing and enjoy it. Everything was a plus for me, it was a wonderful way to go motor racing and so when the chance to gamble came along I said *let's go dry tyres*. The others were frightened to change because it was status quo: while everyone stayed on wet tyres the logic was they'd all come wherever they were going to come. Now to me that was silly logic. Where can I gain an advantage?

"We knew that Sidney Offord was the starter. Sidney Offord was a bolshie old sod – a lovely old man but a bolshie old sod! He was very strict on his starting time. And we left it until as late as we could, until almost the 2-minute signal, to start changing the tyres. We knew Sid would be going absolutely mad and throwing mechanics off the grid but we were ready."

Nor, reportedly, was Offord the only martinet present. *Motoring News* carried this description: "The contenders for the Pace 2000 assembled on a damp track. Clerk of the Course Rick Gorne paced the grid determined to avoid any shall I/shan't I dithering from the tyre changers but all the runners seemed content to start on wet covers; all except, that is, Frank Bradley."

Bradley was fine-timing it. "We waited until just the last second so nobody could respond even if they'd wanted to. In one sense we knew we had them beaten."

Petter Dahl remembers "it was raining, everybody was on wets and Frank decided to go on slicks. I didn't see him change but I did see, there on the grid, that he had changed. It's a long time ago, but I do have an impression that most of the people on the grid saw this – that he had gone on to slicks, that he was really gambling."

This was the grid:

Senna

Fish

Andrews

Spence

Bradley

Cooper

Bradley will never forget this: "when the flag dropped I was far behind immediately. I got away from the line, I got to Riches" – see the circuit map opposite – "and I thought *I have done this wrong*. I had a job just to stay on the road. It was wet and the tyres were terrible, everything was terrible. I kept thinking *I have to stay on the road* and at the same time I kept thinking *you've got egg on your face, Frank, but at least keep it on the road.* They must all have been saying *who's this wally going so slowly?"*

It wasn't egg on his face – more a whole omelette.

Bradley, slipping and sliding, watched helplessly as a rolling ball of spray fled into the distance: all the others on their wet tyres, in a pack, churning water. How much of this Bradley glimpsed is uncertain because, yard by yard, the pack moved further away from him.

"The first five laps were such a nightmare that they nearly lapped me! When I was coming round I looked in my mirrors, saw them at Coram and I had just reached level with the pits before the start line. I was in major trouble and that was after only five laps."

Motoring News reported: "At the start Calvin Fish got away very well to lead into the first corner, a position he held despite the close attention of Ayrton da Silva until lap 5. Then da Silva found a gap and squeezed ahead and quickly established a distinct lead."

Far, far behind this move, which must have seemed the decisive moment of the whole race, Bradley battled on alone. "After those five laps the track started to dry – still no good for me except only that I did stop losing ground as much as I had been and they weren't catching me *at the same rate*. I still thought they were going to come up and go past by lap ten."

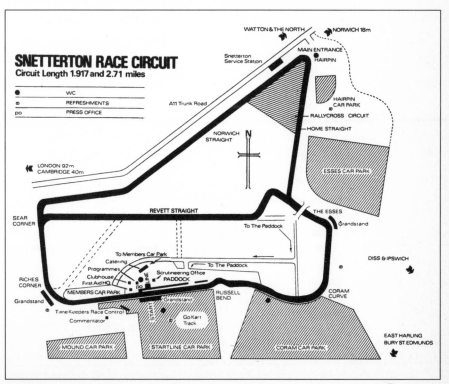

Wrong.

"By lap ten I had started to hold my own. After the tenth lap it started to dry more and then the car started to work."

Motoring News: "Before half distance, with the track drying rapidly, it was obvious that the leaders, particularly da Silva, were intent on conserving their tyres, although Fish, who had closed on the back of the tail of the Brazilian, was not allowing the leader to slow his pace as much as he would have wished. Bradley of course had no such tyre problems ..."

Bradley would catch Senna but not quite yet. "It was just a matter then of how brave I was, and I felt braver and braver because the car felt better and better. It was lap 15 when I started to see them again" – the rolling ball of *lower* spray betraying where the pack was. The gap was reducing. "I was coming round Sear onto the straight and I could just about see something at the end of the straight, though still a long way away."

Because a racing car is so taut and so evenly matched into tiny fractions of time, a huge advantage like wet tyres crosses over into a huge disadvantage when the track dries.

Motoring News: "Bradley began a run from seventh which saw him reach third by three-quarter distance."

Seventh? "I was getting more and more confident and I'm an arrogant bastard when it comes down to it. I was confident in the car and I was confident in what I could do. I was getting more and more grip and they were getting less and less. All I had to do was pick them off and my main worry was that I was going to run out of time to pick them all off."

So Bradley picked 'em off and picked 'em off and was third by lap 15, bringing him to the ultimate problem: Fish's hounding of Senna had drawn the duo clear of the pack *but* the lingering spray wasn't now visible to show where the duo were because the track was virtually dry.

Each yard Bradley covered, counting the laps down towards the finish from around lap 15, was a gain to him. "Because Ayrton and Calvin had gone – they had 20 seconds on everyone else – they were the dot in the distance. When I'd got past the rest I still had this pair miles away."

It moved into a classical confrontation.

"Last two laps they – Fish and Ayrton – were *there*. I'd caught them, but the difference now was that Ayrton was hard, Calvin was dirty. I'd been overtaking everybody else, no problem. I caught Calvin – in my mind it's a fact and I'm not frightened to say it – and Calvin tried to put me out because he knew I was coming through; but, the last two laps, I was eight seconds a lap quicker. *Eight seconds*. It's night and day.

"It's not even motor racing ... it's being in a Ferrari against a Hillman Minx. When I caught Calvin I thought *hold on, I'm so fast that all I'm worried about is that I've miscounted the laps down from 15*. Was there still another lap to go, because if there was, I had to be able to do it. *Nothing's going to stop me unless* – and I'd seen Ayrton before, of course – *he tries to put me off on the straight or somewhere*.

"So what I did, I got Calvin – or I went to do Calvin and he went to put me off. I held back, I waited, just accelerated past him, blasted past him. Ayrton was that bit in front and Ayrton was the one I was more worried about. As I came to Ayrton I thought *be careful, be careful* but I must give him credit: I '*hit*' him so quick and so hard that he surrendered. I think he thought *well …*

"I overtook him at Sear, went straight past. He held his line, he kept in – and, from Sear to the line, I think I pulled eight seconds. That's how quick I was going. I was lapping at one minute 9 seconds, they were lapping at one minute 15 seconds or something crazy like that. Calvin had tried to catch Ayrton during the race but Ayrton was thinking and saved his tyres. Calvin's tyres went, and then he couldn't stay with Ayrton. Ayrton still had a bit of life in his tyres – he *thought* the race whereas Calvin had driven with his balls. And that was it – the only time I led Ayrton Senna, although I nearly had that time at Hockenheim when Cor Euser crashed.

"Afterwards at Snetterton we chatted about it and on the rostrum Ayrton said *well done* and I replied *well, I was lucky*. He said *no, no, you were the best man today, you were the best man*. I replied *well, I chose the tyres right*. He said *no, no, you were the best man, you did it right*.

While Fish looked scornful, Senna was almost laughing."I think if it had been Calvin who'd won it, Ayrton would have been disappointed, but because it was me we saw his sense of humour again: *the Old Man's beaten me!*"

The photographer Mike Dixon was there and offers this judgement. "I've already spoken about Senna's car control in 1981 and how amazing it was. Thinking back to this race at Snetterton, Bradley started way, way back in the field but the track dried pretty rapidly. Every one of the front runners, including Senna, were desperately trying to find wet patches to cool their tyres and there was no way they could do any speed at all because the tyres were going off at an horrendous rate but Senna kept in front of Bradley for a long time, really on sheer determination. Interestingly – if Bradley hadn't got past at Sear – Senna would probably have held him off to the end."

Petter Dahl remains convinced it was a *very* close run thing. "If the rain had continued for two or three minutes more than it did, Bradley wouldn't have made it, because when it started to dry it was drying up very quickly. In the last laps Senna was fighting very hard, the car was all over the track and the tyres were completely gone, no treads at all left. Very bad. Bradley was storming through for the last five or six laps and he didn't beat Senna by much."

Bradley finished at 24m 46.4s, Senna at 3.6, Fish at 4.1s. Fastest lap: Bradley 1m 09.5s (99.30mph).

Thence to Castle Combe, where Senna won, Snetterton where he won, and three successive EFDA rounds – Hockenheim, the Osterreichring in Austria and the Jyllandsring in Denmark. Senna won Hockenheim and the Osterreichring a week later. Dan Partel has an anecdote about that.

"He'd virtually taken the championship in Austria and it was about seven o'clock in the evening. We had quite a heavy conversation, in the sense that it was my first time to concede that he *was* a star. After all, he was now the champion-elect and my influence was over, other than as a friend or a 'school teacher'. There was no reason not to support him. He'd done an incredible job to [virtually] win the championship. I said *you've seen Formula 1, you know what it's really about, is this what you want?* He never really answered the question. It was kind of one of those rare moments that you go through."

The championship was sealed in Denmark. Senna was extremely happy and for once had a drink or two more than he ought to have done. Naughtily, Partel says: "I don't know if it was his first sex outside of marriage, but he was out all night long. I remember another thing. Creighton Brown (a McLaren director) flew in to land on the Jyllandsring and as the plane came in the cars were running on the track, not the 2000s but some other class: a little plane, it was windy as hell and they were crabbing and everything else."

Creighton Brown confirms the hair-raising landing. "Will I ever forget it? I was sitting next to John Watson and I can tell you he was even more scared than I was. The plane flew out from Copenhagen, a single-engined light plane with an exceptional pilot and to be honest I still don't know how he got it down. He was quite extraordinary.

"No, we hadn't gone to look at Senna. We [McLaren] had taken across the MP4 which Watson was driving in the Formula 1 World Championship. It was a time when Unipart was one of our sponsors and I think they were sponsoring a demonstration by the car. So we took the car over and Wattie did a few laps to please the crowd. That was the reason I was there – and of course Ayrton won his championship at the same time, which was very, very nice.

"I had seen Senna before, all season. I'd met him at the end of the previous year in 1600 when he was introduced to my wife, who is Brazilian, and I by Chico Serra, who had raced for us in Formula 2 the previous year. So we met Ayrton then and I saw him race many times in Formula Ford 2000 during 1982 because certainly while he was racing here in the UK he was on the same programme as myself. I was racing Clubmans' Supersports and very often it was the same circuit so, as we got to know him a little bit because of the Brazilian connection, I always made a point of watching him race.

"It was at the end of the year that in fact I went to Ron Dennis and said *look, there's a young Brazilian driver in 2000 who's just absolutely phenomenal and we really ought to have a look at him.* Ron said *yes, I've already taken note, I've seen the results and everything. He does seem to have a remarkable talent."*

Ron Dennis can't remember exactly how he and Senna first made contact. "But however it was, it led to him coming to see me at McLaren to discuss his career. At that stage it was just prior to him starting Formula 3. He explained what he was doing and I offered to pay for this Formula 3 season, conditional on him signing an option to drive in our Formula 1 team. He hadn't driven F3 yet. Amusingly he declined and said that if I guaranteed him a physical F1 drive – paid for, and therefore free to him – he would sign this option. Of course he sat there as a Formula 2000 driver, and I sat there as a Formula 1 team owner, but the only way he would give *me* an option is if I gave him a firm commitment! To his credit, he had the confidence and self-belief – because that is what it was – that he would be able to demonstrate in Formula 3 a level of success that would make him attractive to a Formula 1 team. That's what happened."

Incidentally, it's time to clear up once and for all a backwater rumour that Dennis actually signed Senna on some magical contract so that McLaren could wait for several years while he matured and gained experience, then call him into their F1 team. Dennis stresses that no such contract existed. End of rumour.

Thence to Thruxton, Oulton Park and Silverstone – Senna won them all – and Mondello Park at Naas, County Kildare, for the final round of the EFDA. As with Bradley, to appreciate the full context of the man Senna now faced, Joey Greenan, you need a little bit of background.

"I'm from the north of Ireland and in 1982 I was 33," Greenan says. "I started early but I didn't go into single seater racing until I was about 26. That was in an eight-year-old car and I was immediately a front-runner."

The last days of innocence: During a wet race Greenan noticed that part of the rear of Tommy Byrne's car was "being held together by a wire coathanger!" Byrne visited Greenan in Belfast and "when he sat down the holes in his shoes had cardboard in them. My wife took him up to the corner shop and bought him a pair of shoes." Greenhan remembers Eddie Jordan on the Naas dual carriageway "towing his racing car to Mondello – didn't even have a trailer." Innocent days? Guilty, m'lud, too. Jordan confirms "we used to tow it off the roll-hoop [roll bar], totally against the law, and that's true …"

Into this different world came … Senna.

The organisers of the Mondello event chose a novel way of publicising it. "They decided," Greenan says, "to show everyone the 2000 cars."

It began with a reception at the Mansion House – "which is like the Buckingham Palace or the 10 Downing Street of Dublin – and there was a considerable amount of beverage on board. I would say virtually everyone who attended had a few toots in them, everyone was in a boisterous mood."

After this, the idea was to parade the cars down the main streets, led by the police. Crowds turned out to watch. "It was to be a procession and it turned into … a little bit of a race. The cars were to be in a line. You'd pull out of the carpark of the Mansion House to get onto the main road and, instead of just following you, maybe the driver behind would let you get four or five seconds down the road and then give his car a blast.

"Er … between you and me there would have been a few toots taken but, for me, I wasn't a big drinker." And then of course drinking and driving wasn't the same? "In Ireland in those days if you were stopped by the police for drinking and driving they would literally have driven you home and driven your car home too. No-one was really done for drinking and driving in Ireland at that stage. It was part of the culture."

Frank Bradley (of course) was in the midst of this 'street race.' "Mondello Park were trying to promote the circuit and promote everything, so they closed the streets of Dublin and we all got up behind the police and did a lap. The police were such good fun, they said *let's have another lap* and the second lap we all went like dingbats – Ayrton, everyone – and it was fabulous, we'd never had fun like it. We were going through the streets of Dublin and people were standing at the side of the street and we were going by them like lunatics. The outcome of it was that the police got such a bollocking it wasn't true – but were told *we have to give you a bollocking* [for form's sake]. What a wonderful way to go motor racing!"

When everyone moved on to Mondello Park the next day Greenan got down to business. "Not only did I drive the cars, I was mechanic that weekend too. I had the driving of three cars" – he was also driving Formula Ford 1600s.

"The 2000 practice started, I went out and I was quick. Senna, then seeing the way the whole thing was going, stayed very, very – what could I say? – with a far away look in his eye. He never really spoke as such and many times he sat on the front wheel of that yellow Van Diemen and looked across at my three cars. He'd watch me getting overalls on, working on the gears, even changing an engine, then going out and achieving pole position for the 2000 and 1600 race. Dennis Rushen I had known and also I had become desperately friendly over the days with Ayrton's mechanic, a dark-coloured guy. He and I were real chatty but Senna never became chatty. I use the words *nearly aloof*. He was, however, immediately quick in the car, a works car, of course.

"I knew myself that he was very, very shrewd. He intensively watched every single driver" – the locals and what were described as a *foreign invasion*: all Senna's European counterparts – "and he realised that there was only one danger to him, I felt, and that was myself."

There were two kinds of tyres, one used for the British rounds and the other for the European rounds. "They were," Greenan says, "of different construction. The rear tyre was the same but the front tyre was much larger and, as a result, the times achieved on the European tyres were much quicker. The cars had little extra wings which I hadn't got, so I made up my own from aluminium that we had in my transporter and we were able to get them on. Senna went out and did time, I went out and equalled or bettered it, Senna went out and bettered it …

"We went out for the last session, from memory around tea time on the Saturday. The one thing I knew was that the air started to get more dense because you had the dampness coming in – it was September – and the cars could always pick up 200 revs more.

"Senna was very switched on. For such a young person, he really thought everything through. I remember following him as we went out and I do believe we lowered the lap record at Mondello by over one second. He went across the line first, from memory I think with a time of 56.5 seconds and the record was maybe 57.2 or something around that. I followed him over the line on the same time as him but he, having achieved it first, got the pole position. I was alongside him on the front row. At this point I still didn't think there was a danger, the only thing I did think was that he was backed by the factory and I was a privateer."

One evening – it may well have been this Saturday – an official of the meeting called Alex Sinclair was staying "at the Town House Hotel in Naas and Senna was staying there too, with his parents. That struck me as unusual, because normally drivers just have hangers-on round them. I thought this was a family effort and I also thought *this must be costing them a fortune.* They obviously had money because his mother was dripping with gold and jewellery."

On race day a young lass, Jacky Noonan, was at Mondello Park. "We used to get dragged down as children because my dad would be helping out with the general organisation. There was always a great buzz. You'd feel a little bit important because you were helping out, photocopying and running round with the time sheets down to the pits and paddock. I enjoyed looking at all the cars, but as a 16-year-old I was more interested in looking at the guys.

"I had heard of Ayrton Senna. Everyone was quite excited because his was the name going round as the driver to look out for, and it was the big thing having him there. More than that, the 2000s were the bigger cars so they were the most exciting. My dad sent me off to get his autograph. I was probably one of these annoying kids who gets in everyone's way, actually. I remember I was wearing one of those Indian skirts with tassels all around the end of it. When I went to hand him a time sheet, he said *ah, here comes the girl with the tablecloth dress …*"

On the Sunday, Greenan "had the Formula Ford 1600 race, which I won, and that took place only about one hour before the 2000. The crowds were huge, people wanted your autograph, people wanted interviews, so when I got back to the 2000 car there wasn't much more than 15 or 20 minutes to the start of the race." Greenan suspected his car had weaknesses but no longer had time to do much about them.

"Senna made a mistake on the warm-up lap – actually I seem to remember there were two warm-up laps. He went off at, I think, Dunlop corner [see map overleaf]. It was unusual. He was very tense. I was more relaxed and maybe if anything even a little bit tired because I'd won a fairly difficult race within the previous hour."

When you say he went off, you mean he put two wheels off?

"Oh no, he went right off, four wheels off as we were warming the tyres up. It was even mentioned by Pat Duffy, who was in that race as well, that he thought *God, this fellow Senna is not invincible, there's a chance we'll be able to beat him.* But I always maintained that great drivers are all very nervous. You practise in the morning and you never show nerves because you go out singly, but when you are on the grid with 20 cars around you it's

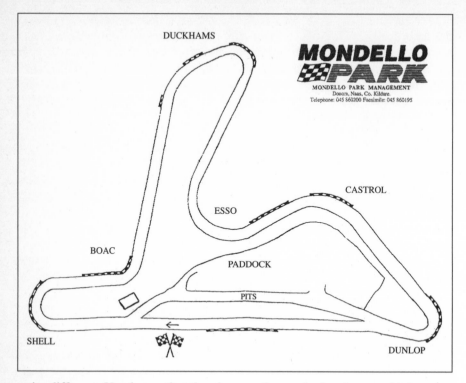

quite different. You know that the chance of a crash, the chance of injury are very high. I am very nervous on the grid. Once I got round the first corner I became calm and collected but when I went to the grid, if I did not have that nervous feeling inside me I knew I wasn't going to have a good day. I'd say it was the same for Senna.

"He was so hyped up and probably he was warming his brakes, maybe he was testing the track, maybe trying a different line. He was special and maybe he did something like that: go to the outer side of the circuit to see if it was *marbley* there or there was grip or whatever.

"Reflecting now, and thinking about what David Kennedy said when he went on a 12-hour flight to Japan and Senna was on the plane and talked for hours of how he was beaten in one race by Calvin Fish – well, if anybody spends hours explaining the reason why they were beaten it shows they were passionate about what they were doing.

"I remember we looked across at each other on the grid and then the flag went down. Senna got a slight lead into the first corner and I absolutely went for it round the outside of him. Into the second corner he sort of drove the car towards me – I think to intimidate me to lift off – but I didn't, I kept my foot in, got round and slid the car across his bow into the lead. I thought to myself *this is it, I've done it*. I also thought it would be a tough race but I knew Mondello well and it was a circuit where, at the sort of speed we were doing, passing was going to be very difficult even without driving defensively.

"He came up alongside on the first lap, pulled out of my slipstream and he actually got half a car length alongside down the straight, braked late, smoke coming from the tyres but then tucked in and I'm still in the lead, still feeling confident despite the fact that this was going to be a long race.

"Second lap I left maybe a little too much room on the inside of Shell corner and he nearly got by on the inside – which I don't even think I realised until I saw it on TV afterwards. We had another good lap, no problems, same thing again – he came up alongside – then into the third lap we come out of the corner which was called BOAC. It was undulating, a circuit very like Brands Hatch. I went for third gear, it missed and if I'd have got it in a second time that would have been OK but three times I tried for it and three times it didn't go in. Senna got by me on the straight. On the TV film you can see him arriving into Duckhams, past me before the corner. Lots of people thought he passed me round the outside of Duckhams but he didn't.

"David Kennedy judged it very well. He says afterwards on the television that he believed I'd have had to make a mistake or something happen to the car because either Senna was mad to try and pass Joey Greenan round the outside or he was bloody good.

"The one thing I knew was that once he had passed I was never going to be able to get up there again. He'd have had to have had an accident or another off and, to be honest with you, I was quite comfortable in second. I'll tell you what it was: I didn't race on at speed because at this stage my mind had started to work towards the weakness in the car. All I was interested in was preserving the gearbox and preserving the car to get to the finish in second place. If anything I was easy on the car. I could have raced on closer to him but it wouldn't have gained me anything. I wasn't going to be able to overtake him."

It finished Senna 19m 32.7s, Greenan at 18.5 seconds.

"After the race, that's the first time Senna had spoken to me. He shook hands with me, he was ecstatic and Dennis Rushen said to me that day *you know Joey, you're looking at a World Champion.*"

David Kennedy remembers "the first time I met Ayrton was at Mondello. I was doing the television commentary and I interviewed him. He was Ayrton da Silva then, just a kid from Brazil but he made an outstanding manoeuvre on the outside of a corner [this, delightfully, contradicts Greenan, above] and you know people just don't go round the outside. In the interview he was a very shy, quiet young Brazilian fellow, no beacon over him, no light over him, you know. There wasn't a hole in the clouds with the light shining down on him."

Yet.

A week later Senna journeyed to Kalmar, Sweden, to take part in the World Karting Championship. It was the one title which had eluded him and that rankled (as it always would). He finished fourteenth and returned to England in a filthy mood for the final round of the 2000 Championship, at Brands Hatch. He and Rushen became involved in a lively dispute over how the car should be set up and, uniquely, Senna didn't seem interested in what happened in the race.

Petter Dahl feels that "one reason was that he had already tied up the championship. No-one could catch him. I remember he was in a bad mood. That race was the last time I worked with him but not the last time I spoke to him. The year after – 1983 – when he was in Formula 3 I met him a couple of times. In those days I used to go to England quite often and I'd be at the British Grand Prix when he'd reached Formula 1. He didn't like to speak too much with people during race weekends if it was not necessary. He said *hello* and we had a chat but he was always concentrating, even in Formula 3. When he was working, that was what he did. He didn't want to get disturbed with things."

Senna started the Brands race from the second row of the grid and, soon enough, was circling in second place behind Fish. Then, Rushen feels, the urge to win banished all memories of Kalmar and arguments over the car. Senna began to go very quickly indeed and it is something many people remember: how he deployed his skill – his balance, the late braking, the economy through the corners, how he wielded the car like a scalpel to cut through back-markers. He broke the lap record but in the end Fish stayed a whisker ahead – 0.8 of a second.

That was not Senna's final race of 1982, however. It would be at Thruxton in a couple of weeks, for a new team and at the next step up the ladder, Formula 3. His career in Formula Ford 2000 was already passing into folklore but before we leave it for ever here are the ruminations of Rushen and Bradley, beginning with Rushen.

"The guy was awesome. It was so easy for him. He could go out round Snetterton, come in and say *oh, my right rear tyre is graining a bit* because he'd looked in the mirror and seen it. He had time to do that. Or he might say *oh, I think this tyre needs a couple more pounds of pressure.* I saw him as a World Champion even then, no question about it. I told people he would be. You see, the driving came so naturally to him that he had time to think about all the others things which were happening. He did not have to think *oh my God, here comes a corner* because he'd instinctively sorted that out the corner before."

Was he complete in every way like Alain Prost?

"It's a difficult one to quantify. Prost always did just enough but Harry wanted it at all costs. He'd do qualifying laps nobody could match and Prost would actually say *well, I can't go that quick* and not worry about it. Ayrton didn't have that sort of mind. If it poured with rain Prost would say *to hell with driving in this, I'm not doing it* which, when you look at it now, was quite smart really.

"Prost knew when to quit. He seemed to have slightly more of the whole picture of grand prix racing, and perhaps more of the whole picture of a life, but in terms of sheer speed it was Harry. Nobody came near him and I don't think they will. I'm not talking in terms of speed but the impact he made on so many people."

A thought from Bradley about Senna's apparent arrogance. "Ayrton was determined to be a professional driver. Therefore he had tunnel vision and while other people would switch off, he never switched off, even in those days. He'd be looking at things, he'd be watching things. This is why I think it annoyed him so much with Calvin: because he couldn't understand how Calvin could stay with him. In theory Calvin couldn't, but he did, so *how is he doing it?* Ayrton was looking at Calvin's car all the time and asking *how can Calvin run an eighth more wing than me and do the same speed down the straight?* That was especially true at a place like Hockenheim because at Hockenheim you used to virtually take the wings off. In fact I think Ayrton was one of the ones who did take the wings off once to try it – completely off!" [The wings, which use the airflow passing over the car to press it to the ground for adhesion, are vital for speed through corners but a handicap along the straights as forcing the car down slows it.]

"Hockenheim is a circuit where you've got the Stadium Section [the snake-line contortion before the start-finish straight] which is a compromise in terms of setting but the rest of the circuit is straights and, by running his wings ridiculously flat – or even taking them off – Ayrton could gain so much down those straights. Calvin used to run with wings. Through the Stadium Section the wings made a massive difference so through there Calvin was that much quicker but it didn't make any sense because Calvin wasn't losing it on the straights.

"Ayrton let his hair down with us but he wasn't a socialiser. He didn't have time to socialise. His English wasn't that good but, again, he was a very astute person, he'd sit and think and work it out. Whereas you and I might answer immediately, he'd think and then answer. His English wasn't as bad as I think he made out, either. When he was racing with us, and he was in the caravan letting his hair down, he was a *person* and he could speak very good English, which makes him cleverer than people assessed even then."

In other words, Senna could use words – or maintain he lacked the words – as the occasion demanded. Socially he was fluent, but in front of the stewards after naughtiness on the track he was *I-not-understanding*. It's only a thought: in all human activity, especially motor racing, if you have a weapon, use it. The others will.

"There was nothing wrong with his sense of humour but in those days there was no such thing as people being groomed for PR. Let's say he was before his time in that respect, clever enough to think about PR as well as doing other things."

What did you think of him?

"Well the thing at the time was that we couldn't make out how he could keep winning. No, I didn't think he was as special as he was because I'd never met anyone that special before and I had no comparison. The only thing I could say was that he won everything, so he obviously was special!"

A postscript from Merrilees. "When Ayrton was doing Formula Ford 2000, at one stage he and Gugelmin had some good fun between them. It was the end of the year and all the racing was done. I think Gugelmin was testing a works 1600 car. He and Ayrton set off together and Ayrton came back with tears in his eyes from laughing. Gugelmin never reappeared and the cars had a whole load of corn in them. They'd been buggering around out the back of the circuit and Ayrton had put Gugelmin off – so there was some fun to be had but that was out of hours, the championships finished, time for a bit of mucking about.

"Senna raced for himself and anyone who worked for him will never have a word said against him. What the public felt was neither here nor there. He was dedicated to racing. Either Ralph or someone else asked him how on earth he managed to set all those pole positions and Senna said *well, I go out, I do the practice, I think about it and I concentrate on one small thing I can change that will have an effect. I make that change then I go out and drive to my maximum.* People inside racing knew what he was like and that's all that really mattered to him – and quite rightly."

Then and now

The interviews for this chapter took place in early August 1998, except the one with Dennis Rushen, which was conducted by phone in 1995 for a magazine article when he was in Florida. That Christmas – 1994 – Rushen had taken part in a BBC TV tribute to Senna and when it was transmitted his wife recorded it for him. He'd found talking about Senna no great problem but even many months later was quite unable to bring himself to watch the video tape, to see Senna again, hear Senna again. And Imola: "I don't think he should have driven at all. I think he knew he shouldn't drive. I think he should have walked away and that's very easy to say afterwards – what if he'd won the race by half a lap? Anyway, I think Prost would have walked away from it in the same circumstances."

August 1998, and Frank Bradley was living, temporarily, in a small house next to the eel business near Heathrow. At 53 he was still hooked on motorsport. "Did the Festival two years ago and I'll do it again this year." The Festival is the FF1600 Festival at Brands Hatch, of course, and it is confined not just to kids but to crazy kids. You should have seen the glorious glint in his eye when I queried why he'd still want to go to the Festival. "To me life is about optimism. It's better to do something and tomorrow be sorry you did it than be sorry you didn't do it at all, because you can't backdate tomorrow." He also said, "I couldn't believe Senna could die. I thought he was too special."

Bradley has directed me towards Peter Merrilees, who now works for Formula Palmer Audi, *a highly competitive series of races run by Jonathan Palmer, the former Formula 1 driver. The headquarters is a cluster of buildings on the rim of an airfield north of Bedford. It has a familiar feel because Thruxton, Snetterton, and Silverstone were hewn from just this: bomber bases. Merrilees has gone out but one of the workers, Sarah Taylor, sits and explains that she was a journalist in 1983, mostly working for foreign magazines. I wondered what she, as a woman, made of Senna. "He didn't really stand out as anybody special from a woman's point of view at that stage but you've got to remember how young he was. Very slight. His physique changed a great deal in the years following that." Palmer appears, much closer to being a middle-aged businessman than a driver who raced in the company of Senna from 1984 to 1989. Merrilees appears, bustling with bonhomie. Later, the talking done, I'm working my way back across the runways and, as if from nowhere, a red Audi on some intensive testing goes past like a missile, the driver taking care not to lift his foot from the accelerator.*

Senna would have understood – perfectly.

Chapter 3

The simple facts of life

THAT LATE AUTUMN DAY in 1982 Dick Bennetts, who ran the Formula 3 team West Surrey Racing, was stumping round on crutches with his leg in plaster. Not long before, the team and their driver Quique Mansilla had been testing at Snetterton prior to the final round of the championship at Thruxton. "We tried an engine tweak and it was good, worth a tenth of a second or so, and we took the decision to leave it in for Thruxton. However, when we got there Thruxton was harder on an engine than Snetterton and it detonated. We had to do an engine change between qualifying sessions and I dropped the crane on my foot. I was in plaster but I thought *I'm not missing the first chance to run Ayrton*. I knew of him because Dennis Rushen and I had had a chat. Dennis rang me to say *this is next year's man, you need this man*. I'd kept an eye on him."

As luck would have it there was a non-championship Formula 3 race, televised by the BBC, at Thruxton on 13 November. It provided an ideal opportunity for West Surrey to offer Senna a drive.

"When I first met him I thought he was very professional, quiet," Bennetts says. "I'd spoken to him a few weeks before we tested and he'd been over for a couple of meetings. He was having his arm twisted to run with other teams but he reasoned that if we could get Mansilla up there – and Senna didn't rate Mansilla – then we must have a pretty good car or a pretty good team, or both. Senna reckoned that if we'd won five races and finished second in the championship with a kid like Mansilla who hadn't done slicks and wings – he'd jumped straight from Formula Ford 1600 to Formula 3, a big transition in those days – then we were all right. That's what was in the back of Ayrton's mind and that's why he wanted to run with us.

"The very first time Ayrton drove for West Surrey was October 28, a dry and cold day. We started at 9.15 in the morning. It was just a test because the race would be at Thruxton and this was a couple of weeks before it, in fact a two-day test, 28 and 29. We'd been there for the final championship round with Quique.

"Now we'd set the car up and we hadn't made any adjustments, because you always do a weather-check run to make sure everything's OK, checking the ride heights – which were an inch and 4/5ths, now they're all metric. Senna did that. Then we've sent him out again and he's dialling himself into the car. If you look at the lap times, [see below] he goes out and we don't start timing until he comes round and crosses the line. He does a very slow recce lap finding his way round – the 1m 33.46s, which appears as Lap 2. Very sensible. Some guys would go a lot quicker than that but he was having a look around, having a feel.

"Then he's down to 1 minute 17 seconds, then he takes three seconds off that and he's found a pace: 14.9s, 14.2s, 14.3s, then he's done a slow lap –

Dick Bennetts' meticulous record sheet of Senna's first drive for West Surrey – testing at Thruxton. (Courtesy of Dick Bennetts)

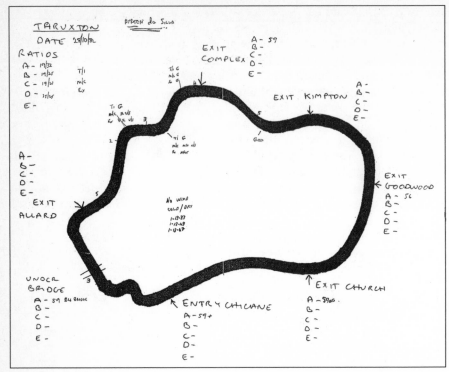

The circuit map of Thruxton – a very visual way for Bennetts to see what was going on. (Courtesy of Dick Bennetts)

ah, traffic. You see the little letter *T* just next to the Laps column – that means traffic, and that's why the 14.3 was a tenth slower. He must have had bad traffic so he's come in. If I spotted it myself, or he came in and told me, I'd put the *T* there. Traffic does make a difference even if you just have to move off line or whatever. Incidentally, I circle each fastest lap.

"Then he went out again and on only his fourteenth lap got down to a 1 minute 13.33s. It's amazing for somebody to be that consistent, especially when they are new to Thruxton, which is not the easiest place. And that time stood because it was early in the morning. As it gets warmer, the times get slower."

Reproduced here too [see above] is an annotated circuit map of Thruxton on this morning when a new world was opening up for Senna. Bennetts explains that he had found such annotations simple, graphic and effective: the driver either filled them in or else talked Bennetts round and he filled them in. This made the driver think and look, and helped Bennetts understand what was going right and wrong.

"I got them to do circuits. It's my writing. You take them round and ask them what problems they have on each corner, what gears, where they're shifting gears and so on. These days you don't have to because it's all on computers" – Bennetts brandishes pages of print-outs, all tight columns of figures – "but then it was the equivalent of the ledger and the quill pen!

"The letters A, B, C, D, E were so you could put different comments. If you wanted to show you'd tried a different set-up on the car, each corner on the first set-up would be A, then if you changed the set-up each corner would be under the Bs etc."

Bennetts also recorded drivers' general observations and gives a typical example from Senna during a qualifying session somewhere: *"the track's wetter* – because all we can ever see in the pit lane is in front of us, we don't know what the track is like elsewhere – *visor smeared.* I'd add a note: *he was on worn tyres, not brand new."*

With all your knowledge, how do you evaluate this map now?

"It's very basic compared to what we have these days. You can't really tell about speed and so on, all you can relate to is his lap times relative to the next guy, and he was already immediately on the pace of Quique. That meant his first time out in a Formula 3 car – apart from when Eddie Jordan had given him a run at Silverstone – well, first time out in F3 at Thruxton, the 13.33s, is blindingly quick, and that's on old tyres."

It can happen in the junior formulae that one bloke's outstanding but it doesn't mean he's going to be a World Champion.

"It doesn't and we didn't know; and in a sense it wasn't really the first test of him because we'd been on the front row two weeks earlier with the same car so therefore we knew it wasn't badly set up. However, he got in that car and the thing which impressed was: new to F3, brand new to Thruxton in F3 – obviously he'd been round in Formula Ford 1600 and 2000 – but to do that time on his fourteenth lap was outstanding."

How could he, straight in, bang?

"I think it's from starting from a very young age in karting. A lot of kids start karting and don't make it to the grade there that he did – it's that *something* you're given, self-belief, raw ability and intelligence all rolled into one.

"To get in the car, to give the feedback that he did, no fuss, just get on with the job, drive it, then get out, sit down and go through things methodically was, I thought for a kid his age, exceptional.

"Then we took him to Snetterton on 9 November for more testing, then it was the actual race. It must have been a one-day meeting, qualifying and race on the one day. [Bennetts consults his sheets] *Ayrton da Silva, Engine number 8211, pole position by seven tenths of a second."*

It was the fastest Formula 3 lap ever driven round Thruxton and Senna won the race easily enough beating a Swede, Bengt Tragardh, by 13.1 seconds. He'd drive for West Surrey in 1983 but now, the 1982 season completed, he caught the plane home for sunshine, his mother's cooking and a chance to meet his friends. A bare 11 months before this, he had virtually abandoned racing after the Formula Ford 1600 season and joined the family business, game over. Now he was but a step away from Formula 1. As he wintered in Sao Paulo it must have been in his thoughts, and perhaps all the time.

When he returned to England for the 1983 season he'd made a decision to change his name. Da Silva is, evidently, a common name in Brazil and he simply lopped it off. He preferred Ayrton Senna, Senna being his mother's maiden name.

A great deal of the story of 1983 remains profoundly interesting, not least this extraordinary glimpse of Senna exploring possibilities which nobody else could. It happened at Brands Hatch in May, at which point Senna had won *all seven* of the opening Marlboro British Formula 3 Championship races. The witnesses included journalist Jeremy Shaw.

"During qualifying I was watching at the bottom of Paddock Hill Bend and about half way through the session Ayrton came flying into Paddock. From my view I could see him zipping over the crest and I thought *bloody hell, this is going to be a big accident*. He got down towards the apex and then realised he was going way too fast and threw the car sideways and aborted the lap. He carried on round but when he reached the pit lane he didn't go in, he came round and did the same again: he entered Paddock way too fast but got a bit closer to the apex, then aborted it. The third time round he'd nailed it. He came through that corner light years quicker than anybody else was coming through there.

"After the session I went straight to the West Surrey transporter. By the time I got there he was just sitting down with Dick Bennetts to do the de-brief – and it was always a very, very detailed de-brief. So I walked in as they were starting and I said *look I hate to interrupt. You know me, and you know I don't normally interrupt but Dick, whatever he tells you about Paddock, he c-a-n-n-o-t go through there any quicker. I don't know what he was doing, but whatever it was, that was it*.

"Senna looked up. He sort of gave a flicker of a smile and slowly said *yup*. I asked him what he had been doing and it turned out he had been taking it in fourth gear and it was definitely a third gear corner. He'd figured out how to take it in fourth and he'd been building himself up to do that. Then he'd done it.

"This is beyond normal people. It's a natural ability. You can't teach anybody that. You either have that extra little bit of determination to make it happen or you don't, and that's what makes the truly outstanding drivers. There's two or three, I'd say, in the 30 years I've been closely involved and I'm not really sure who the others might be. He is the outstanding one as far as I am concerned. It was apparent right from the start in Formula Ford 1600. There was something about him: not a superior air but just an air about the guy that was different, and you *know ...*"

Between Brands Hatch and Round 11 at Cadwell Park on 19 June, Senna raced two rounds at Silverstone, winning the first but spinning off twice in the second. Martin Brundle – driving for Jordan – won. Brundle and Eddie Jordan were applying pressure now and it was beginning to tell.

"At Cadwell in qualifying," Bennetts says, "Senna was very quick and apparently someone timing him in a different place to the official timing points had him four-tenths quicker than pole, but he didn't quite complete the lap. He was so confident up through The Mountain" – a steep hill section beside the paddock – "but he hung a wheel over the side, the right rear. It meant that when he went to turn in to go up The Mountain he didn't have the steering, but – believing the car would come round – he kept his foot hard on the throttle and went straight into the marshals' post." (In 1989, when Senna was checking the manuscript of *The Hard Edge of Genius* where I described how a marshal inside the post "had to be treated for bruises and shock," Senna wrote in the margin *Never realized the situation with marshal!!* The implication was that, had he known, he'd have found out how the marshal was and apologised.)

"Anyway," Bennetts says, "not having spare cars, we had an early bath that night at Cadwell and I was home at 2.15pm Sunday afternoon."

The pressure mounted. He had an accident at Snetterton, won at Silverstone and was second at Donington.

He also tried a Formula 1 car for the first time at Donington – a Williams. "He couldn't wait," Gugelmin says. "That test was unbelievable because straight away he was really fast. Something ridiculous like his third lap he was quicker than Jonathan Palmer [the Williams test driver] had ever been at Donington. Frank Williams called him in immediately and told Charlie Moody, the mechanic working on the car, *put another 20 gallons in that car to keep his value down!* Ayrton never knew this, but they did put more fuel in the car, keeping the car heavy. He went a bit slower and other teams wouldn't try to get him. And on his fast lap he had a problem, couldn't get from second gear to third on the pit lane-straight so he lost another three or four tenths of a second there." In the matter of coping with a Formula 1 car Senna entertained no self-doubts. Gugelmin further insists that in the general matter of driving racing cars Senna never entertained any self-doubts either. He knew he could do it.

He had another accident in the Formula 3 race at Oulton Park.

He couldn't take being beaten?

"No, that was definitely one of his downfalls," Bennetts says. "I had to sit him down and say it was better to finish second with fastest lap and get seven points than chuck six away [six for second place but of course keeping the one for fastest lap]. Yes, he found that difficult to take."

It was a very primitive thing. You go to a race meeting with one idea: pole, fastest lap, victory?

"Yep, and that's a good attitude but sometimes you had to give in to someone if we didn't get the car dead right, or in one instance at Silverstone he arrived late for qualifying – Mr. Gugelmin will confirm that." (Mr. Gugelmin does confirm it but has forgotten why they were late. He explains that, to keep life interesting, Senna would often cut five minutes from a prospective journey. Gugelmin decided he wouldn't constantly nag him to get ready "because I'd have sounded like I was his father. So I went with the flow. Silverstone could have been one of those deals: *oh, yea, we'll be all right.*")

By now it was 1 October and the Championship had become Senna 116 points, Brundle 113, with only this and the final round at Thruxton to come. Not an occasion for rolling up late.

"It didn't go down well with me. They blamed each other – they'd left it a bit late and cut it a bit fine and probably been doing speed on the way up there. The session had started when they arrived. By the time he got changed and in the car, by the time he'd done his third lap, it had already started to rain and he shunted it."

Here Bennetts consulted his records. "The page shows OUT, a lap of 30.67, OFF. Then the times of the others: DJ is Davy Jones, MB is Martin Brundle, AB is Allen Berg, DL is David Leslie, MH is Mario Hytten. Ayrton's time is 30.62 – the 30.67 would be me with the stopwatch, the 30.62 from the official timing.

"This was the race where he started fourth but instantly got up to second on lap one and he just stayed behind Martin. The worst he got was 1.5 seconds behind and as they crossed the line you could hardly measure it: 0.4 of a second."

If you gave him a rollocking, how did he take that?

"He was a bit sheepish. At Silverstone he knew they'd arrived late and here was the championship at stake."

At Thruxton, Senna took pole, the race and the championship, beating Jones by 5.43 seconds and Brundle by 8.53. Sarah Taylor was a freelance journalist. "I sort of got to know Ayrton, but because I knew Dick I tended to go and talk to him more. At that point Ayrton wasn't as confident as he grew to be when he was dealing with English people. He was quite sociable but at race meetings he didn't mix much with journalists. Whenever you spoke to him he was very polite and, I think, genuinely shy.

"Everyone was just amazed by his skill and talent but because the championship was happening in Britain and because there was an up-and-coming British driver – Martin Brundle – obviously a lot was focused on Martin. But you couldn't ignore Ayrton. When they announced that Ayrton had won, it wasn't greeted with instant applause like there would be for a British driver. You felt as though it was held back. Clearly the team were highly delighted and a lot of people did want Ayrton to win but elsewhere you felt a … reticence."

Bennetts nurses other feelings about Thruxton. Senna and Brundle both had Novamotor engines but, Bennetts believes, Brundle's was "a new spec." around mid-year. When Senna got the same for Thruxton "we were flying. That told me something. If we had had that same spec. engine as Martin from mid-year on, Ayrton would have won more races because he wouldn't have had to push as hard as he did."

In November 1983 Formula 1 reached out to Senna. This was the next crossroads. He tested for a small, friendly F1 team called Toleman. The team had been created by Ted Toleman, who owned the largest car-transporter company in Britain. Toleman had won the Formula 2 Championship in 1980 and were now in their third season of Formula 1, running Derek Warwick and Bruno Giacomelli. The man in charge, Alex

Hawkridge, had recognised Senna's outstanding ability as far back as the early days of FF1600 and had monitored him carefully ever since.

This test took place at Silverstone. Rory Byrne, who designed the car, remembers: "I'd heard about him but I hadn't actually met him until he arrived at the factory at Witney prior to that first test. He struck me as a very professional and determined sort of individual, really quite pleasant but totally dedicated to what he wanted to achieve. That was obvious from the first day."

He intended to dominate Formula 1.

"Oh, that's true. Anything other than winning was not on his agenda: it was his philosophy and of that I am sure."

They all think this but the reality is they're simply unable to get into a Toleman and win races. He almost did.

"Yes. Oh yes, yes, yes."

The test?

"It's a long time ago and I can't recall all the details but I do remember that he went out and did a few what I would call exploratory laps, nothing special at all, in fact quite slow. He was getting to understand the car. So he did a series of laps, came in, asked questions and discussed things. That's how he approached it – step-by-step – and at the end he'd put in a time quicker than Derek or Bruno had done all season at Silverstone."

A glimpse of that cool November day. Byrne, wearing a white jumper, has a stop-watch suspended by a cord round his neck. He is standing beside Senna, who has his helmet hanging loose from his right hand, and they're discussing the car. A special six-speed gearbox had been fitted instead of the usual five, and gear-selection problems hampered Senna. Were they discussing that?

Senna still did 72 laps and peaked at 1m 11.54s which, as various people noted, was almost a full second faster than Warwick's qualifying in that season's British Grand Prix (1m 12.528s). Nobody seems to have bothered to mention Giacomelli (1m 13.422s). Giacomelli was too far away from the pace Senna was already setting. Typically, perhaps, Senna reasoned that with a properly functioning five-speed gearbox he'd have gone under 1m 11s.

Senna did not join Toleman immediately. A week after the test he went to the Paul Ricard circuit to test a Brabham. The team were giving promising young drivers a chance (Mauro Baldi, Roberto Guerrero and Pierluigi Martini drove the car too). The track was moist and Senna spun on what he felt would have been his best lap. His next best was 1m 07.90s but, since the test was on the club circuit, no comparisons were valid with times set at the French Grand Prix.

Then he flew back to Britain in Bernie Ecclestone's Learjet with Ecclestone, who was reportedly anxious to sign him to partner Nelson Piquet. There was a typical Formula 1 problem about that, however. Brabham's major sponsor was an Italian company, Parmalat, and they wanted outgoing Riccardo Patrese's replacement to be Italian. This no doubt explains why Baldi and Martini were at Paul Ricard. The notion of Senna partnering Piquet is in any case explosive (Piquet called Senna the "Sao Paulo taxi driver" and once snubbed him, to which Senna retorted "I'll beat the bastard one day"). Anyway, commercial pressures being what they were, Ecclestone told Senna he wouldn't be joining.

Senna confided to Gugelmin that the Brabham had been "pretty hard, the way the turbo boost would come in: really hard. He wasn't thrilled with the car. He said the boost was really strange and he tried to use long gears in certain areas so the boost wouldn't be so brutal – subsequently he found out that Nelson was using different gear ratios."

Did he and Piquet really not like each other?

"Eventually they hated each other because of things that Nelson said, which were totally out of order, and are not relevant now. In the beginning I think Nelson felt threatened by Ayrton and he was quite right to feel so."

The test had been on a Monday. Next day Senna flew from London to race with Bennetts in the Portuguese enclave of Macau, just across the bay from Hong Kong. Various forms of racing had been held here since 1954 but this was the first for Formula 3.

Bennetts insists that Senna matured as a man over the year. "He was very mature for his age when he joined us but I can confidently say that when he left us he was more so." This was well demonstrated at Macau, because it was unknown territory. "The tyres were new to us, Yokohamas, the track was new to us, team and drivers: a four-mile street circuit and tricky, oh yes. To clear off and win the first Heat by six seconds and the second Heat by five and a half, five and three-quarters, was something; but he was up to six and a half at one stage, never forgot it was an aggregate race and he backed off knowing he'd be safe.

"What impressed me was his last lap of the first Heat: he'd done 2:21.65 on lap 8 and, just to rub it in, did 2:21.59 at the end. He was showing them *the car's good, I can push harder if I want to,* he was sending a message to the others. He was happy to have won because we'd had a late night on the Friday and he was a bit under the weather on the Saturday. He'd arrived jet-lagged because he'd been testing the Brabham down at Ricard – arrived late, didn't even get a chance to walk round the track, which all the other drivers had, and which is always helpful; and he was against the pressure of all the top Europeans."

One of those Europeans, Roberto Guerrero, said he couldn't believe what Senna was able to do on cold tyres.

"That was one of his abilities. In a lot of the races, if he had qualified second or third, lap one was always one of his fortes. It was raw ability. Cold tyres are difficult and you need a very fine feel when the car's losing the grip."

Do you think he was a better driver at the end of your year than before?

"He had learnt a lot more on sorting a car out, developing a car, whereas in junior categories you don't tend to. Formula 3 is still the first category where you've got a proper racing car [smooth tyres for adhesion, adjustable wings]. The driver can make a difference. He learns what does what. The

	FUEL	LAP	LAP TIME	P	DRIVERS COMMENTS	Tyres YOKO	ACTION TAKEN
HEX	14	1	2·29·81	1	AB NC GB DJ EE GM TB	bini PHT.R	
	13	2	22·51	1	2·83	SG2	
	12	3	22·46	1	+		
	11	4	22·25	1	+4·6 AS LG GB DJ EE		
	10	5	22·81	1	+4·95		
	9	6	23·10	1	+4·2 AS LC GB DJ TB EE FK AB MH·		
	8	7	22·00	1	+5·1		
	7	8	(21·65)	1	+7·0 - - - - · · - ·		
	6	9	22·98	1	+6·6 - " " DJ TB EE		
	5	10	24·6	1	+5·4		
	4	11	22·15	1	+6·1 AS· LG GB DJ TB EE		
	3	12	22·44	1	+6·0 - " - · ·· "		
22·1	2	13	23·09	1	+5·1 - - - - · · - AB MH·		
	1	14	22·31	1	+5·1 - " " " " " A		
	0	15	*(21·59)	1	+6·0 AS LG GB DJ TB EE		
		16			%+ -2½	O·	
		17			· O 11·	··12	

The destruction of Macau. Senna wins Heat One – and surprises even Dick Bennetts who'd circled lap 8 as the fastest before Senna had completed the final lap, 15. (Courtesy of Dick Bennetts)

junior categories – the Ford 1600 and 2000, the Vauxhall Lotuses and so on – have been good for a driver's learning curve because you don't change the car much. Therefore, as a team, you just get it to where it's best for the driver and he drives it, but in Formula 3 you have dampers, cambers, ride heights and so on. It's a small Formula 1 car. Formula 3 is a very good training ground.

"What also happens when you have a driver as good as Senna is that you tend to try things which you wouldn't with a driver who can't give you the feed-back. A guy like Senna would tell me if something is working *before he'd done a full lap*. He'd just come back in if it was no good. If it was any good he'd do another couple of laps, then come in and say *it's got potential*. With this feed-back he is helping the team to develop the car in a way it might not be able to do otherwise."

Bennetts believes drivers should be given equal treatment, and if they feel they haven't he puts on a demonstration by getting another driver to make their car go fast. Senna helped with this once, and it's revealing because it happened in 1984, when he'd reached Formula 1.

"It was at Snetterton and he'd come back to help us, do a few laps for us. We put him out in Carlos Abella's car because Abella felt it wasn't right. Ayrton did five laps, stopped and said *leave me to re-adjust back to Formula 3 because in comparison to Formula 1 it's so light on the steering, so light on the brakes and it's got no horsepower* – he'd jumped out of the Belgrano [the nickname for the Toleman]. *Don't touch the car, let me re-adjust my brain.* He sat there for five minutes, head in his hands, then went out and immediately was half a second quicker than the times Carlos had done. Then he said *for my driving style it needs a bit more downforce on the front.* We gave him quarter of a degree of front wing, or half a degree, and out he went again, went another two or three tenths quicker. He said, on the quiet, *there's nothing wrong with that car, I could have gone even quicker.* We had

Carlos back in and he went a few tenths quicker, but he still couldn't match Ayrton."

As we leave 1983 journalist Jeremy Shaw provides an instructive footnote. "I had a fabulous working relationship with Ayrton and he was always wonderful but it's funny, though, because he got upset at the end of that Formula 3 season. I did the *Autosport* review of the season and in those days we didn't really rank them 1–10, we gave them all stars. The article was laid out so that you knew what the rating was. Well, I gave both him and Martin Brundle five stars and because *B* came before *S* they put Brundle ahead of Senna on the page.

"As far as Senna was concerned I had put Brundle ahead of him, which wasn't my intention. Clearly he was the outstanding driver that year, won the championship and deservedly so. He was the better of the two drivers but Brundle had raised his game so much during that season that I thought he was deserving of an equal ranking, and he'd pressured Senna into mistakes, he'd kept the championship alive until the last round.

"But when Ayrton saw the story in the magazine he was cheesed off, no, really angry. He said *how the hell can you rate him ahead of me?* I explained that it wasn't a question of rating Brundle ahead of him, it was just the way they laid out the page and if it had reflected the way I'd written the article the order would have been the other way round. Senna said *yes, but he's nothing like as good as me blah blah blah*. He went on and on – and didn't speak to me for about a month. Sulking? Yeah. Then he forgot about it, but he couldn't accept that anybody was better than him and that was really his only fault, as far as I was concerned. He couldn't accept when he had made a mistake. His way was the right way, end of story. However, I do think that's one of the things that makes these people stand out in all sport, and in business, and in everything."

So Senna joined Toleman. Although his name had been linked with various teams only Toleman were prepared to give him a contract. "They really believed I could learn with them." It was early December, and the week he signed there was testing at Silverstone.

Brian Hart made the engines which Toleman used. He remembers, "I was on the Silverstone pit lane wall with Rory Byrne [the designer] discussing something and Alex Hawkridge came along with this young lad that I'd heard all about. Alex said *have you got a minute, Brian? I'd like you to meet next year's driver.* We shook hands and talked for a bit. Senna looked at the car and asked a few questions. I think Alex had the Toleman helicopter up there and they whizzed off in it. I thought *Christ, how did Alex manage to sign him?* Here was, in most people's opinion, the next coming man and somehow Alex had got him. I think that Alex was at the height of his entrepreneurial powers and here he was: he'd blundered his team through Formula 2, been champions in 1980; in 1981 we'd done the impossible and gone from having a useless little car – it took until Monza to qualify for a race – to getting to the brink of breakthrough in 1983. This was all through Alex's motivation and stubbornness. He believed it could be done and he obviously said to Senna *yes, this can be done and you've got to become a part of it*. And here he was."

After the test Senna returned to Brazil to talk to sponsors.

Toleman had many strengths, not least an experienced and firm team manager in Peter Gethin, a former racer himself. But they had three disadvantages: of being small, and therefore vulnerable; of running a very old car – what they styled their 183 – at the start of the season; and of being on Pirelli tyres.

Everything which happened at Toleman is hugely significant. Hawkridge will never forget during the negotiations to sign him Senna said if he was not in a winning team he would simply walk away from Formula 1. Being second held no interest for him whatsoever. Hawkridge, who remembered the negotiations with the clarity and exhaustion of a man who'd been put extremely slowly through a wringer, formed an astonishing opinion: Senna was only interested in *dominating* Formula 1 – quite something for a slender young man who'd yet to actually cover a race lap in a Formula 1 car.

It is useful to examine the season in detail, especially the start, because it shows how quickly Senna had to accept – and try to master – the unexpected storms and flurries of Formula 1. This was quite a culture change from the nicely dramatic Formula 3 struggle against Brundle, which had been essentially straightforward. Toleman was to be torrid, tempestuous and maybe the making of the man. If you want to understand Senna, these early days repay close scrutiny. The dates here are in bold type to emphasise the sheer intensity of the workload.

He'd partner Johnny Cecotto, a Venezuelan who had driven the previous season for the small Theodore team and recorded a sixth place, at Long Beach. Cecotto had been a World Champion on motor bikes, winning the 350cc title in 1975.

Ayrton Senna came to the insular, insulated tribe of grand prix racing as a stranger, a name, a curiosity loaded with promise, maybe a cocky kid looking for a comeuppance. A decade later he left this same tribe lost in the bewilderment of their emotions; left them in a sudden, silent void, and in his leaving remained somehow a stranger.

Monday to Saturday, 16 to 21 January. Senna drove the Toleman at the traditional tyre testing at Rio. All the teams went except four and Senna finished tenth – faster, incidentally, than Alain Prost and Niki Lauda in the McLarens, although that wouldn't mean much as the season proper began.

Brian Hart kept notes and of this test he wrote a description which captures the future with uncanny accuracy:

So far Senna has been quite good, very analytical, but he lacks experience and certainly is not fit [underlined]. On Tuesday after an initial few warm-up laps he would be knackered after 4 or 5 [underlined]. Senna is obviously very bright and to keep him we will certainly have to produce more power and certainly a better car in the 184 [the new Toleman, not yet ready]. By the European races at least, Senna's ability will be apparent and I'd imagine teams would have little problem finding the money to break the contract (this is an opinion Peter Gethin and I have formed independently). We have to get on top of our production and machining problems and make components in sufficient quantities.

Overall ... I feel that Toleman's new car will be significantly better. In the long run the only way to keep a driver who has the capabilities and determination that Senna has, is to provide him with the equipment – and unless Toleman and ourselves do this, my feeling is that he will move on to another team for '85. We must keep organised and keep the pressure up, most of all if we can find that little bit extra of performance by the time the new car is running and the car itself has achieved the designers' increase in performance over the 183. Senna's ability will undoubtedly do the rest.

Autosport reported that Pirelli arrived with a "bewildering selection of new sizes, compounds and constructions, but using a 'reference' tyre Senna worked his Toleman-Hart round in 1m 39.31s. Ayrton's biggest problem, we understand, appeared to be finding a *race* tyre which would do more than five laps." That was early in the week.

Friday 20 January. In broiling heat – and incidentally Senna had never driven the Rio circuit before – he did a 1m 33.43s, worth that tenth overall. "I feel comfortable in the car, I don't feel lost at all. I just feel frustrated when I see such a big difference between the equipment" – meaning the Pirelli tyres against the Michelins.

Nigel Mansell went second quickest at Rio in a Lotus-Renault and the designer of that car, Gerard Ducarouge, was there. Ducarouge was an innovative and highly-regarded designer. "Senna came to me and what he said was very straightforward. *I well know what you have been doing at Matra and everywhere* – that I'd been to Ligier after Matra, and Alfa Romeo after that, and all that lot. *I want to work with you,* he said, *I am going to work with you I'm sure.* This was far, far before we did come to work together and it's very strange because the man knew the details of my professional life. It gave me a clue about his attention to detail because he knew everything so precisely: not just where I'd been but all the drivers as well. I even thought he must have been talking to a few of them in order to have that kind of information. Yes, a strange but beautiful story."

Or perhaps it happened like this: when Senna and Gugelmin talked, talked, talked Formula 1 in the house they shared, *everything* was discussed and dissected; and if you intend to get into Formula 1, the team you go to is all-important; and a significant part of that is the man who designs the car. Bad cars are a very bad thing for a young driver – for old ones, too. Perhaps there's another meaning to Senna's conversation with Ducarouge. Although just at the threshold of Formula 1 racing, as yet untried at this level, Senna was already looking beyond Toleman.

Cecotto hadn't met Senna before 1984. "Initially we had a good relationship. Sometimes we travelled together and it was OK, very fine. When we travelled we had a good time. We spoke to each other in a little bit of Portuguese, Spanish, Italian also because he spoke that – so it was mostly Italian, or English because the team was British. Then the season started and things, well … they didn't go as fine as I thought. It was difficult because he was being pushed within the team by Hawkridge and so he had the priority, he had a different car, he had the new engines with the electronic fuel injection, I still had the old ones with the mechanical fuel injection. So there was a difference in speed and performance. I do remember one time at Donington we were testing the same day in the same car. The rest of the time he was doing all the testing, and I was just testing on Friday mornings at the grands prix."

Did that change the relationship?

"Well, yeah. He was getting more and more cold and we didn't spend much time together, just met at the grands prix and no more. So this didn't make things better. It was difficult for me because I didn't get the possibility to improve my car by testing it and the car was not performing the same as his car. It was a bad season for me. I didn't have a reliable car and I didn't finish one single race."

In his career he saw each team-mate as a threat and he tried to destroy them.

"Yes, that's right."

Did you feel that?

[LONG PAUSE, SIGH] "Yes, more or less. As I said, he had the whole team, and especially Hawkridge, who was the boss of the team, on his side and he was getting everything, the best car, the tests, everything. Nothing was on my side."

Monday to Saturday, 27 February to 3 March. In testing in South Africa, Senna revealed the car was better than at Rio where "after three laps it was frightening." He did a 1m 07.83s, seventh overall. Cecotto, who had the car for one day, did 1m 11.03.

Friday to Sunday, 23 to 25 March. Senna made his debut in the Brazilian Grand Prix at Rio, qualifying sixteenth but retiring after eight laps with a turbo boost pressure problem. In his notes, Brian Hart wrote:

First day's practice was not very successful, it being impossible to balance the cars on the new Pirelli tyres. Generally the feeling was that although the tyres may have worked in the South African tests they certainly weren't performing here. This allied to the fact that the car is 15 months old was obviously a considerable disadvantage.

Two things stand out in my mind: after first day's practice, the ability of the major teams to respond and change their cars under a heavy development programme and, secondly, this has made an even larger gap between the major manufacturers and ourselves. I feel that this can only possibly become a bigger gap as their sheer physical and financial 'clout' carries them through the season.

Senna finished in 22nd. position and Cecotto finished in 17th. position. Unfortunately we had an engine failure on Senna's car, almost certainly a dropped valve. The qualifying tyres were an absolute disaster, delaminating after 2 or 3 corners. In short, the tyres and the inability to get the chassis working put the whole team further down the field than we deserved to be.

On Saturday, Senna managed to find one set of tyres which appeared to be better and these just managed a lap.

Thursday to Saturday, 5 to 7 April. In South Africa, Senna qualified thirteenth and finished sixth. "That was the only race where it was looking good for me," Cecotto says. "I was behind him but I was faster than him" – Cecotto was behind Senna from lap ten to lap 26. "I was trying for a long time to get through, to pass him but he didn't want to let me past.

"After a while I had a rear tyre explode, at the end of the straight. I managed not to have an accident but it destroyed the car. I had to stop. And that race he finished very well – sixth – so this could have been a good race for me also."

Lauda won, completing 75 laps in one hour 29 minutes 23.430 seconds. Senna, three laps down, crossed the line after one hour 29 minutes 54.794 seconds. It represented an extreme test of his body because a Formula 1 car makes such demands that the driver needs to be extremely fit.

"I'd known Peter Gethin for years," Hart says, "because we used to race together. After the race we couldn't really believe it, because in Brazil the engine went before Senna's physical condition was discovered. At Kyalami a combination of the altitude and the temperature left him completely knackered. Peter and I had gone up to the car and of course there weren't the medical facilities then that you have now. We poured some water over him. Peter had a bit more 'clout', I was just an engineer, and Peter got him to the medical centre. You suddenly realised what a young and slender man Senna was."

Two relevant factors, however: early in the race the Toleman lost part of the nosecone, making it even more exhausting to handle – even so, he set his fastest lap (1m 12.124s) on 71 out of the 72, a feat all by itself.

He was taken to the medical centre suffering from what Professor Sid Watkins, Formula 1's resident doctor, would describe in his book *Life at the Limit* as "serious and agonizing cramp in his neck and shoulders." Senna evidently didn't know what was wrong with him and was "creating a fuss." Watkins, a man of considerable physical and mental stature, explained the facts of life, which were that a) he wasn't going to die and b) what was happening to him was his "physical chemistry." Senna then became rational again. Though neither man knew it, this was the beginning of a friendship which, in terms of integrity and depth, was among the strongest Formula 1 has known.

Hart wrote:

Without going into details, Thursday started off badly with Senna losing oil pressure. If one summarised the weekend, the old 183 is bloody old now and, allied to Pirelli's overall problem, we really are pissing in the wind. Senna's lap times came partly from Senna; a higher percentage, shall we say, from increased engine performance; but the race performance of the cars was appalling with the Pirelli tyres, and something drastic has got to be done there.

South Africa represented the next crossroads. If Senna was to become World Champion he'd have to move through three intermediate stages: finish races, which would mean muscle-building; get on to the podium, which he could probably make the Toleman do once he'd tackled the muscles; then learn how to win races, which he'd do somewhere else if the Toleman simply couldn't.

Hart says that after South Africa we "came back to England and we talked about his fitness. I said *you've got to get fit. These guys train* – not what they do these days, but even then they did train." Hart remembers Gethin was even more insistent.

Did Senna accept this when you told him?

"No, you wouldn't get a reaction like that from Ayrton," Hart says, "but what you did get was that he took it in, he was listening, it got logged and he wouldn't forget. So next time he went back to Brazil he started to do it – but you couldn't tell him which direction to go in, he had to decide for himself what was best for him."

Was that the secret of handling him? You make people like that think they are discovering things for themselves.

"You insert the idea and you rely upon their intelligence – and, as we all know, he had extraordinary intelligence."

(In Sao Paulo he'd contact a physiotherapist, Nuno Cobra and, using the city University's 400-metre running track, begin the laborious process of making his physical frame into that of a strong man. Cobra has said that, in 1984, "we had a skinny, highly-motivated young man." At first Senna had difficulty completing ten laps of the track, but in time he could "run 40 or 50 laps with incredible endurance." Beside the track was a metal gantry painted red and Senna used that to limber up, stretching his legs fully before the running. It is still there. Cobra has recorded how, to his astonishment, Senna could complete each of more than 30 laps *in virtually the same time – to within one second.* "I witnessed all that and I couldn't believe my eyes." On a more prosaic level, Senna himself would explain that he was wearing out running shoes at a rate of a pair every two months. Hart noticed how Senna's arms and chest developed. Soon he would fill out into the shape of a strong man.)

Between Tuesday and Saturday, 10 and 14 April. Senna briefly tested the new Toleman 184 at Brands Hatch and then at Zolder. The car, reportedly faster than the 183, was described by *Autosport* as "much more orthodox in appearance than its predecessor." It was also tested at Silverstone and Snetterton.

Peter Merrilees remembers these early days. "When Ayrton joined

Toleman he turned up at Snetterton to test the 184. We went down to say hello. He was sitting in the car chatting. As he pulled out of the pits I said to the two people with the car *how are you getting on then?* They said *he'll be all right but he's got a bit to learn.* I thought *you're the ones who've got a bit to learn!* It was so early in the piece they obviously didn't realise how good he was."

Friday to Sunday, 27 to 29 April. Still using the 183, Senna qualified nineteenth and finished seventh in the Belgian Grand Prix at Zolder, subsequently elevated to sixth because a Tyrrell was disqualified. By now Toleman had decided to change to Michelin tyres but for political reasons would not do so until after the next race – San Marino in deepest Italy, and Pirelli an Italian company, of course. Hart wrote:

Having been privy to the secret of the 'M … deal' it was clear that it would be hard to make a 183 go well on Pirellis and the 183's handling problems. However, the team did well and we produced sufficient engines. Everything ran very smoothly, brakes and tyres being the major problems. The race was fairly uneventful, Cecotto screwing his clutch on the line. Senna managed to come through, despite being of the opinion he was not able to last the distance with the car, to finish in seventh position.

Friday to Sunday, 4 to 6 May. Senna did not run in the San Marino Grand Prix at Imola because Toleman's relationship with Pirelli touched crisis. Hart wrote:

At Imola one can summarise the weekend fairly quickly. By now everyone knew of the Michelin quote "secret" and the reason for not running the 184s was more apparent: political hassles with Pirelli, which needn't be gone into, prevented us running until Saturday and only Cecotto qualified (Senna again having a Toleman fuel problem).

Monday to Wednesday, 7 to 9 May. From Imola, Senna drove up to Dijon with Toleman publicity man Chris Witty to test the 184 with Michelin tyres. Hawkridge was euphoric with what Senna could do, Senna was certain the team had made the right decision to switch to Michelins, and Michelin were deeply impressed by him. Hart was more circumspect, as befits an engineer:

There was a brief Dijon test with the 184 chassis on Michelin tyres. It's now clear that this was not the best circuit for us to choose to debut the car. However all went fairly well although a great deal of time was lost with the weather, Cecotto going off and a turbo being lost.

Saturday 12 May. Senna then contested the Mercedes-Benz Cup celebrity race at the Nurburgring. We may surmise that he calculated his future with precision and decided that only one man might prevent his domination of Formula 1. The leading drivers in that era were Lauda and Prost, Elio de Angelis (Lotus), Keke Rosberg (Williams) and Piquet (Brabham). Mansell, partnering de Angelis, had not won a race and many doubted he ever would. In the normal evolution of a driver, Senna would be approaching the point where he could dominate in another three or four years. By then Lauda would certainly have retired, Rosberg would be at or near the end, so would Piquet. Senna surely believed he could handle de Angelis. Therefore, Senna concluded, Prost is the potential enemy.

Prost has recounted a revealing anecdote about that (talking to Nigel Roebuck in the October 1998 issue of *Motor Sport*). The celebrity race was to mark the opening of the new Nurburgring. A wide selection of drivers had been invited, including Stirling Moss.

"I was coming from Geneva to Frankfurt on a scheduled flight," Prost told Roebuck, "and Ayrton was due to land half an hour before, so Gerd Kremer of Mercedes asked me if I would bring him to the track. On the way we chatted and he was very pleasant. Then we got to the track and practised the cars. I was on pole with Ayrton second – after that he didn't talk to me any more! It seemed funny at the time. Then, in the race, I took the lead – and he pushed me off the track after half a lap. So that was a good start ..."

John Watson was in this race and remains convinced that Senna regarded it as a chance to advance his reputation, whereas the other drivers saw it more as a celebration and a time to enjoy themselves within the context of good, swift racing. Senna (who won, from Lauda and Carlos Reutemann) clearly did not share such sentiments and had taken the opportunity, *already,* to set out the ground rules for a full decade of struggle against Prost.

Monday 14 May. Toleman were testing at Dijon again – the next grand prix was there. Hart wrote:

> Again bad weather thwarted the tests. BH/PG/ASH [Hart/Gethin/ Hawkridge] going by plane on Tuesday. It became apparent there would be a considerable learning curve with the Michelins whilst they gain confidence in us. All in all, the 2 days were quite successful, we were lucky to catch a retainer failure and were silly not to twig the turbine housing distortion problem – which subsequently caused both cars to stop in the race. Overall the car is better, lighter, more handleable and now we have to find more performance. One odd problem was water temperature rise on the straight, and Senna now still sees .1 bar boost drop. The car's first race will therefore be at Dijon.

Hart unravels these technical mysteries. "Retainer failure was in the valve gear – and we had turbines touching the exhaust housing, and we didn't realise what it was."

Friday to Sunday, 18 to 20 May. Senna qualified thirteenth for the French Grand Prix at Dijon and retired after 35 laps of the race when a turbo failed. Hart, almost anguished, wrote:

My original estimation of how much we'll need to catch up on power once the car is sorted – and the pace of development – showed itself clearly when in race trim Senna was quite unable to match the top cars at max. straight line speed, commenting that, despite understeer, the chassis felt quite good.

All in all, Senna's talent and the new car amply aided by Michelins really are going to force the issue about power. I imagine we will have to make some effort to rectify this. The [engine] management system should be tested in a 183 at Donington after the race weekend.

Thursday 24 May. Toleman took the 184 to Donington to test this new electronic management system. Reportedly it went so well that Toleman were working at full speed to have a race version ready for Monaco on 3 June. Senna was delighted with the improved throttle response. Hart wrote:

Initial testing by Senna was excellent, there being no misfires, interference or installation problems. In short, the car ran so well it was decided to fit up 184/01 [the 184 car with the 01 chassis] in a panic so that it could be tested in practice conditions at Monaco. What was slightly alarming was the high fuel consumption, about 3.5mpg: that indicated the amount of work that is going to have to be done – but it was a promising test, Senna commenting on low speed response and power, but was unable to confirm any distinct top end advantage!

Thursday to Sunday, 31 May to 3 June. And he came to Monaco, a place where, as Rory Byrne points out, he had never driven before. "He went round and I remember it was incredible, he must have spent about eight or ten laps driving round slowly. We thought *what's happening here?* Anyway, he just drove around and obviously he was looking for all the details round the circuit – like if there were any manhole covers, that kind of thing – just really absorbing all the circuit's peculiarities, which the other drivers had gained over the years. He had to gain it in ten laps. So he went round and he was *really* slow and suddenly at the end of the laps *booom*, he put in a time which was pretty respectable. His trait was to think the thing through first before he really committed himself."

Monaco is especially taxing for the newcomer to its dubious embrace. It travels up and down, in places it is bumpy and everywhere it is tight, narrow, taut. If the ambitious newcomer tries to kick Monaco into submission, Monaco kicks him back and much, much harder. Senna 'felt' his way round in the first morning's untimed session. Hart, who for the rest of the season decided to abandon his retrospective notes for the bare facts of each session, filled in a sheet of columns. They included:

Chassis No	Engine No	Boost	Ambient Temp	Comments
184/01	961	3.0	19C	Car problems
		3.05		U/S Grip

Senna switched cars for a second run, giving

184/02	947	2.9	19C	Grip OK
		3.0		

Senna had taken his race car and the spare round, had a variety of boosts, and either solved or watched a problem being solved.

He faced the daunting hour of qualifying. As a yardstick, Michele Alboreto (Ferrari) would finish it quickest with a lap of 1m 23.581 and Corrado Fabi (Brabham) slowest on 1m 31.618. (In fact Manfred Winkelhock's ATS was slowest on 1m 52.889 but he was beset by so many problems that he, the car and the time didn't really count.) Senna ventured out and spent two laps – 2m 14.312s and 2m 01.642s – re-absorbing the circuit before stretching the Toleman to a 1m 36.236s: nowhere near the pace but headed towards it. Then he came in.

Hart wrote in the Comments column: *Seems OK. Driver says much better off boost?* This almost cryptic reference would assume heroic (and epic) proportions during the race itself. Hart's own question mark betrays a certain ambivalence about Senna's thought processes.

His next run – in the other car – was proportionately quicker all the way through: 1m 55.950s, 1m 31.896s, 1m 28.562, 1m 27.865 – his fastest time of the session but he stayed out because each moment of learning was invaluable. He covered three more laps – 1m 33.979, 1m 28.281, 1m 37.607 – and we cannot know now whether this was due to traffic or just the learning by looking. We do know what happened at the end, however. In the Comments column Hart wrote *Hit Armco, so use 01.* Hart then recorded how much distance the engine had covered: 60 miles.

On his next and final run Senna had achieved consistency: 1m 49.675s, descending to 1m 29.381, 1m 28.075, 1m 28.226, 1m 29.349. He was fifteenth at the end of the session; and thirteenth after second qualifying, with a lap of 1m 25.009s.

He learnt quickly.

The race has passed directly into folklore. Prost led in heavy rain, Senna coming up through the field wielding a combination of bravery, ambition, sensitivity to movement and the most delicate finger-tip control. Monaco was a dark, dank, drowned swimming pool of a place. Senna floated across it. Later he told Angelo Parrilla he had discovered that the more he turned the boost down the more control he had.

Since the boost was entirely designed to create speed, let's look at that. "Bearing in mind that the turbochargers were only in their third or fourth years," Hart says, "and we hadn't quite reached the giddy heights of electronic control, Rory and I realised something quite extraordinary. He drove the car not on the rev counter but with the boost gauge! He could tell by *noise* – Rory said it was incredible. We'd give him 3.2 bar and then he'd ask for more power and we'd try it because when we'd got the turbochargers working properly the engine was strong enough to take boost.

He'd say *no, no, no, I've got wheelspin now. I don't need that much more power.* In those days we put a bit of white tape over the gauge and said *don't take the needle past this!* And often he'd not be anywhere near it. So at Monaco as the deluge got worse – and it almost became when are they going to stop it? not if – he was able to turn the boost down because that gave him more traction. You couldn't turn it off but you could probably get down to half a bar, which is very little at all." And, Hart reveals, Toleman gambled that the race wouldn't go the distance and put less fuel in, "so the car was lighter and Senna could throw it around more".

The race director, Jacky Ickx, decided conditions were too dangerous and stopped the race on lap 32. Senna was catching Prost so fast that as they crossed the line, Prost slowing, Senna thought he'd won. He hadn't, because officially the race ended on completion of lap 31. Hawkridge turned to Hart and said: "He does think he's won"!

It's easy to forget that Stefan Bellof in the Tyrrell might well have got past Prost *and* Senna and won if the race had gone on longer. It's easy to forget because that season Tyrrell were ruled to have illegal weight distribution and their results were expunged from the records.

Monaco finished	Prost	1h 01m 07.740s
	Senna	1h 01m 15.186s
	Bellof	1h 01m 28.881s

That of course was at the end of lap 31 and we know that during lap 32 Senna gained almost *eight seconds* because as Prost crossed the line to complete the lap Senna had caught him.

Ken Tyrrell remembers all this vividly. "First of all, there were only 20 cars allowed to start at Monaco in those days and Bellof qualified twentieth. He had the only car there with a normally-aspirated engine. He was lying third and Prost was in some difficulty with brakes and every time he came past the start line he was waving his fist at Jacky Ickx to tell him to stop the race! Bellof was catching Prost and Senna and it was a tremendous drive.

"However, perhaps what one has to bear in mind is that for the circumstances and on a circuit like Monaco he probably had the ideal car. The reason I say that is the turbos at that time – in fact most of their times – were very difficult in the wet: when you put your foot on the throttle nothing happened, then all of a sudden you'd got 1,000 horsepower. With a normally-aspirated engine he could ask for what power he wanted. Bellof didn't have the maximum power that they had but in those conditions driveability was so much more important.

"So that is one of the reasons why he came through the field – but he did come through the field and, you know, at Monaco where it's so difficult to overtake he passed the whole bloody lot of them except Prost and Senna – and was catching both of them … and bloody Ickx went and stopped the race! Prost and Senna were both in difficulties because of the type of car they were driving. Bellof was a star of tomorrow and in my opinion he would have been the first German World Champion of the post-War era."

Did Rory Byrne think Senna had won?

"Well," Byrne says, "I remember in the warm-up it was raining and Michelin only gave us the hard rain tyres. There were accusations of McLaren preventing us getting them but I don't know. Anyway, the reality was Michelin gave us the hard wets – really just to see how we'd get on." Senna did ten laps with a best time of 1m 59.892, seventh fastest overall. "He staggered them with the time he did on those tyres and so for the race they gave him the real thing – because of the time he'd done. And they may not have had that many of those soft wets. Really what I think they were doing was [literally!] testing the water to see how quick he was going to be and they were pretty impressed ..."

McLaren were a major team and Toleman were a minor team.

"Yes, but in this game you just get on and do your job, don't you? There are plenty of other people to worry about who's responsible for what. I just concentrate on doing the best I can with what I've got."

What did you make of him as a man, because by Monaco you were getting to know him?

"Well, as I person I really liked him. He was straightforward, honest, had a sense of humour. The thing you couldn't forget, though, was that he was absolutely committed to winning, so people who weren't professional in their approach he suffered pretty badly."

Did that lead to problems within the team?

"No, not really, because people respected him. He had a few contractual issues with Alex over his contract for the following year – I kept away from all that, I wasn't involved – but the mechanics who worked on his car had tremendous respect. It really lifted their game and their efforts and certainly I never had a problem with him at all."

Wednesday to Thursday, 6 to 7 June. There was a general test session at Brands Hatch, where Senna was fourth (1m 12.35s against Mansell, quickest, 1m 10.86s – Rene Arnoux in the Ferrari sixth on 1m 13.82s). Senna had been second fastest on the Wednesday with the Hart engine management system. This was removed on the Thursday – for a service! – but he still managed that respectable fourth without it. Next day Senna sent Hart a handwritten letter on his headed notepaper.

Ayrton Senna da Silva.
11 Chelsea Close, Kintwood, Tilehurst, Reading RG3 6EP, England.
Tel: 0734 415018

BRIAN,
Many thanks for helping Toleman and myself on our success at Monaco. Hopefully we will do well in other events to come.
After the Brands test, I am sure that your electronics work well and also give more power. That conclusion was on the second day of testing – we had a normal engine on the car.

This picture was given to me by Ferrari and they were really impressed with your four injectors per cylinder!!!
See you in Montreal.

Regards
Ayrton Senna
08.06.84

This photograph is reproduced on page 150.

Was there a moment when Hart fully realised the talent they were working with? He felt it was the test at Brands. From the Rio testing on 16 January to these two days embraced a period of just under six months. In that time Toleman had vaulted to the point where they were pushing the front-running teams and were arguably poised to become one themselves; and Senna had vaulted from being a novice to a potential front-runner. He had done this despite the uncompetitive tyres, the lack of fitness, the unfamiliarity of Rio and Dijon and Monaco. With all these details now established, the rest of the season can complete itself without the intensity of days and dates in bold type.

In Canada he qualified ninth and finished seventh; in the USA East at Detroit he qualified seventh and retired after 21 laps (hit a tyre wall); in Dallas for the United States Grand Prix he qualified sixth and retired after 47 laps when the driveshaft failed. He fell out with Gethin because he went out with the track breaking up when Gethin had told him not to.

Senna said that, starting around the time of the Dallas GP, he began to doubt the team management's ability to give him what he wanted – the championship. He didn't doubt the mechanics or the car.

"We were a small team," Byrne says. "You know, let's face it, we were showing potential and, from when we started in 1981 to what we were doing in 1984, we'd come a long way but it was still a small team with a small budget and I think he felt that to be a World Champion in Formula 1 he needed to have pretty big backing in terms of technical resources. I don't think he left Toleman because of any one person. He'd set his sights on being World Champion and he didn't think in the short term we were going to do it. He obviously thought that Lotus could, so he signed for them" – itself controversial because this involved a wrangle over a buy-out clause in his Toleman contract.

Hawkridge was so enraged that he took the car off him at the Italian Grand Prix as punishment. This was, Hawkridge judged, the only punishment which would hurt (and Hart confirms Senna's anguish). By then Senna had driven a round in the World Sportscar Championship (with the Joest Racing Porsche team, partnering Stefan Johansson and Henri Pescarolo; they finished eighth), and come third in the British Grand Prix at Brands Hatch.

During the Friday morning untimed session, Cecotto crashed heavily and injured his legs and feet so badly that his grand prix career ended. Senna, Cecotto says, "was one of very few drivers who didn't come and see me in hospital after my accident. I don't know if it was deliberate, I didn't understand the reason – but as I said, he was getting more and more cold, if I can use this word."

I say that Karin Sturm, a journalist who wrote a perceptive book on Senna (Goodbye Champion, Farewell Friend/Motor Racing Publications) *had pointed this out to him years later and he acknowledged his reaction had been mistaken.*

"Really? I don't have anything against him because of this – but it was strange to me."

Did you feel he was going to be a World Champion?

"No, not really. I didn't think so because, OK, I know he was a very fast driver but he was risking very much. This was my feeling. After my accident I was watching the races and this is what I was thinking: OK, he's very quick but not 'reliable'. Of course he improved later in his career."

I wonder if South Africa was the moment when he thought you were a danger, and the coldness began.

"Well, I can remember that we were testing together – the same day, the same car – at Donington, and at that time I was a bit faster than him. And he was not happy at all. I can tell you that. This was around the start of the season."

Maybe that's when the coldness started?

"It's possible."

Lauda won Brands Hatch from Warwick. (When I told journalist Maurice Hamilton I was due to interview Warwick, he said "be sure to ask him about Brands because I think Senna turned to Derek on the podium and said *I could have been second!*" Warwick didn't remember that happening, but it would certainly have been typical of the early Senna and his ravenous ambition.)

He qualified on the fifth row in Germany but crashed after four laps; was on the fifth row again in Austria and retired after 35 laps when the engine failed; was on the seventh row in Holland and retired after 19 laps when the engine failed again. This was the weekend when Lotus announced they had signed him for 1985.

And Hawkridge took the car off him for Monza, next.

The European Grand Prix at the Nurburgring was explosive. Rosberg had been in the Mercedes race, of course, and was in this one too.

I always felt, watching Senna when he was young, that there was going to be a big accident and he was going to be in the middle of it.

"Yes, absolutely. The Nurburgring, the start, he flew over my car and left tyre marks on my helmet. He took five cars out! First corner! And I was not surprised, definitely not!"

Did you talk to him?

"So what should I have talked to him about?"

Johansson said at the time that he'd raced this new Nurburgring in sportscars and there was always an accident at that first corner so he decided to be extremely prudent.

"Everybody knew! Everybody knew, but Senna didn't give a damn. And he would never have come up and said *sorry, I made a mistake.* Never. It was always somebody else's fault."

Rory Byrne is more benevolent.

How do you estimate his progress that year?

"Obviously he learnt a lot," Byrne says, "but I think the biggest progress he made was his stamina. When he finished sixth at Kyalami the doctor wouldn't let him fly back to Europe that night because he was absolutely exhausted but, by the end of the year, he had improved a lot in terms of mastering the sheer effort of driving a Formula 1 car. He was sharp, he realised that that was a shortcoming and so he set to and obviously got some people involved to give him the right sort of guidance in training, in diet, in lifestyle and all that sort of thing.

"He had improved a lot by the end of the year although I remember the last race, the Portuguese at Estoril. It was Ayrton and Stefan Johansson driving at that stage for Toleman. Stefan finished eleventh because he'd had a coming together with, I think, Niki Lauda somewhere in the race and he had to stop and change the nose. I remember Ayrton getting out of the car – he'd finished third – still looking pretty tired, then old Stefan got out, sort of came wandering over and lit up a fag! I just couldn't believe it but, you see, Stefan was so much more used to it. Anyway, I think that was the biggest change in Ayrton: he developed the stamina that was required to race for 100 per cent of the race."

What about the feed-back?

"Bearing in mind in those days there were far less sophisticated data acquisition systems, a driver's feed-back, and accuracy of feed-back, was really important and he was excellent at it. It wasn't only his feed-back, it was his attention to detail. At Estoril in that last race Ayrton was third on the grid and it was pretty cool so the radiator blanking [to make the engine run hotter] had to be worked out. We'd run in the warm-up at a certain ambient temperature and I'd made a note of it all [Lauda quickest, 1m 25.313s, Senna fifth, 1m 26.147]. Just before the cars went out on the formation lap I went up to Ayrton's car to check what the radiator blanking was, because I knew it would have to be changed for the race – the temperature had changed. You always wait until fairly late, close to the time, to check the ambient temperature. When I got to the car, the radiator blanking had been changed – but changed to precisely what I was going to change it to.

"I said to the number one mechanic *how come you changed it to that?* and he said *Ayrton told me to change it to that,* so the bloke, in spite of all the other things he'd done and had to do, had worked out mentally what the blanking should be and told them. I was staggered. He was involved in that level of detail."

Do you think his feed-back and his driving improved over the year?

"Oh yes, but it's something that obviously improves gradually and it's difficult to notice – and the whole thing, the team, the driver, everything improved over the year. When we first ran the Michelin tyres, at Dijon,

Ayrton qualified thirteenth. We were in a sort of qualifying band of tenth to fifteenth and by the end of the year he was on third spot. So obviously relative to everyone else, he improved – and yes, the car was better, the engine was better. At the end of the day, if you go from thirteenth on the grid in your first race [on the Michelins] to third on the grid – and then finish the race third – you've improved. It doesn't happen in this day and age, not to that extent."

Is this ability to remember all the details God-given or is it something God-given and you work on it, or what?

"To a certain extent I think it is God-given. Some people can do it, some people either can't or aren't particularly interested in it, anyway."

And to his level of detail?

"Aaaah, no. That's reasonably special. There are not many people around that can both drive quickly and attend to that level of detail. There are a few and – surprise, surprise – they're the World Champions."

Schumacher's another one?

"Oh, yes, yes. Precisely the same."

In 1984, Senna drove 14 races for Toleman, finished second at Monaco, third in Britain and Portugal, and sixth in South Africa and Belgium. This gave him 13 points, worth joint ninth place in the Championship table with Mansell.

This year of 1984, Gugelmin married Stella. "I'd never met Ayrton before," she says, "although Mauricio had known him for years. He came to the wedding. We were living at Attleborough and we were hoping to rent a house so Ayrton said *why don't you come to my house while you're looking around?* We kept on looking at houses and we couldn't find anything we liked. Then he said *if you come, you have to stay!* We said *no, no, only until we find a house.* He always wanted us to stay – and we did end up doing that, but because we couldn't find anything we liked. He was in Formula 1 already and we shared the rent, shared all the costs: heating, lighting, gardener, housekeeper, everything we needed. He was travelling all the time, and he went home to Brazil whenever he could. After that he bought another house [in Esher] and we stayed together until he moved to Monte Carlo.

"He was a very nice person and very professional. That was impressive about him, the way he dealt with his career. He was a soft person inside, and many people didn't know about that because he held his professional face in front of himself. Very nice person, very caring, really nice."

Did he do any housework?

"I did most everything! I was doing the housework for Mauricio so I may as well do it for him too. We were all living together."

But why didn't you make him do the dishes?

"Because it was a Brazilian way of life, you know. We lived like that. He used to help me sometimes and Mauricio used to help me sometimes but I didn't make that an obligation and as soon as we moved to the other house we had someone to help us."

What was he like on his own?

"He was happy and he was quiet. If he felt comfortable with you he'd make jokes and, yes, be happy.

"Curiously, perhaps, we didn't spend much time together because the season was from March to November and he was gone most of the time and we were travelling too. We all had very busy schedules so we didn't spend a great deal of time together but the little bit that we did I found him friendly. He was very involved with his career, very intense. You could see that. Then we all went back home to Brazil when the season was over. He was one of those who missed Brazil a lot and he was very, very close to his family. His mother used to come sometimes and she'd cook all the things he liked."

You have a woman's intuition. What did you make of this man who appears in many ways strange?

"When you are in the public eye it's very difficult because people all have different opinions and they all look in different ways. It depends how much you know him. I think, as I said, he was very intense in his work and he was serious at the times he needed to be serious – really focused on what he was doing – but at home he was fine, he was doing the things that normal people do: jokes, listening to music and so on. I think the way he was can be put like this: his profession required that he was intense. Formula 1 is very, very intense for any driver, very competitive. You can be gone in two minutes if you're not careful. And when you are at the top it's very difficult to stay at that level for a long time. So you *have* to be intense, you *have* to work hard because such a life doesn't come *just like that*."

Brazilians by repute find relaxing very easy. Did he?

"It all depended which way his racing was going. If he was doing well, it was easier for him and if he was having problems it was a little bit more difficult."

Alex Hawkridge, who in 1998 was working for Reynard cars, says: "You feel privileged that you had the chance to work with the guy and to be a part of his career."

Was it inevitable that Toleman would never be able to keep him?

"Oh yes, no doubt about that, because it's more of a reflection of the status quo in Formula 1 and how hard it is to change it than anything else. I think Ayrton would have been very happy if the team had got a good package [for 1985] but, you know, he was absolutely not going to have a second best if he could have a first best."

You were making terrific progress together.

"Yes, and he was a big fan of Rory and the team generally. A lot of the improvement during the year, to be fair, was down to getting Michelin tyres instead of Pirelli. They were year-old Michelin tyres but still a hell of a lot better than Pirellis. That was another thing that wound Ayrton up. Why did he have to have the second-best Michelins, why couldn't he have the same as Alain Prost? The fact that all we could do was deliver him second-best solutions made it inevitable. So I had no doubt that we were going to lose him. On the one hand, I expected it and on the other I was really shocked with the way he went. I thought he was far more honourable than that. I'm a racer, he's a racer. I have to say that if the roles were reversed I'd have done the same thing but I might have done it differently – given that we gave him his chance in F1 and took a hell of a risk ..."

... because he was a novice and this was the only chance he had?

"Yes. The other teams all talk about it now like they and he were big buddies – but they all wanted to have a good look, nobody wanted to buy anything. I think everybody in the team would say he was a phenomenon and from the very first time he tested the car at Silverstone we knew he was something different. It was a great experience for everyone there. I mean, he *was* phenomenal. There's no other word."

Senna did not leave Toleman immediately after the Portuguese Grand Prix because the team were staying on at the circuit to test several drivers – Palmer, Roberto Moreno, Manfred Winkelhock, Jan Lammers and Ivan Capelli – and Hawkridge asked Senna to go out on the Monday and set a time so there would be a yardstick to judge the others by. (Hawkridge also felt the fact that Senna agreed to do this demonstrated the relationship between driver and team had healed after the eruption of Zandvoort–Monza.) Around the loops of Estoril, Senna now proceeded to give another sort of demonstration. He had the spare car. He had soft Michelin race tyres, which were by definition slower than qualifying tyres. On them he set a time of 1m 21.70 seconds – compared to Piquet's pole time (1m 21.703s) in the mighty Brabham-BMW in the grand prix and set, of course, on qualifiers.

Brian Hart sensed that what Senna was going to do would be special and hastened to the part of the circuit behind the paddock – the tricky downhill section with a corner – to witness it for himself. Each time Senna came through the section at real pace (the 1m 21.70s was the fastest of a clutch of fast laps) he was able to raise a gloved hand from the steering wheel and wave to Hart, who found it astonishing that anybody *could* do that. Senna later confessed that he'd gone over the limit – one of the few times he'd ever do so. He also said he had thoroughly enjoyed himself.

And then Senna was gone, gone to find the rest of his life but only after he'd visited the factory to say good-bye.

And wept.

Then and now

Dick Bennetts is as he was yesterday, florid, softly spoken and barely an ounce heavier. It's autumn 1998 and there's a transporter outside his new factory. It bears the name Nigel Mansell, who Bennetts is running in Touring Cars. "On the team full-time in '83 we had myself, Dave Stevens and John Goodwin, a Kiwi mate who came and helped us." The team had just moved from lock-up premises to a modest but more fitting base.

In 1998 they came to this new factory, within echoing distance of Heathrow. "On the race team we now have 22 people and an extra nine working on associated projects. The floor area is 16,000 square feet and it's custom built: it used to be a warehouse but we've had it all designed." Down the corridor five people in the design department gaze at computers. "The lock-up garage? Didn't have computers in those days. It was all done by the seat of your pants."

Bennetts has a nice photograph of Senna and "you know, I never did get him to sign it. I always meant to but never got round to it – like somehow people don't get round to doing things."

On one of the circuit maps – mid-season at Donington – Senna has written, in his neat script, that he was "tugging." I asked Bennetts about that. "You know what it means," he says, giggling naughtily. "He was trying to say that he was not driving as well in the afternoon as the morning. 'Tugging. I'm tugging.' He learnt that from Gug—, I don't know who he learnt that from!"

Jeremy Shaw lives in Ohio and has found the best of both worlds. He follows CART racing intimately and likes its structure – the constant overtaking – just as he watches and likes the more drawn-out tactics of Formula 1. He remembers when Senna tested a Penske at Phoenix in 1992 – and might have gone to witness it. "I couldn't but I really wanted to because I only saw him once a year when he came over for the grand prix. Whenever he saw me he would always make a point of coming over and we'd chatter away for a while. When he did this test they had a media teleconference afterwards. I called up and asked him a couple of questions, then at the end of the conference everybody hung up and he said 'wait a minute Jeremy' and we had a long chat about the whole thing."

Johnny Cecotto had won the German Super Touring Championship for BMW a couple of weeks before I spoke to him. (Do you want me to call you champion? "If you like!" Do you want me to call you Johnny? "If you like!") We'd never spoken before but I seemed to remember reading that in his motorbike days he could be difficult. If that was true then, the years seem to have smoothed it away. He's 42. Like Bennetts, he's a gentleman.

I spoke to Ken Tyrrell during the week leading up to the Japanese Grand Prix, climax of the 1998 season. Tyrrell wasn't present, his team had been sold and was to be renamed for 1999 – the first season since 1970 without them. Tyrrell had just returned from a holiday in Australia. Are you happy in retirement? "No. I'd rather be working."

Brian Hart is quiet, immensely informed and just plain good company. We were sitting in the corner of a proper English pub outside Harlow, Essex, where his factory is. Much good laughter, especially when his secretary Jane claimed Senna had had an operation for reasons of vanity: on his ears. "You compare photos of him and when he was older his ears were smaller!"

Chapter 4

You must remember this

THE GRAND PRIX CAREER of Ayrton Senna exists in three dimensions now: memory, statistics and, if I can put it this way, the elusive statistics of memory. You might remember an overtaking move but can't place the circuit or the year, might remember a qualifying lap which seared and sizzled the tarmac but was that Silverstone in 1989 or 1990 or 1991? You must remember the crashes and bitterness but was that with Mansell or someone else? When were those farces at Suzuka with Prost? Didn't Schumacher confront him somewhere and it nearly came to blows? And Donington that time in the wet: did he really lead by a whole lap?

In the briefest of space, to settle the statistics: Four teams – Toleman, Lotus, McLaren, Williams – between 1984 and 1994, 161 grands prix, 65 pole positions, 19 fastest laps, 41 wins, 2,982 laps in the lead.

Another century of grand prix racing contested by generations yet unborn will not diminish this monument that Senna left as a legacy. The monument is too enormous and, even if greater drivers are drawn to the race, there won't be many and their monuments might or might not be as high; it turns on the human body and what, between its early 20s and late 30s, that body will tolerate as it is worked so hard. But 65 pole positions from 161 races will take some overtaking.

If you want it all again, race by race, as a fossilised recital of the career – you know how it goes, highlights and lowlights butchered into the language of race reportage – then look elsewhere.

This chapter and the next are an examination of the stranger as he moved into the main body of his Formula 1 career, from Lotus, the team he joined in 1985, to McLaren and the great days from 1988 to 1993. It is loosely in chronological order, but only loosely.

As we have seen, Senna had a small house near Reading which in 1984 he shared with Mauricio and Stella Gugelmin. They now moved into a larger house in Esher, and there will be more about this in Chapter 9, "Hearts full of passion".

"You've got to remember that at the very beginning of our relationship – not when I was signing him, because I'd been in contact with him for 18 months – he went home to Brazil after he'd signed for us," Peter Warr, running Lotus, says. "He came back from his holiday with Bell's palsy and one side of his face was paralysed. It may have been caused by a virus which attacked the facial muscles. I sent him off to Sid Watkins."

Watkins has recounted how not only did Senna have this paralysis but he couldn't close his eye and his mouth was "down to one side." Watkins put him on steroids and he made an almost complete recovery. Watkins remembers Warr ringing up several times to be sure Senna would recover.

As Warr says, "Sid Watkins sorted him out but even to the end of his days you could see a slightly lop-sided look and when he smiled one corner of his mouth didn't go up as much as the other side. So in those early days he had an additional burden he had to carry around with him as a very public figure. The reason he came to the factory that day [after his return] was to have the official photograph taken in his driving uniform in the sponsor's colours. It was as much as we could do to get him to stand in front of the camera. I can't blame him for that, absolutely not, but it had to be done because there was a deadline. Happily we got him off to Sid Watkins in double quick time and for whatever reason – whether it was dealt with quickly enough or it wasn't that severe a case or what-have-you – by the start of the season Sid got him back in halfway decent shape."

Nigel Stepney, a mechanic (who in 1998 was with Ferrari), remembers the first day. Senna "had an enigma about him. People like him are normal people, but they come with this something about them. They have a look, they know what they are doing. Same with Michael Schumacher. They are very calm, both of them. They put an air of confidence into the people working around them. Some drivers come along and think *I am the driver, you have to do this for me or that for me*. When those two, Senna and Schumacher, came along they were the best in the business but they didn't portray themselves as something superior to other people. I can name a few who think they are superior because they drive a Formula 1 car and those ones, I'm afraid, you just forget about. I have no time for them. Ayrton was – and Michael is – very, very similar and not like that at all.

"That first day Ayrton was paralysed through the thing he'd caught. He was very shy at the time, but he couldn't speak because his left-hand side was paralysed. He stayed shy through even to the end, although he wasn't in front of people he knew."

Designer Gerard Ducarouge remembers Warr recounting that Senna had told him during the negotiations *I will not come to Lotus if Gerard is not there* – "because he knew McLaren were after me and several people were after me. Now on that first day I remember Warr knocking on the door of my office and Ayrton was standing behind him. Warr said to Ayrton *there you are – Gerard is there!* And of course the relationship was so easy to build because somehow he trusted me immediately and he had a lot of respect for me, and I had a lot of respect for him when I saw what he was going to do in Formula 1. We had a fantastic *complicity* to start with. [Ducarouge speaks the most excellent English but here he is using complicity in the French sense – participating together.]

Trevor Foster wasn't a contemporary (he worked for Lotus much later) but recounts the folklore passed down to him. "Basically when he first signed there was a buy-out clause in his contract with Toleman and everybody was amazed that it was $100,000 or something – a very low figure – and obviously Lotus were happy to pay that. As a buy-out clause, $100,000 was nothing really and I think that although Toleman had a contract they'd overlooked the buy-out. So that was pretty smart dealing on Senna's part.

"I remember the stories people told me. Senna went round the factory introducing himself to everybody and making very clear to people what he expected from them. One particular department was gearboxes. The conversation he had with one of the personnel there was: *do you realise that if you screw up more than so many times, and I don't finish races, then under my contract I am free to go.* It's a hell of a thing to say to somebody, isn't it?

"It was interesting talking to the people who'd worked with him, the mechanics and so forth. They remembered that he used to be literally wound up because in those days you had turbos and you could wind the fuel on and wind the boost on – obviously if you put more boost on you need more fuel. In certain parts of a race the team used to wind up the boost depending on how much fuel load they'd got left to play with. This was in the days before refuelling, so you had to make whatever fuel you had last to the end.

"One of the stories they told me was this: they decided to put a fuel 'counter' on, like the front wheel calibration gauges which used to click over: a very simple sort of thing. Senna finished a race and when they pumped the fuel out he still had 20 or 30 litres of fuel on board – but this counter showed zero. Apparently they realised afterwards that because of the bumps on the track surface the car was jumping" – and whenever it left the ground the counter stopped, resuming again when the car landed.

"So he thought he'd got less fuel than he had, but when they got the system working properly he would finish and feel he'd done the job absolutely right if he crossed the line and ran completely out of fuel within something like 100 yards. If he'd got much more left, he'd misjudged the race.

"I remember the stories too of how he'd go out very early on in a practice session and work entirely on the race set-up. He'd be able to come in and say to his engineers *right, these are the five problems I've got with the car, but those are the two we must concentrate on because these are where the biggest time gain is. We'll sort the other three out later on, so don't try and fix all five, just try and fix those two.* In those days they knew when the car left the workshop that if it was any good round the circuit he'd be on pole and if it was rubbish he'd still be about fifth!"

He was like Schumacher in that he could find time from within himself.

"Oh yes. You watch these guys over and over again, and that's what they do."

It's difficult to remember that when Senna joined Lotus he had driven only 14 grands prix, had yet to be on the front row of a grid, had yet to win a race and had scored a total of 13 points. Everything remained to be proved. He didn't waste any time doing it.

Interestingly, he and Warr gave an interview to Reginaldo Leme of *TV Globo* on the day he signed in London. "I was the only journalist there and it was embargoed," Leme says. "He told me he had gone to Lotus to get the first win, not to be World Champion. He thought Toleman couldn't give him it, and Lotus would be the initial step." Was he already looking beyond Lotus?

The team went to the traditional pre-season tyre testing at Rio. "I've said that people like Senna have a difference about them, and also they earn respect," Stepney says. "Every driver you listen to says *there's something wrong on the car* or whatever, but when the good ones speak you listen to them and when you look into it something *is* wrong. I remember Brazil and the testing – and this is actually how I came to work on his car. During a run Ayrton altered one of his brake balances, which was a little bit strange because we hadn't touched the car" – so the brakes ought to have been performing exactly as they had on his previous runs. "He said we had to change the brake balance and he added *there must be something wrong because something is different*. We thought *definitely a bit strange*. We looked round but we didn't twig straight away. It wasn't until some time had elapsed before we found what it was: something had happened on one of the roll-bar systems.

"So out there he'd had this problem, he'd changed the balance of the car to suit him and driven around the problem. When he came in he explained about changing the brake balance but he didn't know why he'd had to do it. Once we found what it was we put it right. He came over to the car and asked *what about the brake balance?* We said *we've already adjusted it back*. He was surprised, because the team he had worked with before wasn't at the same level."

Three weeks later the teams were back in Rio for the 'proper' pre-season testing which, ironically, coincided with the announcement that Toleman were withdrawing from Formula 1 because they couldn't get a tyre contract with either of the suppliers, Goodyear or Pirelli. Michelin had withdrawn.

In Rio, Senna produced a lap of 1m 27.9s, an outright lap record which also, as someone pointed out, totally eclipsed the pole time of 1m 28.39s set by de Angelis in the Lotus in 1984. In the grand prix, on 7 April, he qualified on the second row but retired with an electrical problem. Two weeks later in Portugal he took the first of 65 pole positions and, in a deluged race – the track like sheet ice – he beat Michele Alboreto (Ferrari) by more than a minute. While others slithered and skated, he lost control of the Lotus only once. It took him off the circuit and when, later, people fawned over how perfect his drive had been he contradicted them by pointing out that not only had he gone off but he was helpless when he did. Only luck enabled him to get back on. The win, the first of his grand prix career, forcibly suggested that Lotus would remain a front-running team and that he had become an authentic front-running driver.

Brian Hart was there and when he heard the weather forecast – rain – he said to everyone within earshot *you might as well go home now. Senna will win.* "You remember the race, cars slithering off everywhere, Prost doing a pirouette on the grass along the start-finish straight. I watched Senna's face when he brought the car back to the pits and the look was a sort of response to all those who had ever doubted him. I tried to get into the garage to congratulate him but I couldn't. It was completely full of photographers. I did meet him about an hour later, I did congratulate him and he just said *well ...*"

Lotus were discovering Senna's quite astonishing mental capacity. This was the era of fuel conservation and, Stepney says, "you had to drive the car accordingly. Fuel conservation was a war and everything depended on driver ability and tyres and so on. These days you can push to the maximum because you can use what fuel you like [as much as you like]. Relying on computers, Senna knew how much fuel he had and where he had to conserve it and how to conserve it. He also knew whether he was up on fuel or not by points on the circuit where the fuel meter changed. He had a fuel counter and when he went under a bridge, for example, he'd know if it changed before the bridge or after it. Now imagine you're trying to think about that at the speed he was doing – trying to watch the little digital display on your dashboard at three points or whatever on the circuit every lap. He knew at the point where the figure changed whether he was up or down in terms of what he ought to have to finish the race. He was driving on that sort of margin."

At Imola he took pole but in the race ran out of fuel; at Monaco he took pole but the engine failed; in Canada, de Angelis took pole from him and he had turbo problems. A week later he was in Detroit for the United States East Grand Prix. To recapture what Detroit was really like requires a leap of the imagination: picture a cluster of tall buildings, some abandoned, and, rising immense from them a hotel-cum-shopping centre-cum-who-knows-what called the Renaissance Center, sheer as a cliff, shimmering in the heat. A couple of streets away the brothers played soul music loud as you could take it *and man I ain't never heard of no Formuhlawan. Does it suck?*

It sucked all right below the RenCen, sucked all round the geometrical streets and 90-degree corners – ordinary everyday streets, ordinary everyday corners – which was the race track. Around this you'd do well to average 85 miles an hour and when the brothers heard that they said *maaan, I do more' n that on the freeway.*

What the great drivers like Senna have, Stepney insists, is a total competitiveness which translates into a total grasp of detail. "I remember people used to try and hide stuff from Ayrton. In Detroit he arrived on the dummy grid and he'd run over a manhole cover" – Senna complained that they were even worse than the year before. "He said *have a look underneath.* So I had a look. Basically we'd lost two lugs off the gearbox on the oil tank but there was no oil leaking. The engineer said *don't tell him this, tell him everything is OK.* After the race he said *you saw something underneath* and I admitted that I had. *Why didn't you tell me* he wanted to know. I explained about the engineer. He said *you should have told me, because I wouldn't have gone over that manhole cover again, I'd have driven another line.* Suddenly you have an enormous amount of respect for a person like that and you never try and conceal anything from them again. You're absolutely straight with them. Like Michael [Schumacher] today: they find the people who give them the correct answers – and you can't hide anything from guys like that. Anyway, at Detroit after Ayrton had spoken to me he spoke to the engineer ..."

If Senna had foreseen that he could handle de Angelis, 1985 provided evidence, because de Angelis – much more experienced and in his sixth season with the team – finished with five fewer points, saw which way the world was revolving and departed for Brabham. This brought a strange by-product and one which somehow reinforced the notion of Senna as a stranger, a name, a curiosity, a cocky kid looking for a comeuppance (although in fact he was 25).

It was a strange, strained, turbulent run in to the autumn. In mid-September there was testing at Brands Hatch for the European Grand Prix, due at the circuit on 6 October. Senna was having a couple of weeks' rest in Sao Paulo, where he was quoted as saying he would not go to South Africa for the grand prix on 19 October because of apartheid. One press agency report hinted that Senna had come under pressure from the Brazilian government to boycott the meeting.

De Angelis had an ear infection so Derek Warwick was released by Renault (who weren't there) to drive the Lotus in the Brands testing. He was happy to do this and liked the car although, because the team were more interested in work on the suspension and aerodynamics than in outright speed, he wasn't given the chance of a blistering lap on qualifying tyres. He *still* managed a respectable 1m 11.70s (Prost in the McLaren did a 1m 09.30s with, reportedly, qualifying tyres on the rear). Anyway, who could have imagined that such an innocent afternoon would detonate, within a few short weeks, into a feud lasting years?

There was an unashamed hardness about the young Senna in Formula 1 and the initial year with Toleman seems to have sharpened that rather than refined it.

He won the Belgian Grand Prix at Spa – a wet-dry race – despite an engine misfire which he thought might be the exhaust breaking. The week after, he went to see Warr at the factory, taking Gugelmin along with him. Warr naturally congratulated him on a superb drive and said he was World Championship material now. Senna, as Gugelmin remembers, interjected hotly that he had *always* been World Championship material – it was the team that had to be brought up to that level! Gugelmin, sitting behind Senna, tried to make himself very, very small.

Keke Rosberg, 1982 World Champion and himself a tough guy in a cockpit – but entirely fair and never foolhardy – encountered Senna's hardness twice, at the Nurburgring celebrity race in 1984 (as we have seen) and the 1985 European Grand Prix.

"It was the race that Nigel Mansell won," Rosberg says. The grid:

> Senna (Lotus)
>> Piquet (Brabham)
> Mansell (Williams)
>> Rosberg (Williams)

Senna led from Rosberg as the race settled. *Autocourse* reported that "the Williams was quicker than the Lotus through the fast corners but Senna's advantage lay in the ability to brake late and deep." Cumulatively all this left Rosberg "with no option but to try a risky move under braking for Surtees on lap 7."

By then Senna had been openly blocking Rosberg, who said at the time: "After eight years in Formula 1, it seems I need to go back to Formula 3 for a month to learn how to drive race cars. You get big eyes when someone starts weaving at 180mph – you're not used to that. I'll admit it, I don't have the balls to start banging wheels at that speed, and that's what it would have led to if I hadn't backed off on occasions when I was going to go by."

If you are unfamiliar with Brands Hatch, Surtees is the sharp uphill left at the end of the straight which runs along behind the paddock.

"Surtees was always a very wide entry, I went inside and he cut over and cut my tyre," Rosberg remembers. "I had to change it, pitted, and I emerged from the pits just when Nigel and Senna were coming so I put myself between Nigel and Senna and made sure that Nigel would win the race. Senna was very upset – but he'd just cut my tyre, I wasn't going to do him any favours. *I* would have won that race otherwise. How did he take it afterwards? Oh, we never discussed it. No. Senna wasn't a man with whom you could discuss things like that – especially with me. We'd had other, similar incidents."

Did you ever speak to him?

"I don't think I really did. That was for a very simple reason: I was already on my way out of Formula 1 and he was on his way in, and he was hungry for it, crazy for it. Crazy is really the right word at that time. So if I may call myself the old generation at that time, I didn't really have a lot of time for him because he was too crazy in our opinion. I mean, he ran into the back of me at Adelaide. You remember I was leading the race, I was going into the pits and yes he ran into the back of me. He went off and destroyed his race and I won it. A bit similar to Schumacher at Spa [in 1998 when he ran into the back of David Coulthard] getting over-excited. Of course there was a bagful of talent. Everybody knew that, but I think he was dangerous in those days. I don't want to see this as a headline, ROSBERG THINKS SENNA WAS DANGEROUS, but in the right context – and admitting to and agreeing with the fact that he had enormous talent, and recognising his enormous commitment to his profession – he was.

"That said, we've had people – like Niki [Lauda], then the next one was probably Prost, and maybe the next one was Senna – who have raised the game to a different level. And the next one is Schumacher, who's brought a new idea of fitness into motor racing."

Senna, as we have just seen, took pole at the European Grand Prix. On the Friday morning after the untimed session he said that the car felt completely safe, which had two meanings: in the testing it had not, but now that it did he felt liberated and empowered to bend Brands Hatch to his will. It would be an astonishing performance.

Interestingly, Lotus were pre-heating their tyres because that got them to their optimum pressure sooner than using the traditional method of going round the circuit using the friction of the tyres on the tarmac to do it. "This was another Ducarouge thing," Warr says. "He'd done a bit of that with Matras in sportscars and we had these things made by a guy in France. They were real Fred Karno* compared to what they are today with all the digital controls and so on. The guy in France whizzed them over and we used them to pre-heat the tyres. As a team, I think we were still very innovative – we went on from there to the active suspension and all sorts of things that other people hadn't thought of. We were always prepared to have a go if the logic and the reasoning was sound. *Yeah, yeah, give it a go.* And sometimes it came off and sometimes it didn't."

In first qualifying Senna set fastest time but he was briefly baulked by Ivan Capelli (Tyrrell) and so he knew there was more to find. As the moments melted towards the end of the qualifying hour Piquet (1m 09.204s) and Rosberg (1m 09.277s) had overtaken him. Senna watched, absorbed and then with exquisite timing went out for a last run. He circled for two slow laps, the black and gold Lotus cold as a predator. Coming round the languid loop of Clearways that second time he was travelling faster and faster; and crossed the line to begin the lap. *He* felt that at two points the car was "not that precise." Watching, you were totally unaware of that. Here was the will bending the circuit.

1m 08.020s.

It scattered Rosberg's lap record (1m 09.540s) set in 1982, of course, and scattered Rosberg's and Piquet's lowering of it this same session. It left a momentary sense of disbelief when he crossed the line and eased into Paddock Hill Bend, shedding speed. He had scattered Piquet's provisional pole by more than a full second. Then this amazing human being explained

---

* *Fred Karno's name has become synonymous with complete disorganisation. Karno had a troupe which toured British music halls before the First World War – in one review Charlie Chaplin played a clown.*

about how he had lacked absolute precision in those two places and mentioned – not complained, mentioned – that he'd had a touch of understeer. The car, he said, was the best it had been all season but the implication remained: *I can find more*.

And he did. Lotus had been pre-heating their tyres, remember, and in second qualifying Williams did too, enabling Rosberg and Mansell to dip into the 1m 8s. Senna responded with 1m 07.786 and returned to the pits. Now Piquet – all his career a very, very fast driver and at instants a supremely fast driver – put in a mighty lap, forcing the Brabham BMW to 1m 07.482s. Game over? As Piquet crossed the line – doing, incidentally, 296kmh (184mph) – the black and gold Lotus circled again.

Then the hammer: at Paddock, he'd say, he went a fraction wide but we must be talking of balancing *centimetres* against his vision of the *perfect* line, then pump-pump-pumping up and round Druids, descending, running breathless along Cooper Straight, corkscrewing uphill at Surtees Bend, then the long downhill surge into the country, the dense woods flicking by but, as he approached Hawthorn – a right feeding a tight, alarmingly fast loop – he came upon Prost touring.

There were many virtues about Prost, not least that he fully intended to complete his grand prix career with his body having exactly the same number of parts as when he began it – yet even in the act of making sure he did not impede Senna, and thus avoiding a crash, he could not dissolve either himself or his McLaren. Senna, reaching him with ferocious speed, ought instinctively have lifted his foot off the accelerator – a reflex action of self-preservation, however slightly he lifted, before pressing the foot down again.

He did not lift.

He went past Prost like the wind.

As the loop released him at Westfield Bend and he prepared for the run to Dingle Dell, Stirling's Bend and Clearways – he put a wheel wide: utterly trivial, normal and unremarkable except in the context of the perfection of this one lap. He carried the ferocity of speed full to the line, averaging 225kmh (140mph) for the lap. Nobody had ever done that before.

1m 07.169.

And this amazing human being wondered aloud if he'd got the most out of the car …

On one of these laps, probably this one, Senna came upon John Watson, deputising for Lauda (ill) in the other McLaren. Watson's words have appeared before, so I won't quote them all again – just edited highlights to give you the real impression of Senna at speed and at close quarters. Watson was, like Prost, on an 'in' lap and therefore concentrating on keeping out of the way. He was at the dip at Dingle Dell and as Senna came by "it was as if he had four hands and four legs. He was braking, changing down, steering, pumping the throttle and the car appeared to be on that knife edge of being in control and being out of control." Watson had begun in 1973 and this was his 152nd grand prix meeting. He had never seen anything like it before.

A question to Peter Warr: what was it like being in the pits when something like that was going on?

"To start off with in 1985 it was very, very nervy but later on when we got to know him better we realised that it was all part of the master plan and the team got pretty relaxed and spent time on the pit wall or looking at the monitors enjoying something you weren't likely to see again for a while."

Senna finished second to Mansell (this was the race, incidentally, where Prost became World Champion for the first time). Next: South Africa, and it must be said that in the apartheid era all contacts with South Africa were controversial and major sports no longer went there – although Formula 1 had visited Kyalami every year from 1967 except 1981. The arguments for and against all this are largely – and mercifully – buried now in the prehistoric place where apartheid belongs, but to go to South Africa in the mid-1980s troubled some teams (in 1985 Renault and Ligier refused to go) and troubled some drivers, Senna among them.

At Brands Hatch he stated that he was still considering the matter and Warr was quoted as saying: "I think he is still hoping the race will be called off, but it's not a matter of his making up his mind. We are under contract to race at Kyalami, and he is under contract to us." Now let's reflect on this – in 1998.

You pointed out to him – or everybody within earshot – that you had a contract to go to Kyalami and he had a contract with you and if you put the two together he was going to Kyalami.

"Yes. That I think was the public position of what one wanted to establish: the employer-employee relationship without saying it to his face. In point of fact I think the way I persuaded him more than that was *this is the only international sporting event that is allowed to happen in South Africa and by taking part you are showing support for South Africa, not disapproval, of the people there. You get down there and you'll see that 60 per cent of the people watching the race are coloured anyway.* It was a point of principle because he was a very principled man, but he had an over-riding sense of duty and obligation. You hear all these stories about him being arrogant but they are just totally unfounded. I never had a situation where, if you went to him and said *look, we'd like to do this, what do you think about it?* and he said *yes, I'll do it,* there was no question about whether he would or not. It was always *if I said I'll do it, I'll do it.*"

Between Brands Hatch and Kyalami he had another important engagement, watching Gugelmin win the Marlboro British Formula 3 Championship at Silverstone. That week de Angelis announced that he was leaving Lotus and Warwick became favourite to replace him.

One report implied that Senna was "less than keen" on having Warwick as a team-mate and tried to persuade Warr to give Gugelmin the seat. "No," Warr says. "I think that some of those stories arose because at that time he was living with Gugelmin down at Esher and very often when I went to see him it was at the house. People put 2 + 2 together and got something like 7."

The sponsors, John Player, would never have agreed to two Brazilians –

they'd have stipulated at least one Brit, as they had done in 1983 when Warr
wanted to replace Nigel Mansell.

"That was a different case. Elio was on pole at Brands and Mansell was third and I had Ayrton in my office ready to sign for $50,000 for the following year and I told Peter Dyke [promotions manager of John Player] *you've got to do this* and he produced the British newspapers on the Sunday morning and the Christopher Hiltons and the others of this world who were pandering to their editors had got headlines MANSELL THIRD! They completely omitted the fact that Elio was on pole in the same car. So that was the justification for keeping Mansell for the following year. But then Mansell had to go to make way for Ayrton and, if you remember, Ayrton came in on the basis that *I don't want to be number one, I'm quite happy to drive with Elio and learn my trade – you know, make some progress.*

"I thought this was very mature of him, and then the following year it was perfectly obvious that he was number one anyway on performance and he had the opportunity to say *now hang on a minute, I want this team set up the way I want it set up.* I was disappointed that we didn't have Warwick because I felt that Warwick at that time would have been a fabulous Eddie Irvine of today [1998, partnering Schumacher at Ferrari] – you know, a very, very solid number two, reliable, uncomplaining, always give his best, probably produce some jolly good results for us and I think the team would have benefited from a bit of two hands-on experience rather than one hands-on experience.

"Of course we signed Johnny Dumfries and, lovely lad that he is – and although he was quite quick on occasions – first of all everyone was measuring him off Ayrton and second of all he was very, very hard on the transmissions of the cars. That meant a lot of Did Not Finishes. I don't think we'd have had that with Warwick. I think Warwick, with his experience of having been at Renault – and he was well liked by the Renault people – didn't create trouble, nice guy to have around, always a bit of a laugh even when things are going badly. It would have been a very, very good mix.

"In those days, what people didn't realise was that when Ayrton said he wanted something you said *whatever you say, Ayrton.* It was perfectly obvious that he knew which way was 'up'."

The perception of Senna hardened within his own hardness. Toleman were a popular team (who'd also launched the Formula 1 career of Warwick, incidentally). Senna was perceived to have been less than honourable with them. Elio de Angelis was an effortlessly accomplished and popular man. Senna had usurped him. Warwick was a sort of English yeoman, open and disarmingly honest and approachable and amusing. He was extremely remote from airs and graces. His father once told me "if he starts anything like that I'll kick his backside so hard he won't come down for a fortnight," and this when Warwick was in Formula 1.

Ayrton Senna exercised a veto on Warwick joining Lotus.

"At the time the Press were very much pro-Warwick," Warwick says. "It was not at the peak of my career but it was when I needed to make the right choice because I'd just come off the back of a bad year with Renault in 1985. I had talks with Lotus and then I had a contract with Lotus. We'd agreed terms and everything was fine. I was going back up there [Ketteringham Hall, the team's Norfolk headquarters] just before Christmas to sign the contract and when I got there I was greeted with *I'm sorry but the deal's off.* I don't think it was Peter Warr who told me, I think it was Fred Bushell [the financial director].

"He said *Ayrton has considered it, he's spoken to the sponsors, he's put a lot of pressure on the sponsors for you not to come here. He feels that you would be too much of a* – what was the word that they used? – *too much of a problem* because he knew that my forte was getting a team to work, getting the mechanics to work for me and he didn't want that. He wanted to be kingpin. He was not at the beginning of his career but he was still trying to establish himself. He thought that Lotus could only run one works car – one number 1 car. He wanted to have the other car [the spare] to himself. He stuck to his guns and got absolutely destroyed in the British Press but he still stuck to his guns.

"Several things come out of that, and one of them is that you have to admire the guy for holding to what he knew was right. I think he was right for him – I'm not sure it was right for the team, but I'm sure it was right for him. He was hated by a lot of fans and he was hated by a lot of the Press but he did still stick by his guns and those are the traits of a real champion, I believe.

"I was destroyed and I think with reflection it destroyed my career because I ended up in 1986 with no drive. I signed for Jaguar [in sportscars] with Tom Walkinshaw and ended up getting a drive with Brabham when unfortunately Elio de Angelis was killed. But from then on my career took a bit of a side step and then in 1987 I signed for Arrows and that was a slippery slide. So my career really stopped.

"I would not have done that to another human being but that's probably why I'm not a great champion.

"At the time I understood what he was doing even though it destroyed me. There are people within my family that will never forgive him for that, because they know that Derek Warwick's career took a big slide but if I look at it now, it's my belief that he did it for the right reasons – and that was for him. I spoke to him again afterwards. Well, we spoke about it and he apologised to me but said that he believed it was the right reasons for him *and* the team. Now, with history behind us, you have to say it probably was. He wasn't afraid to face me, no he wasn't afraid to face me.

"Let me tell you something very special that happened to me that maybe had a bearing on all this, because he was such an open person. When I went to Brazil for the funeral his mother, who I greeted after the body was laid to rest, came up to me full of tears and said *you know Derek, Ayrton always had a special place in his heart for you* and then wrote me a letter – and I've still got it today – so I think he knew what he did to me and my career but still felt it was done for the right reasons. I don't know whether he was awkward with it or whether or not he just knew he had to squash something in order to survive himself. With hindsight I don't bear him any malice for that. I'm actually more angry with myself for not being tougher in certain situations but, you know, I am my character and I'm proud of what I am – but that went against me at the end of the day."

Senna regretted the thing had happened at all, because up until then he and Warwick had what he described as a "good relationship". He expressed public sadness that Warwick was without a drive. Senna pointed out, however, that he had signed a contract in 1984 to join Lotus in 1985 and that the contract stipulated the team would "concentrate" on its leading driver – Senna, of course. He had been with Lotus a year now, was in a position to judge its strengths and weaknesses, and suspected that if they tried to cope with two front-runners they would, in his own words, find themselves in "compromise situations."

Senna went to South Africa. That was a time of uneasy compromise and, on arrival at Kyalami, observers noticed that several cars no longer bore the names of their sponsors.

I never spoke to Senna about this, and never heard him speak about it either. We cannot know what his views were although it seems reasonable to infer that as a human being he found apartheid repugnant and perhaps more so coming from a multi-national, multi-cultural and multi-coloured country like Brazil. By a seeming paradox, when he arrived at Kyalami he said that "without a doubt, this is the most relaxed grand prix of the year" – meaning the whole atmosphere was rather laid-back, especially if the championship was no longer in play. Nigel Roebuck struck a lovely phrase when he wrote that it felt like being at Snetterton on a midweek day.

Mansell took pole and won, Senna out with an engine problem; in Australia, final race of the season, Senna took pole and suffered an engine problem again but not before he'd tried an ambitious move (as they say) on Mansell and made contact.

In 1985 he drove 16 races for Lotus, taking seven pole positions, winning Portugal and Belgium, finishing second in Austria and the European Grand Prix (the debacle at Brands Hatch with Rosberg) and third in Holland and Italy. This gave him 38 points, worth fourth place in the Championship.

In 1986 Senna drove 16 races for Lotus, taking eight pole positions, winning Spain and the USA East, finishing second in Brazil, Belgium, Germany and Hungary, third in Monaco and Mexico, fourth in Portugal, and fifth in Canada. This gave him 55 points, worth fourth place in the Championship.

Perhaps this is a good point at which to seek the evaluation of Gerard Ducarouge on Senna the driver and Senna the man.

You have seen or worked with nearly all the great drivers …

"Well, I've seen a lot, yes and I've had good relationships with very great ones, although some only, but for a few months, like for example with Mario Andretti. I worked with him for a short time, maybe six months. He was a great driver and a great man. I remember reading an article in the

States where he said he was amazed at the six months we passed together, and the quality of the relationship."

This was the sort of depth Ducarouge and Senna found in their own working relationship but it lasted three years.

Senna could see everything in slow motion.

"It's true, it's true. I remember when we had turbos and we had a lot of parameters to check and that man was able to remember even in a qualifying lap what was the exhaust pressure – which at that stage was one thousand one hundred and twenty for example. Plus the water temperature, plus the oil pressure, plus so many other things. Bernard Dudot [Renault engine man] was just looking at him ... just looking at him ... with big eyes. The checking in those times: we had of course some data acquisition on the car but you had to do the pick-up of that at the end of a test – it was not direct [in the way that telemetry is transmitted from the car to the computers in the pits electronically every lap]. And Ayrton was right! He was never wrong! There were so many things like this which were frankly unbelievable and he was the only one who could do it.

"I'll give you another example. In qualifying he'd make a first run and let's say he was 1.7 seconds behind the fastest. We would sit down with a piece of paper with the circuit on it, we were talking about it and he was thinking about it corner by corner. He'd say *last time I missed three-tenths there* and after that *I didn't position the car well there, too much understeer but next time I will gain two-tenths there.* He completed the full lap like that and we arrived at a [potential] total of him going two seconds quicker" – an immense amount to gain in qualifying. "So he'd jump in the car and he did go two seconds faster. It was just something which you cannot believe.

"I was in trouble. We were making this pole position after pole position after pole position and I had a good friend at Williams, Patrick Head. Patrick came to me and he said *Gerard, you're cheating!* And he was telling everybody. I was fed up with that because we were not. I went to the FISA [governing body] and said to their people *you stop the car just before it comes back to our pit and you check it for one hour and you make all the measurements you bloody want. Patrick and anybody else who thinks I'm cheating can be there, even though I'm not too happy with them seeing all the details of the car.* I was going on and on because I was so upset. I said *don't lose any time any more checking the bloody car just after we've been making a pole position. If you want to disqualify something, disqualify the bloody driver because he's just too fast.* Nobody understood that it was not out of the car that we got these performances, it was out of a driver.

"Yes, it was a good car, a quick car, but he was the talent to find the tenth of a second he needed to be quicker than everybody else. It looked so simple but you knew the man was putting in *everything* he had. Some drivers would find a tenth then Ayrton would find something else. I don't know where – but I do know he had extra somewhere. It was inside him, for sure. Very special."

Many people claim to have been his friend but very few were.

"Very, very few were friends, he had very, very, very few selected friends. He was a kid and like all the kids of 20-whatever he was at that time, 24, 25, 26, I remember he loved to play! I had the privilege of being with him on days of holidays" – lovely expression – "in the *Club Med* in Mauritius and I guarantee you he was playing like a kid all the time, making jokes and so on, but that was only when he was surrounded by a few of the friends he had. There were one or two people from *TV Globo* who were very good friends, and myself, and he was absolutely going crazy for everything, doing sport, flying the little aeroplanes, and the jokes. That was the man that no-one [outside] had been able to see. It was great to have that privilege, to follow his real moments, I would say. In the car or at the circuit he was a totally different man. But on an island like Mauritius he could say *now I'll have fun, now I won't be criticised for what I'm doing, nobody will write silly things in the newspapers about this, deforming the truth, not telling it.* He was feeling completely free, you know, to do what it is normal to do when you are 26 and you should be enjoying yourself a bit."

Something of the naughty boy remained in him, even now in his third season of grand prix racing. Perry McCarthy, who once upon a time almost became a cult figure for his hilarious (and worrying) attempts to qualify a car called an Andrea Moda, remembers 1986.

"I had injured my leg earlier in the year and I was just on the way back. I was driving in a support race to the French Grand Prix at Paul Ricard. I'd already seen Ayrton there to nod at, because I knew him from a few years before anyway – not well – and also Mauricio Gugelmin. Karen my wife was with me and after my race we stayed to watch the grand prix and left. We got hideously lost and found some kind of country road in the middle of nowhere, a farm-type country road but tarmac. Then we saw this moped – a motor scooter – over to the side.

"I thought *I recognise those crash helmets*. It was Ayrton and Mauricio Gugelmin standing by the side of the road. I thought *well, they wouldn't stop there for a laugh* so I pulled up and asked *what's wrong boys?* They said *oh, it's broken down.* [Today Gugelmin seems to remember they'd run out of petrol.] I said *can I give you a lift anywhere?* They said *it's ok, we've already sent for a guy who's bringing a car.* I said *look, I'll hang on in case he doesn't find you.* Within two minutes the guy turned up – and they left that poor bastard there with the scooter and commandeered the car!

"Ayrton was driving. I've now pulled away and I've got them behind me, and all of a sudden Ayrton's right on my rear bumper so I've said to Karen *right, here we go. We are now going to race with Senna.* We've gone absolutely flat out down these lanes. We did have big visibility – wasn't blind corners or anything – *but* we were overdoing it, screeching the brakes, screaming the tyres, putting the car off the tarmac onto the dirt. Every time I looked in the rear view mirror of course Senna is stuck to me. I was kidding myself if I thought I was going to lose Senna, wasn't I? But by the same token I was keeping him back.

"So: he was back there, just there, in the cloud of dust I was kicking up and we were having a great laugh. I'd glance in my mirror and he and Mauricio were cracking up laughing. Karen looked like an eight-year-old on a roller-coaster ... terrified. I was really enjoying myself! Great!

"This must have carried on for about three or four minutes, which is quite a long time driving like that, and all at once we were approaching a town. There was a big build-back of traffic and I could see it leading to a blind corner. I said to Karen *watch this*. I pulled up and I knew he was going to do it: he came past and they were waving and shouting and laughing, pipping the hooter, and Ayrton *went straight on the outside of this traffic queue and vanished round a totally blind corner*. By the time we had crept up to this corner and got round it ourselves I wondered if we were going to see their car looking like a dustbin lid up against a juggernaut – but no, Ayrton got away with it. I was laughing – but it was insane.

"Mauricio once told me a story about when Ayrton had a brand new Mercedes and he was trying to take the slip road off a motorway – a very curved slip road – *flat* ..."

(Gugelmin neither confirms nor denies this, contenting himself with a broad smile, a rumbling chuckle and "Ayrton tried to take a lot of things flat.")

During this season Senna drove in the Spanish Grand Prix at Jerez and what happened there during first qualifying allows Peter Warr to explain what he meant when he said Senna made the team nervy. "He had a habit, and the best example I have got of that is Jerez. He went out there and did a time and he was like 1.7 seconds faster than everybody else. Those were the days when we used to have to go out very early in practice because we had to change the turbos between the runs. With the exhaust waste gates blocked off, the turbos lasted a lap – but you didn't half get some 'grunt!' They were red hot and it took quite a lot of time.

"So he went out and he did this stunning time, we changed the turbos and it got to 15 minutes to go. He said *I want to go out again*. I said *no, no, no, don't be silly. You're 1.7 seconds quicker than everybody*. He said *no, no, I want to go out again*. I asked him *why, Ayrton? There's no point*. He said *I can do a 16.9*. I said *I beg your pardon?* He said *I've been thinking about it, I can do a 16.9*. That was a mind-blowing time in the context of what he'd already done. He got in the car and sat there with his helmet on his chest and his eyes closed. He was thinking his way round the lap. It got to about ten minutes left, maybe five minutes left and he said *right, I'll go now*. I said again *are you sure, it really isn't necessary, no-one's going to beat your time* but he repeated *no, no, I'll go*. So we let him go and he went out and did a 1m 16.9."

Because he was actually in competition with himself.

"That's right. And once you got used to that, when he said something like that, of course you sent him out and immediately you said *right, lads, everybody round the monitor because this is going to be mind-blowing*. And sure enough it was. So, as I said, to start off with we were a little bit nervy but later on the whole team was pretty damn relaxed knowing that we were going to have a fantastic show. The opposition weren't privy to what we knew – we knew what he was going to do. The other thing you've got to remember is that it was the heyday of qualifying tyres and 1300 horsepower – *and* when he'd been to McLaren and was at Williams he said the Lotus 97 was the best handling car he'd ever driven. We had this magic way of setting it up. D'you remember it used to spray sparks out of the back like crazy and everybody thought we had some trick cheating device – and it wasn't anything to do with that: Ducarouge had worked out the parameters for a qualifying run.

"Latterly, of course, Ayrton didn't have to do that quite so much. He had to go quick but you weren't into the unlimited horsepower and you weren't into the super sticky gumball qualifying tyres. You were on a set of race tyres which were part of your allocation for the weekend. You try and do a quick time but then you bring them in and save them because you need them for the race. Put it this way: the 1980s was the era of conspicuous consumption and Ayrton helped us consume ..."

In 1987 Lotus, true to the Colin Chapman tradition of spectacular innovation, produced a car with active suspension. As Peter Warr says, "Ayrton won two consecutive grands prix in it: Monaco and Detroit. If it had worked consistently it might have taken the other teams at least a season and a half to catch up and in point of fact that in itself was a stunning story because we went testing in Rio in January, a month before the race, with what we called a conventional car – a 'sprung' car – and the active suspension car. The active suspension car was part of the development that we'd promised Ayrton we would follow – and with a bit of luck, if it went right, we would have it by mid-season. He got in the conventional car at Rio and did some laps, he got in the active car and drove that, came back and said *this is what we've got to have for the whole season, from the start of the season – and nothing else.* What he'd omitted to take note of was the fact that the special valves and the very tricky hydraulic stuff were on 26 weeks delivery from the manufacturer in America. Yet we turned up a month later for the Brazilian Grand Prix with an active suspension car. But it was Ayrton's *drive* [in the other sense of the word: his push], his enthusiasm and his uncanny instinct for what was going to be good, and what wasn't, which forced the issue and made us get on with it."

In 1987 he drove 16 races for Lotus, taking one pole position, winning Monaco and the USA East, finishing second at Imola, Hungary, Italy and Japan, third in Britain and Germany, fourth in France, and fifth in Austria and Spain. This gave him 57 points, worth third place in the Championship. Lotus were now sponsored by Camel, all the overalls and livery bright yellow.

Stepney is trenchant in his feelings about the active suspension. "I have to say we won with the Camel Lotus in Monte Carlo and Detroit and it was very satisfying to win in those days with the active because we're talking about the late 1980s. If you think of what we had then in computers compared to the technology and computers today we were happy to win those two races – but also we had Ayrton Senna and on those sorts of circuits he was literally streets ahead of everybody else."

Do you think the car was before its time because it was too complicated?

"Lotus had had the very first active car long, long before. If you speak of innovation, you can't say you are too early. How can you say you are too early? It is an *innovation*. You have got to make it work. You look at Williams: they are probably a good example because they stick with something, work at it, work at it and do well when it is proved. You don't just drop it. A lot of teams years ago started things and did drop them. You are always looking for small advantages and you can't just pick up something for five minutes. I don't know if learning is a lot harder now but you have a lot more equipment to measure everything ..."

Ducarouge judges that Senna "was very patient with the active car, I have to say. With that kind of car we were all a little bit confused because it was so complex to analyse all the parameters and for him, he had to work out what was doing what and why and so on. He didn't spend a thousand hours to try and understand but he was very patient and we won two grands prix. The car was of the future but for him it was something very difficult because the quality of a good driver is always to make some anticipation of what's going to happen in the corners. With an active car you are not doing that, the car is doing that for you – and that makes a lot of confusion in the way you tell the engineer about it, and even in the way you feel it: with an active car, the parameters are changing with each centimetre of the road according to the programme of the computer."

And perhaps worse for him because as a driver he was so sensitive to the car and the track and everything.

"Yes he was, and that was something else which was unbelievable. I'll tell you a story which was the bad story! We were talking and he said *you set the car up exactly the way we have been discussing – which is exactly the way it was last time* and I said *yes, of course, Ayrton, you know that.* He went out and came back in after one lap. *Look Gerard, it's wrong,* he said, *you did change something and I think it must be a shock absorber. I want to check with you.* He was correct: something was wrong. It was all the way down to very, very small details.

"Being in contact with so many of the big drivers, starting with Dan Gurney [American grand prix racer between 1959 and 1970] and Jack Brabham – but I don't want to make the list, because I think it's something like over 60 drivers and, of course, a few World Champions in the middle of it. I do say of Ayrton that you cannot make a comparison with anyone else. You can talk about talent. OK, Schumacher is a great talent, Ayrton was a great talent, but that's it.. You can not say any more, because all the other ways you are going to try to make the comparison between the two you will never, never be right. Never.

"Ayrton was not like anyone else. No chance that he had something in common with someone else, even the great Prost. I'm not talking about the numbers, or the World Championships: the human being was very different than all the others. And he himself knew how to be different people. In a matter of seconds, or a matter of minutes, he was not the same man at all: always professional when he was driving, always a young boy away from that, enjoying himself and knowing the right way to do it. He was *right* when he was playing, he was *right* when he was driving, he was *right* everywhere ..."

Trevor Foster says, "I think it was Hockenheim and he had a problem with the active car. It used to have those little 'helper' springs. At a period during the race the active suspension failed and the car went down onto these helper springs – which was a system employed to get the car back to the pits if the active suspension did fail. Evidently they saw from the telemetry that the active suspension had died so they kept saying *come in, come in.* I think he was running second at the time but obviously the car went further and further backwards because it was on these very soft, minimal springs – and he finished the whole race, third! He got four points out of it and when he came in after the race he said *you'd better have a look at the brake pedal because it was going 'long' for the last four or five laps.* When they looked at it, the floor was worn away because the car had been running so low and all the pedals were coming out of the bottom! In other words, when he said the pedal had gone soft it was actually hanging out underneath and he *still* finished third."

At the end of 1987 he left Lotus to join McLaren and partner Prost. Peter Warr is in no sense, I suspect, a bitter man but just this once his voice moves towards it. "I took all the (expletive) after Ayrton left about *oh well, Team Lotus is nothing without Ayrton, it'll never be anything again, it's a shadow of its former self.* I didn't notice them saying that when Ron Dennis lost him and McLaren turned to rubbish and I didn't notice them saying that with Benetton when Schumacher left and so on – but it's just the way it is. If you've got a Jimmy Clark, if you've got a Niki Lauda, if you've got a Prost, if you've got a Senna, they as much as anything drive the team."

And presumably when he went to McLaren there was nothing you could have done to keep him?

"No, because he'd done a deal with Honda to take the engines to McLaren and he was totally in love with Honda and their way of working, and Honda were totally in love with him. If he said *I want the Honda in the back of a Sinclair C5* they would have said *yes, how many do you want and where do you want them delivered?* He had an enormous pull with Honda."

Mr. Honda liked him a lot.

"It was a mutual relationship. Ayrton had an infinite admiration for the way Honda went about their business – I did, too – we had a wonderful working relationship, but mine with Honda went back earlier. Ayrton came to it fairly fresh and in the year that we ran Senna and Nakajima in the Camel car [1987], we did 16 grands prix, two cars in each grand prix so that's 32 starts and we finished 31 times, which is extraordinary."

Warr is right about the void a driver like Senna leaves when he departs any team. After he left Toleman in 1984 the team only ever finished one more grand prix; after he departed Lotus in 1987 the team never took another pole position or won another race – and they continued competing until 1994; after he departed McLaren in 1993 the team did not take another pole position, or win another race, until 1997. You see the way it is: the great driver earns millions because, without him, the team spends millions for very little purpose. To create, maintain and prepare a Formula 1 racing car requires the harmonised skills of several dozen experts in completely different fields, but out there on the circuit the driver *is* the team. This is the razor blade of greatness. When a team has two great drivers, and they both have the razor blade, you get a lot of blood on the floor. It is fair to say that when Senna joined McLaren to partner Prost, many foresaw this. They were not wrong.

Then and now

Keke Rosberg was interviewed at Monza (he was there as Mika Hakkinen's manager) and he has made no concessions to the years – except that his son is in karting and evidently serious and good. Rosberg remains explosive social company: a bubbling concoction of humour, trenchant opinion, shrewd judgement and machine-gun bursts of laughter, intermingled with hammering German phrases into his mobile phone whenever it rings. This is the man who took on Senna at Brands Hatch and didn't give him an inch and you know, if it all happened again today, he still wouldn't be giving him an inch.

Trevor Foster has an open-plan office at the Jordan factory and there's a warmth about him. You'd want him as a favourite uncle. He delights in the folklore of motorsport but he talks quietly about it because he's naturally a soft speaker. He has an old-fashioned dignity which you don't always find in Formula 1 now – and didn't always find yesterday either.

October 1998 and Derek Warwick had just returned from the Bathurst 1000kms in Australia, where he and co-driver John Cleland finished fifth despite a misunderstanding during a pit stop when Warwick set off too soon and spilling fuel caused a fire. I caught him on the phone in Jersey. He was mulling over retirement, no regrets really, and I suggested he might at least consider an annual drive at Le Mans (a place he enjoys) just for fun. No, he said, that's not how he's approached motorsport and he won't be changing now. His two daughters, who skipped and scampered round Silverstone on British Grand Prix weekends when Senna was still a hungry young man, are now competing on horseback at Badminton.

The Peter Warr interview was done in October 1998. "I invited Steve Hallam up here last night for a cup of tea after he'd finished the testing at

Silverstone with McLaren. He's a lovely guy, I brought him into racing and he was Ayrton's engineer at Lotus. He was saying 'you know, Hakkinen's got to go off I think tomorrow or the next day to China to help them sell cigarettes, but I suppose the plus side is he'll get a bit more used to the time change just before a very, very telling grand prix' – Suzuka, the deciding race of the season. He said 'you wouldn't believe the schedule and the [expletive] these drivers have to put up with.' Well, all of that sort of thing started in the Ayrton era with us when the demands of the sponsors were becoming fairly severe – but if I sat down with him at the beginning of the year and said 'look, we need you to do this, this, this, and this' and we agreed the timetable, he would be there on the dot, properly dressed, charming as the day is long, and carry out the duty 100 per cent just like he did his driving."

Chapter 5

A sigh is
just a sigh

ALL THE EVIDENCE leads to this singular point, and it is one Alain Prost himself shares: Ayrton Senna intended to destroy him – not outmanoeuvre him, not win more races, not establish some sort of dominion over him but *destroy* him. The domination of Formula 1 would logically follow from that. Not that it was personal with Prost. Thus far he had destroyed Cecotto at Toleman, following up with de Angelis and Johnny Dumfries at Lotus – and, initially anyway, he had liked de Angelis, holidayed with him, frisked around on the beach or whatever. He destroyed them because that was the way it was. They represented competition, they were a comparison with him. He destroyed Warwick before Warwick could even become competition. The next enemy was quite different: the next enemy was the prey he had stalked these four years since the Mercedes race at the Nurburgring.

Perhaps, in his most personal moments, Senna could see through a door to beautiful, sunlit places where he was an absolute champion of all he surveyed and everything he had done with his life – *all* of it – was utterly, utterly vindicated; but a small, wiry figure stood in that doorway blocking access. He was the son of a furniture maker in a French town so anonymous hardly anybody had heard of it. He had shaggy hair and a wonderful nose, often broken. No demons possessed him. He spent *his* life practising the rational, which in his case was winning championships with as little risk and fuss as possible. If he made a single mistake per season it was slightly more than his average.

Prost was so good that his resistance to destruction threatened to destroy parts of Formula 1 itself.

Jo Ramirez, who has spent a lifetime in motor racing and worked at McLaren – so he saw it from the inside – has hammered out these words (in *F1 Racing* magazine): "From the very first time Ayrton drove the car, he had an obsession about Alain. He wanted to know what rear wing he had, which front springs, which tyres. Every time he came in to the pits, the first thing he would ask is what time Alain had done. All the time. He didn't care about anybody else. Alain was the number one and, even before becoming World Champion, beating him was Ayrton's obsession."

It's easy, endlessly easy, to produce evidence which gives a completely different aspect to Senna from the one Rosberg has given, or the public perception of him deserting Toleman, or working over de Angelis and vetoing Warwick, or preparing to launch his assault on Prost.

Here is one aspect from Peter Merrilees who had known Senna since FF2000. "Ayrton was always interested in the people he met on the way up. An example. Somebody who worked for me subsequently went on to get a job in the McLaren design office and when he arrived Ayrton was going round. Ayrton would remember who'd been in the design office and if he saw a face he had not met – because from time to time they'd call in contract draughtsman – he'd go up and say *I'm Ayrton Senna, I hope you enjoy your stay* and all this kind of thing.

"When he noticed the chap who'd worked for me, a New Zealander called Hugh Moran [now with Benetton], he asked *where have you come from*? Moran said *Swift and Frank Bradley.* Senna said *how is Frank? Has he still got the Lambo*?"

Moran, an engineering designer, remembers that "it was a Saturday afternoon, believe it or not. When Senna first signed for McLaren he came in quite a lot to begin with, so he just came round one Saturday because we were busy doing the 1988 car and we were pretty late with that one. This was the end of 1987. There were about five or six of us. I was in a corner and he came and plonked himself on the chair and the conversation went exactly the way Peter Merrilees has described it."

What did you make of Senna?

"He was a hell of a driver, I tell you. He put all his cards on the table. I'm a bit of a motor racing anorak and as a kid I remember reading about Ronnie Peterson and Lotus and so on but the thing about Senna was that he was just so dedicated and so committed."

People say he wanted to know everything about a car.

"There are people who talk about that but from a purely professional point of view it is not possible, definitely not possible. Even the design staff nowadays don't know everything that's going on because it's too complicated. For example, if you get on to the electronic controls – I'm not talking about traction control, I'm talking purely about data collection – the electronics guys would lose me in ten minutes. It's so specialised. I never went to the circuits, I was stuck up in the drawing office but Steve Nichols went to the races and the one thing he'd tell us was that Senna would do a few laps, come back in and remember each corner, engine temperatures, oil pressures and all that, could literally rattle them off."

In 1988 he drove 16 races for McLaren, taking 13 pole positions (a record), winning Imola, Canada, the USA East, Britain, Germany, Hungary, Belgium and Japan, finishing second in Mexico, France and Australia, fourth in Spain and sixth in Portugal. This gave him 94 points (90 counting) and the World Championship.

In Rio he took pole but was disqualified (for changing cars after a re-start to the race) and Prost won; at San Marino, he took pole with a lap of 1m 27.148s, Prost next on 1m 27.919s. Ramirez insists that up until then Prost had been very relaxed about any threat Senna might pose, but the Imola second qualifying – when the fast times were set – altered that. In the truck they were changing and Prost scanned the split-times to see where Senna had gained on him. To Prost's bafflement he still couldn't find where. He had his back to Senna and murmured something earthy about Senna's speed. Senna heard and winked at Ramirez; and Ramirez thought Senna was on the way.

Monaco was the race after, and here Senna reached the next crossroads. Starkly put, he led but lost concentration on lap 67 and butted the barrier just before the tunnel. He retreated straight to his apartment and was so distraught that when Jo Ramirez of the McLaren team rang him that *evening* he was still crying. All this is well known but consider the aspects of it.

Nigel Stepney, long in racing and wise in the ways of it, says: "Drivers are *fractions*. That is the difference between winning and not winning. Ayrton was leading at Monaco by a big margin and he shunted it. He shunted it because he lost concentration *because* he was lifting off. Drivers drive at 100 per cent. Not many can lift off in a race, slow down and get away with it. Different drivers have different methods of trying to achieve this and I think that, after Monaco, Ayrton found his method. You talk to, say, Niki Lauda about it and he'll tell you that the driver stays at 100 per cent while he's only using the engine 90 per cent. You understand? The driver has to keep his mind working at the 100 per cent even when he slows to using 90 per cent of the engine, cuts his revs by a thousand and so on. At 100 per cent he maintains his concentration."

Mentally he is at a constant racing speed.

"Some drivers do it like that, not all of them, depends who they are. I think Michael Schumacher has just gone through that [the 1998 Belgian Grand Prix, clouting the rear of Coulthard's McLaren]. Michael didn't make a mistake but there was something to be learnt from what happened. And he learnt. Whenever he is in that position again it won't happen like that again – for the rest of his career."

Senna felt Monaco was a "fundamental turning point. I spent some time trying to understand what happened to me that day." He'd explain that of course he was new to McLaren, was adapting to the team, straining to do well for it and thus allowed "exterior influences to become too great."

He told Anne Giunti of *L'Equipe,* the French national daily sportspaper: "It influenced my position in the team and my style of driving, but I hadn't understood all of that before the stupid mistake at Monte Carlo. Afterwards I had to understand how such a thing could have happened. We all make mistakes and that is normal but the important thing was to know how I had let it happen. I really had a black-out [mind went blank]. And then I found the way to get out of the situation. Some of my family helped me. Little by little I returned to top form, but only slowly and carefully. I needed a full two months. Viewed from the outside I don't think people noticed it but it was a major part of my development."

People didn't notice because they couldn't. Monaco had been 15 May so the "full two months" lasted approximately to the British Grand Prix at Silverstone on 10 July. While he was regaining top form, this is what he put together: Mexico, pole, second to Prost; Canada, pole, victory; Detroit, pole, victory; France, front row, second; Silverstone, second row, victory. The McLaren-Honda was a beautiful car, but even so ...

Monaco seems to have confronted Senna with his own fallibility and its possible consequences. He had made an unforced error, in terms of the race situation: Senna had been leading by as much as 49 seconds, Prost trapped behind Berger. On lap 54 Prost finally squeezed past Berger. On that lap he'd done 1m 29.817.

Prost reasoned that with Senna so far ahead, the situation was lost, all lost – but, hang on a moment, there is a possibility. Prost did not drive a Formula 1 car by emotion and, as a master strategist, he saw a strategy. He did not yet know Senna but he knew of Senna's intensity and had played upon it at their first test session before the season, sitting in the only McLaren available, pretending he wouldn't hand it over to Senna, who was hovering, desperate to get into it. He was aware of Senna's obsessive attention to detail, and the 30-minute debriefs which Prost had been accustomed to were now three hours and more as Senna tried to dissect *everything,* however impossible.

And this narrow, maddening, bumpy circuit of Monaco punished any error.

Prost could not seriously hope to pull back the 40-odd seconds to Senna and even if he did he'd have no chance of overtaking. So, he thought, let's hammer in three fast laps and send a shock wave up to Senna via the McLaren radio and see what happens next. *I'll try,* Prost thought, *to fluster him: maybe he'll fall over a back-marker.* Prost knew a message would have been relayed to Senna from the pits informing him that Prost was now past Berger and informing Senna of the gap.

"I hoped that if Senna saw the gap suddenly coming down by even a second a lap something in him might say *I have got to respond.*" Prost thought Senna probably wouldn't but it was worth a try. Prost dipped his foot on to the accelerator ...

Lap 55   1m 28.157s
Lap 56   1m 27.451s
Lap 57   1m 26.714s

That was relayed to Senna, who did respond:

Lap 57   1m 26.921s
Lap 58   1m 27.339s
Lap 59   1m 26.321s (new lap record)
Lap 60   1m 26.698s

Prost noted the gap no longer coming down and assumed his strategy had failed, Senna responding and making no mistake. Prost eased off. Ron Dennis now relayed to Senna that Prost had eased off and was lapping in 1m 29s and 1m 30s again. Dennis told Senna to ease off himself. Senna did: his 1m 26.698s on lap 60 went out to 1m 28.278s next time round, then out into the 1m 29s, then out into the 1m 30s on lap 65 – but his concentration waned. He was about to be undone by this *third* change of pace and began making what journalist Maurice Hamilton described as "elementary mistakes": almost missing a gear at Casino Square and brushing against the barrier. Then the crash, lap 67.

When Prost reached the scene – it was Portier, the right-hander before the tunnel – and saw Senna's car head-butted into the barrier he couldn't believe the strategy had worked. Prost had assumed that if Senna did make an error it would be committed at the limit making his response, not when they'd both eased back. Winning at Monaco *is* a big deal, Prost said later, but Senna had done it the year before in the Lotus so that particular imperative was already achieved.

Here was the next crossroads. Senna had moved through the intermediate stages – developing his muscles, getting onto the podium, winning races – but the championship would require a completely different level: consistency, and he'd have to achieve that without sacrificing his audacity or his flair. It was the only way to beat Prost – Prost armed with the same car, Prost so prudent and precise *as well as fast*. After Monaco, Senna drew conclusions about making "stupid mistakes" and prepared to move up to the ultimate level. He'd say later "I learnt a lesson that day, and the big lesson I learnt was that what you really have to watch out for is when you're cruising, because your concentration is just not the same. I learnt this from Prost: do not allow anything to disturb your rhythm. I'd been going along in the lead quite happily, then I speeded up in response to him, and then Ron said slow down so I did – the third change of rhythm, and more to the point I was coming down from a high."

This background was easy to miss because by the Italian Grand Prix in the autumn Senna led Prost by 75 points to 72. Early on at Monza, Prost had a misfire and reached – again – for the only strategy he could try. Prost reasoned that if he accelerated before the misfire finally claimed him Senna would respond and use precious fuel he'd need at the end of the race. Prost dipped his foot on to the accelerator ...

He accelerated from laps of 1m 30s into the 1m 29s on lap 24, peaking with his fastest of the race – 1m 29.642s – on lap 27, then a 1m 30s, a 1m 29s and a 1m 30s before the misfire worsened. Senna responded. On lap 27 he dipped into the low 1m 30s and two laps later he was down into the

1m 29s. He didn't ease back into the 1m 31s until lap 35 – a lap after the misfire did claim Prost.

By the end – two laps to go – the Ferraris were closing on Senna and at the first chicane he crashed into Jean-Louis Schlesser (Williams). Was that desperation to get through, desperation to try and maintain a gap to the Ferraris because of the fuel? Senna said it was no such thing and we'll have a powerful witness to corroborate that in a moment. Was being so close to Schlesser another "stupid mistake"?

It didn't cost him the championship, which he took in Japan. He stalled on the grid, completed the first lap eighth then worked through the field, caught and passed Prost for the lead and won the race.

Gordon Murray, one of the great racing car designers, was at McLaren working with Senna. [Murray had been with Brabham in 1983 when Senna tested at Paul Ricard but can't remember anything about him being there! More amazing still, Brabham were also testing Mauro Baldi, Roberto Guerrero and Pierluigi Martini and Murray *does* remember them.]

"I was his chief designer and chief engineer for two years – 1988 and 1989. My first car was the 1988 and I worked with him on race strategy that year. I loved the race strategy in particular and so did he. He just left Prost standing, basically. Race strategy was completely different to what it is now and 1988 was a disaster [for everyone] because we had the fuel limitation" – in 1985 it was 220 litres, down to 195 a year later and then a meagre 150 litres in 1988. "So you had to juggle it the whole race and you spent all of practice working out how you could best get a lap time and use the least amount of fuel. Then you had to adjust that with the driver over the race. It was *so* complicated – it's relatively simple now. We had a similar sort of mind on strategy which was good. We didn't often argue, whereas I used to argue with Prost a lot and force the issue sometimes with Prost on tyre choice or strategy.

"Senna was excellent at that. It's where he had everybody beaten and we used to have a little thing where I'd stand on the pit wall and talk to him on the radio for qualifying to try and find a clear lap and he was brilliant at that as well. We'd always have a good laugh about it. I'd watch who came in, who'd gone out, who was going quick and he *always* managed to pick a lap. In my book, as a racing driver there hasn't been anybody since Jim Clark that comes anywhere near."

Including Schumacher?

"Oh, yes. Oh. Christ yes. Senna was in a different league. Oh, bloody hell yes. I mean, Schumacher just makes so many mistakes. Senna had a ruthless, absolutely ruthless attitude towards lapping people and we'd talk about it. It was odds-on that one day he was going to get caught out like Monza, for instance. That was the one race McLaren lost in 1988."

Was Senna low on fuel? Had Prost made him use too much?

"No, he still had it pretty much under control. Anyway, it was odds-on he was going to hit somebody one day but, on the other hand, if you look at the number of mistakes he made and then think about Schumacher this year

[1998] – Schumacher has a whole catalogue of them. The last lap at Monaco [where Schumacher lost his front wing].

"Senna wasn't like that at all. Senna was so *together* in his head. He used to get very angry but the red haze didn't exist. He was a very cool guy under pressure, very, very cool. Funnily enough, he used to get incredibly emotional but it didn't come out in the driving – he just used to go faster! He didn't do what Schumacher does and fall off the road."

Jo Ramirez once told me that Senna would come on the radio shouting and swearing but another part of his mind remained perfectly cold. Do you think the two feed off each other?

"They must do if you get that emotional about something. He was Latin American for a start, but not typical Latin American. He had a calculating coolness, a slow-motion aspect to him which ran alongside the emotion and although one drew on the other I am sure he could separate them. That's what you need to do. I remember talking to Jackie Stewart in the 1970s and I asked him *how the hell do you come round a racetrack two seconds in the lead? How do you do that?* and he said *you slow stuff down, your mind just slows stuff down* – and I think Senna had the ability to do that as well."

Did you go to the championship decider in Suzuka?

"Yes."

Was he wound up before that?

"He was pretty wound up but I say again he could handle it. I used to talk to him for hours and hours and hours. I loved working with him. He was a much more complete driver than Prost was."

That's a very controversial statement.

"Well, I think he was and I worked with them both."

For Senna to win at Suzuka has to be one of the great drives.

"Oh yes, absolutely."

And what was he like afterwards?

"He was so different from any other racing driver I have ever worked with, and I've worked with most of the good ones. He handled stress differently, he handled joy differently, he handled winning differently, qualifying differently. I just haven't ever worked with anybody quite like that. I'm really glad I worked alongside him. I had much more fun with Nelson [Piquet] and as much success but I'm really pleased I spent two years engineering the car for him. It's something that will be with me for ever. I'd have loved to have worked with Clark but obviously never got the opportunity.

"You can't compare different eras and cars and so on but you do get a feeling for drivers at the time and, since Clark, I haven't had a feeling about a driver – the *way* he won – until Senna. Schumacher is Piquet level and Senna's was really – well, I don't want to be unkind to Nelson because you don't win three World Championships unless you're a good driver, but you know what I mean. Senna was another level, and Clark was another level."

In 1989 Senna drove 16 races for McLaren, taking 13 pole positions again, winning Imola, Monaco, Mexico, Germany, Belgium and Spain, and finishing second in Hungary. This gave him 60 points, worth second place in the Championship – to Prost.

The destruction of Prost began at Imola where Senna proposed a gentleman's agreement. The details are well known: because the McLarens were so superior, whichever one took the lead at the green lights would maintain that lead through the first corner – Tosa – and only thereafter would the dicing and racing between them begin. [Interesting perhaps that Tamburello, between the start-finish line and Tosa, wasn't regarded as a corner at all but a curve, and therefore was not included in the agreement.]

Senna took the lead and Prost followed him through but Gerhard Berger's Ferrari had gone off at Tamburello and burst into a fireball. When the race was re-started Prost led but, into Tosa, Senna scampered through – seemingly a clear breaking of the agreement, and this by a man who insisted his word was his bond and publicly deplored anyone who ever behaved to lower standards.

Prost told Nigel Roebuck: "Afterwards, he [Senna] argued that it wasn't the start – it was the *re-start,* so the agreement didn't apply. He had his own rules, and sometimes they were … well let's say strange."

On the original manuscript of *The Hard Edge of Genius,* Senna wrote: "The agreement has always been that no overtaking manoeuvre would happen under braking at a first corner. My overtaking was initiated by slip-streaming Prost during the straight and by the first corner we were side by side!" Elsewhere Senna said the overtaking began well before Tosa and asked "what should I have done? Lift off in a straight line because I was going faster than him?"

This *was* what he should have done under the agreement.

Because it was the start of what Roebuck has described as "the most bitter feud in motor-racing history" it bears examination. From the re-start Senna tracked Prost through Tamburello and, just after mid-way along the straight between Tamburello and Tosa, flicked out. Tosa was a sweeping right which tightened to a 90-degree left and Senna flicked to the left – which meant that he had the crucial inside line when they reached towards the left. For good measure he positioned himself in mid-track forcing Prost out into the elbow of the left as they prepared to go round it.

Senna won the race – from Prost. Whatever the motivation of the two men at Tosa, and whatever their thought-processes, the feud now existed. Soon after, however, Senna apologised but, as he wrote under the paragraph in *The Hard Edge of Genius* describing that, "the apology was only made to help bring things to a possible working relationship." The destructive process, which was to last in its most virulent form for another three years, had begun.

By Japan, with the championship still at stake, it had reached such a pitch of intensity that Prost (who led by 16 points) vowed he would not be governed by his usual rational behaviour, meaning if Senna came barging along Prost would not move out of his way to prevent a crash. "As far as I was concerned, Senna thought about himself, and that was it."

Senna tracked Prost and, after 46 of the 53 laps, tried a lunge down the inside at the chicane. "For me," Prost says, "the way he did it was impossible because he was going so much quicker than usual into the braking area. I couldn't believe he tried it on that lap because, as we came up to the chicane, he was so far back. When you look in your mirrors and a guy is 20 metres behind you it's impossible to judge and I didn't even realise he was trying to overtake me." Simultaneously Prost reasoned that he wouldn't grant Senna even a "one-metre gap. I came off the throttle, braked – and turned in."

At the time, Prost was quoted as saying: "Ayrton had a small problem. He thinks he can't kill himself because he believes in God and I think that's very dangerous for the other drivers." I set this quotation at the head of a chapter in *The Hard Edge* and Senna did not cross it out. Instead, above it, he wrote: "That's his own thoughts, his own conclusions and words. They don't reflect my thoughts and my beliefs at all."

And that was the crash of '89.

In 1990 he drove 16 races for McLaren, taking ten pole positions, winning the USA, Monaco, Canada, Germany, Belgium and Italy, finishing second in Hungary and Portugal, and third in Brazil, France and Britain. This gave him 78 points and the championship.

Nor, it must be said, did the championship disturb the private Senna. "People know of my passion for model aeroplanes," he'd say, "but I also adore all aquatic sports: jet-skiing, water-skiing, fishing! At Sao Paulo, I like to relax at home with friends, and go to the cinema."

Joey Greenan – the temporary hero of Mondello Park in 1982 – searches out ways and words to describe Senna. "We had a man who – how can I say it? – used his aloofness or his distance from you as an intimidation, an intimidating factor. He did not allow himself to get friends with you. In racing, if you are racing against your friend there are many times that you make room for him and do things that you wouldn't do. Senna I'd say was totally dedicated, he was a different type of driver and I don't think there was anyone before him who ever had what he had.

"The other thing I noticed came when I got older and I'd been over to England with Martin Donnelly when Martin was in Formula 1 and Senna was there playing with his little computer games. It was the 1990 grand prix at Silverstone. My daughter walked up to him and got his autograph, and believe me he was very talkative to her, but in the racing – I'd seen him a few other times and I always heard the same thing from other people – he distanced himself even in Formula Ford 2000. He was very intense over the springs, the roll bars, the set up of the car. I even heard that when practice was over Senna came back to the awning where the mechanics were working on the car thinking over everything ..."

This love of children was a sincere constant in Senna's life. It stands as yet another contradiction to what he could do on the track, in this case create the crash of 1990 when, in Japan and with the championship at stake again, he took pole from Prost (now Ferrari) but wanted the physical position of this pole moved to the left, where he judged the track surface more favourable. Jean-Marie Balestre, the FIA President, refused to move it and, secretly, Senna vowed that he would give the McLaren full power and if Prost got in the way, too bad.

There are many dimensions to this. Senna was prepared to risk his life, and that of Prost, for something an official would not do; he also brought the whole activity of grand prix racing into disrepute – made it a subject of mockery rather than majesty. But, even more astonishing, two weeks later in Adelaide, Senna held a Press Conference and resolutely blamed Prost for the crash. There was no mention of moving pole position, the tantrum with Balestre, or hammering into turn one of the race regardless of where Prost's Ferrari was. Senna presented it as a simple motor racing accident caused because Prost left a gap and he – Senna – was fully entitled to go into it.

After the race Brian Hart was sitting beside a heap of tyres drinking a cup of tea. He looked, as someone has noted, "shattered" that Senna, who he held in such high regard, could have done something like that. Today, reflecting, Hart finds evaluation slightly awkward. "I got to know JC [Jim Clark] because when I was racing we drove across the Continent together a bit and he was a genuinely soft-spoken, mild-mannered man – until he got in a racing car. Then he went hard. He would beat everyone into the first corner because he was a winner and they weren't. You have to have this. All the great winners have had this. Clark – Jochen Rindt – Prost, yes, when he was young – Senna – Schumacher. Take a great tennis champion. They slaughter an inferior opponent and next day they're booed for doing it. And *they don't care*. They are like that."

British television commentator Murray Walker was present at the Press Conference. He nurses great admiration – and no doubt affection – for Senna but also feels the truth must be told. "I remember that impassioned outburst in Adelaide and I realised long afterwards, having been won over by his sincerity, that he was lying through his teeth – but I believe that, in some convoluted way, he *was* somehow utterly sincere in what he was saying. A bit like Bill Clinton."

Prost saw it all a different way and equated Senna to Islam where "death is a game."

These many years later, Prost reveals that after he had retired he and Senna spoke about the crash of 1990 and Senna "admitted to me … that he'd done it on purpose. He explained why" – the tantrum with Balestre.

Prost also says these ominous and hugely significant words: "He was extremely religious, and he used to go on about that, about speaking the truth, about his education, his upbringing, and everything else. At the time, I used to think that some of the things he did on the track didn't fit with all that, but now it seems to me he really didn't know he was sometimes in the wrong. He had these rules, he played by them, and he wasn't interested in anything else. Looking back, I really think he believed he was always in the right, always telling the truth – and on the track he was exactly the same way."

No doubt this explains a great deal, because Senna represented a *fortress totality* unto himself. This, for example, is what he said at the Adelaide Press Conference: "I wish I had won my second title by winning the race, but a fact is a fact and what happened in Japan wasn't the first time and won't be the last. It wasn't just me; it's happened to others," and more in the same vein culminating in this tirade about Prost: "He has complained so much since 1988. He's complained about me, about Honda, about Honda again, about me again, he attacked me, he attacked McLaren. Then he left the team badly, went on to criticise Goodyear this season saying we had different tyres, then he attacked me again, then Gerhard, then Alesi, then his own team management and his own team-mate. At least it is not boring for you!"

After that, Senna was interviewed by Jackie Stewart on Australian television – Channel Nine – and it descended into acrimony. This was reinforced when Senna saw Stewart in the pit lane and berated the quality of the interview, adding: "I'm never doing another interview with you. I am not designed to come second or third, I am designed to win." (This interview is reproduced verbatim in Chapter 10.)

Later still Stewart was quoted as saying: "I know Ayrton believes totally in everything he says, but so did Hitler ..."

Senna was shown an aerial photograph of the crash and it showed the gap he'd tried to put the McLaren into wasn't really a gap at all. He scanned the photograph and said "that's a lie!"

In 1991 he drove 16 races for McLaren, taking eight pole positions, winning in the USA, Brazil, Imola, Monaco, Hungary, Belgium and Australia, finishing second in Italy, Portugal and Japan, third in Mexico and France, fourth in Britain, and fifth in Spain. This gave him 96 points, and the championship.

This was his second season partnering Berger, and there is no doubt that the partnership educated – and enriched – both men. Senna began to understand that you could live a little bit outside the fortress totality, and the fact that you were beginning to find other aspects to life meant you might be an even better driver – you had an overall context now; Berger began to understand that while living life was what he had been placed upon the planet for, the only way to succeed at motor racing at the Senna level was by beginning to construct something like a fortress mentality of his own. They were both finding that however intensely you set off in any given direction, real harmony can only be reached by compromise.

One of the particular forms of compromise which Berger dealt in was compromising photographs pasted into other people's passports. Senna discovered the image of a dusky, well-endowed topless lady inserted where his own photograph should have been, and a customs official at Buenos Aires airport murmured demurely *Mr. Senna, we don't think it's you*. For this and other wonderfully disgraceful tales, see Chapter 9.

By now, of course, Senna had grown into greatness as a driver and I'd

(Picture by David Hayhoe)

Above *The race of champions at Interlagos. Chico Serra is at the front; Senna, wearing pink, third. Look just beyond him in the crowd. The man in the white pullover with his arms folded is Senna's father Milton.* (Picture courtesy of Tche)

Right *The shy, slender teenager would become so gigantesque his image embraced a whole country. This is Brazilian wall art.* (Picture by Mats Larsson)

Below *Chico Serra, the Brazilian racer friend of Senna, who answered the question "when is The Fast Man coming?"* (Picture courtesy of Petter Dahl)

Tche today, with reminders everywhere in his office. (Author)

Below *This is his visiting card, Senna winning at Interlagos and Tche himself waving the chequered flag.* (Picture courtesy of Tche)

Right *The house on the hill and you needed nerve to kart down there.* (Pictures by Mats Larsson)

Two striking studies of teenage Senna in class. Almost everyone is smiling except him and the whole world would come to know this stern gaze. (Above, taken by Azarias de Carvalho Gianvechio, the school photographer; below courtesy Colegio Rio Branco)

Right *The entrance, the celebrated pupil and the gym.* (Pictures by Mats Larsson)

The Director General of the Colegio, Primo Pascoli Melare who remembers Senna as a boy who just did enough.

The school report wouldn't have been worth framing if it hadn't been his. (Pictures by Mats Larsson)

Priceless pictures that capture the very beginning. Following Alfonso Toledano through Druids at Brands Hatch in his very first race.

Another view of Druids with an unidentified driver close behind.

The first racing car victory of his career, Brands Hatch, 15 March 1981. A driver called Steve Lincoln is directly behind, and where is he today?

Riding the kerbs at Snetterton. (Pictures by Fred Scatley)

Previous spread *The 1981 Formula Ford 1600 race at Brands run under a doom-laden sky, with Senna and Andy Ackerley on the front row. Years later Senna signed it "So what happened to you?" meaning to your career. Ian Dickens, who took this picture, has long worked for Olympus Cameras – Lotus sponsors in 1985. "I dug it out and said to Ayrton 'sign it with something which will wind my friend Andy up …'"* (Picture courtesy of Andy Ackerley)

Above *The South American connection in deepest Norfolk: Toledano left, Enrique Mansilla right.* (Pictures by Mike Dixon)

Left *Frantic action and victory at Snetterton.*

A wink at Zolder.

*Waiting,
Silverstone.*

*Talking to
Reginaldo Leme
of* TV Globo,
*Emerson
Fittipaldi
listening.*

The other-worldly concentration before a race, here at Snetterton.

If anybody tells you he didn't smile much, show them these.

(Pictures courtesy of Petter Dahl)

Right *The drivers had to attend a group photograph at Hockenheim in 1982 and Frank Bradley (holding helmet) always liked centre stage – then he found Senna thought the same way.*

Below *The drivers mill around and joke waiting for the official picture.* (Pictures courtesy of Frank Bradley)

Below right *The struggle of 1982: Senna leading Calvin Fish at Snetterton.* (Picture by Fred Scatley)

Above *The greatest moment of Bradley's career after the most outrageous gamble at Snetterton in the wet. He overtakes Senna to win – a sensation in 1982.* (Picture by Mike Dixon)

Right *Here is Bradley, the only driver on dry tyres, cutting through the field like a knife.* (Picture by Fred Scatley)

Overleaf *The picture Senna sent to Brian Hart in gratitude for the engine which almost took him and Toleman to victory at Monaco in 1984.* (Picture courtesy of Brian Hart)

A word (or two) from Jackie Stewart. Senna doesn't seem impressed. (Pictures courtesy of Brian Hart)

Signing autographs at Estoril.

The new Toleman, the 184, offered rich promise. Here Senna tests it at Silverstone. (Pictures courtesy of Brian Hart)

Toleman driving force: Rory Byrne, Brian Hart, Senna.

The start in Canada. He finished seventh.

A pensive look at Dallas, where it all started to go wrong with Toleman. (Pictures courtesy of Brian Hart)

The British Grand Prix at Brands Hatch, where he finished third behind Niki Lauda and Derek Warwick. This is preparing for the lap of honour.

Above left *The ride on the storm at Monaco in 1984. Pulling on his overalls.*

Above right *As he clambered into the Toleman, the team were telling him (Brian Hart swears): Dry your feet or they'll slip on the pedals!*

Below *A magnificent study of Senna in the wet, here overtaking Elio de Angelis who must have been taken by surprise – look at the posture of his Lotus.* (Pictures courtesy of Brian Hart)

Top *Qualifying in Austria, 1987.*

Above *Monaco 1987 and victory in the active suspension Lotus.*

Below *Driving force at Lotus: Steve Hallam, Senna and Gerard Ducarouge.* (Pictures by David Hayhoe)

As time goes by: Portugal 1986 ...

… Silverstone 1991 …
(Pictures by David Hayhoe)

… Donington 1993.

The pal: Gerhard Berger. This is at Silverstone, testing in 1992.
(Pictures by David Hayhoe)

Left *Senna leads Monaco in 1990 on the road but not on the screen.*

Below left *Settling in at McLaren, 1988.*

Below *The Senna–Prost duel at Silverstone, 1989, but Senna spun off with a gearbox problem.* (Pictures by David Hayhoe)

Left *He always showed agility at Silverstone.* (Picture by David Hayhoe).

Above *He showed agility there in the car too, especially in the wet. This is 1988.* (Picture by David Hayhoe)

Below *Charisma at Hockenheim.* (Picture by Andreas Stier)

Above *His final victory – at Adelaide – 7 November 1993. Alain Prost was second, Damon Hill third.* (Picture by The Motor Sport Shop, South Hurstville, New South Wales)

Right *Yes, yes, the drivers can't stand each other, never have a natter, never smile …* (Picture by Andreas Stier)

Below *Not far from the madding crowd, Hockenheim.* (Picture by Andreas Stier)

The sublime moment: Senna cuts past Prost to lead the 1993 European Grand Prix at Donington. (Pictures by David Hayhoe)

Above *Senna's sister Viviane at the 1998 Autosport Show, National Exhibition Centre, Birmingham. She runs the Instituto in Sao Paulo helping deprived children. (Picture courtesy of Darryl Reach)*

Above right *The worn-out running track at the University of Sao Paulo where Senna built his body into manhood. He used the red-painted metal gantry under the trees on the right to stretch his muscles before running. (Author)*

Right *The infield of the running track is used by one of the Instituto's programmes. Here boys and girls play organised football. (Author)*

Above left *Senna's Bible, passport and briefcase at the Autosport Show. His passport did not expire until 19 November 1997.* (Picture courtesy of Martin Zustak)

Above right and below *They waited between 15 and 30 minutes to see the wonderful exhibits, like this McLaren.* (Pictures courtesy of Martin Zustak).

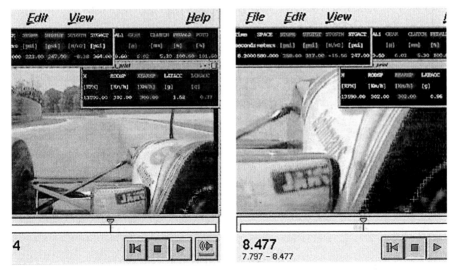

How CINECA put together the telemetry and the on-board images from Imola. Note the green and red arrows and between them the famous yellow button on the upper left of the steering wheel. CINECA have made all this available on the World Wide Web.

Above left *The dignified entrance to Morumbi.* (Picture by Mats Larsson)

Below left *A friend of Sue McAleese (see overleaf) at Senna's grave. She's called Savanah, she's entirely typical of those who come, and it could have been taken any day.* (Picture courtesy of Sue McAleese)

This page *Morumbi.* (Pictures by Mats Larsson)

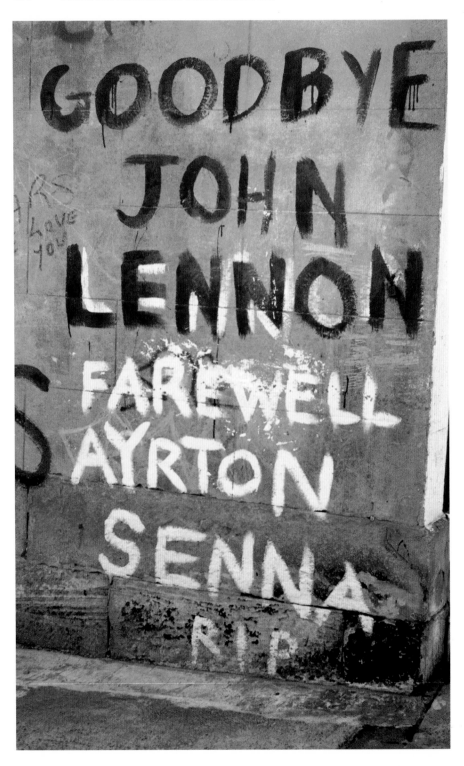

Left *After Tamburello, another wall, in Australia.* (Picture by The Motor Sport Shop)

The other side of the wall. Outside Tamburello. (Pictures courtesy of Sue McAleese)

like to give you a couple of examples of distance and proximity. His English teacher from the Colegio Rio Branco, Paulo Torres, went to Silverstone for the British Grand Prix of 1991, and would again in 1992. "I couldn't speak to Senna because we were very far away in a grandstand. I had a lot of students from the school with me, about 35 – Senna didn't know we were there. We decided we wanted to see the race, we hired a coach, we went and … Mansell won! Ayrton did not finish and at the end he was sitting on top of his car looking disappointed. He was a man of victories."

In 1992 he drove 16 races for McLaren, took one pole position, won Monaco, Hungary and Italy, finished second in Germany, third in South Africa, Imola and Portugal, and fifth in Belgium. This gave him 50 points, worth fourth place in the championship – the lowest he had been since 1986.

Ken Tyrrell has a revealing anecdote about the second race, Mexico – Tyrrell who had been in such close proximity to him for years but had barely had reason to talk to him. "At the drivers' and team managers' briefing everyone was complaining about the bumps on the circuit. The circuit was built on a swamp – the whole of Mexico City is on a swamp – and there was subsidence, so the track became bumpy. Senna said *something ought to be done about the bumps before we come here again* to the Clerk of the Course, whoever that was – in those days it would have been a local guy. When he said that I made the point that what he needed to do was raise his car a couple of inches and he wouldn't notice there were any bumps – but, of course, in doing that he loses a tremendous amount of ground effect and nobody wanted that, did they?"

He laughed, did he?

"I don't think he did …"

And this is how a great driver thinks. The anecdote comes from Martin Brundle and is about the Canadian Grand Prix. Brundle, then at Benetton, was team-mate to Michael Schumacher, itself no comfortable position.

"I had just overtaken Michael for second place, Gerhard Berger ahead of us in the McLaren: so McLaren first, Benetton second and third – and my car broke down at exactly the same place as Senna's car had broken down. It was around the back, coming out of turn five. I ground to a halt, marshals pulled me back in and there's Senna's car and Senna still there. He hadn't broken down much earlier and he was watching the race.

"He knew that that was my best chance of winning a grand prix, that I was catching Berger really quickly and his first words were *it's tough, isn't it?* In other words, *I know how much it hurts when you can win a race and you lose it through mechanical failure.* I said *yeah* – I was destroyed because I was trying to hang on to my Benetton drive and I knew this was crucial, a turning point in my career.

"Then he started looking round my car, starts inspecting the tyres and gets on the radio to his pit – because now, of course, it's Berger in front with

The picture Sue McAleese took of Senna and her son James. Senna liked it so much he asked for a copy. (Picture courtesy of Sue McAleese)

Schumacher behind him. So Senna's instant thinking was to give the team information on my tyres because the condition of Schumacher's tyres was going to look very similar to mine" – invaluable information for Berger.

"As it happened, Gerhard had buzzed his engine early on in the race and was on a wing and a prayer for it getting to the end, because he'd put a huge number of revs on it with a sudden downshift problem. I don't think Senna knew that but the team certainly appreciated the information. It demonstrated his lateral thinking: *here is something we can turn to our advantage*.

"I realised straight away when he was looking at my tyres what was going on but I couldn't stop him looking. In a single-seater like a Formula 1 car everyone can see them! Anyway, a motor bike came to take us away and he left on it first because he'd been there the longest. So I took his steering wheel off, jumped in his car and had a good look round it – where all the switches were, which switches he'd got, what they might do and I had a general poke round."

Nor should we leave Canada there. What follows is instructive because it gives another insight into how a great driver thinks. It also shows how isolated teams and personnel can be from each other even within the confines of the paddock. Ken Tyrrell had been running his team for *generations* and, of course, had been in all those paddocks since Senna began with Toleman. "I knew Senna a little," Tyrrell says, "but I only had one lengthy conversation with him [the distance and proximity again]. That was in Montreal at the time when everyone was getting these automatic gearboxes, well semi-automatic. He asked me what did I think about it and I said *it takes a lot of skill away from the driver.* He made the point that one of the reasons he won so many races at Monte Carlo was that he was able to look after his gearbox. With so many gearchanges it's easy to knock the corners off the 'dogs' you see, and if you do that it jumps out of gear. It's very difficult then because you've got to jump a gear every time, and what happens then is that you knock corners off the other ones.

"It required a great deal of skill to change gear when we had normal gearboxes. He said the semi-automatic affected his competitiveness if drivers were all going to have gearboxes where you could change gear when you liked because it didn't matter. These days all you do now is press a bloody button and it goes into whatever gear you want. That's the only lengthy conversation I had with him ..."

As we have seen, in December 1992 Senna flew to Phoenix to sample a Penske on the Firebird circuit. It had been organised by Emerson Fittipaldi, who told the *Los Angeles Times:* "Ayrton and I have talked about this for a number of years over dinners in Brazil during the off-season. Firebird is very small, with very slow corners, but it gave Senna a bit of a taste. I told him to be very careful, that an Indy car is quite a different breed from a Formula 1 car – but in only a lap or two he was very quick. It was beautiful to watch him drive, to see how much he was enjoying his work. He was very smooth going into the corners ..."

In a celebrated quotation, Senna explained that "it was like having a new toy. There was so much to learn, to understand. It was a tremendous challenge and I think it has rejuvenated me. For the first time in some time racing was fun again. Formula 1 – the people and the politics – had drained my enthusiasm for racing this past season." He explained that he had no commitment to IndyCar racing but he was thinking about it. He never drove an Indy car again.

In 1993 he drove 16 races for McLaren, taking one pole position, winning Brazil, the European at Donington, Monaco, Japan and Australia, finishing second in South Africa and Spain, fourth in France, Germany and Belgium, and fifth in Britain. This gave him 73 points, worth second place in the championship.

Berger had returned to Ferrari and Michael Andretti came to partner Senna from IndyCars, with Mika Hakkinen the test driver. Andretti arrived with his father Mario's experience guiding him (Mario, World Champion with Lotus, 1978) and a reputation of his own for incisive, fearless racing. He arrived, too, with the hope that some of the North American openness and approachability might come with him: fresh air down cob-webbed corridors. Andretti didn't last the season. In the midst of this, and with an ordinary, uncompetitive Ford engine *and* – grumpy about the whole damn thing – only agreeing to drive race-by-race, Senna led the championship towards mid-season before Prost and the absolutely superior Williams overwhelmed him.

Only a maturing man could conceivably have led the championship against Prost, or rather only a great driver maturing into a great man.

Each of the words in that sentence has been chosen very carefully.

Hugh Moran says "one experience that sticks in my mind was when Michael Andretti signed for us. I felt sorry for him in a way, because he was down to do extensive testing at Silverstone and I gather the electronic control of the engine wasn't working properly. Andretti hardly got a few laps in, and when he did the car was pretty slow. He and Hakkinen were driving, and when Senna arrived he was straight on the pace ..."

It is time to consider Andretti, who drove 13 races in 1993, "left the track" (as one statistical book puts it) six times and finished in the points three times, with a podium finish – third – at Monza.

You were joining a leading team but you were pitching yourself against the best driver in the business.

"No question. Having Senna as a team-mate was maybe the toughest of all time to have as a team-mate."

You came to Formula 1 with a reputation as a man unafraid.

"I was glad to be compared to the best. There were times that I ran pretty well during the year and I was comparing myself to the best of all time – and I wasn't that far off at places where I was feeling comfortable."

What places were those?

"Donington. I felt good at Brazil, where I wasn't that far off of Ayrton – he qualified third, I qualified fifth and I felt that if I hadn't crashed there I would have run well: certainly as well as Donington. And at Imola he crashed his car so he had to jump into my car. I'd been out and qualified right away with both my sets of tyres early in the session, then he got in my car and was seven tenths quicker so that wasn't too bad for me considering that I was still learning."

He had a reputation for destroying team-mates. If he felt in his guts that the team-mate was a threat, he set out to destroy. Did you feel that was happening to you?

"No, he was really good to me. He was a great team-mate. He was probably the only ally on the team, the only guy who I felt was seeing what was going on and didn't like it. He was on his *outs* with the team anyway and I think he saw how unfair the whole deal was. After I was let go he had a Press Conference just to tell everybody, and that's the kind of guy he was. We hit it off really well. We became friends out of it and when I won my race he was the first one to call me – that was Australia, my first race back in IndyCars. He said he'd been up in the middle of the night watching the race and how happy he was for me. That was the very next day."

Maybe the fact that he liked you overcame the tremendous competitive sense he had to destroy.

"Maybe. I don't know. I just got along with him very well."

What did you make of him?

"The reason I probably liked him was that he was straightforward. What you saw was what you got. He told it like it was and that's pretty much the way I am. A lot of times I get in trouble when I do that and a lot of times he did as well, but I like that in a person 'cos they're real. He wouldn't tell people what they wanted to hear – just tell them the way it was, good or bad. A lot of times it really backfires on you, it brings trouble, but you can always sleep at night and look at yourself in the mirror. He could always look at himself in the mirror. I can too – and go to sleep at night – so that's what I really liked about Ayrton."

But to go into Formula 1 against Senna?

"That was good, you know. If you're going to do it, you might as well compare yourself to the best. That's what I was wanting to do."

He was legendary about the de-briefs, he would go on talking for ever …

"… yes, he would …"

Had you encountered this before and how did it compare with IndyCar racing?

"We would spend the same amount of time de-briefing [in F1 and IndyCars]. That was the same but what it came down to is I would listen and try to follow what he was doing and I really could not drive his type of race car. That's where I was making mistakes for a while, where I was following him a little bit too much on the set-up – and it wasn't working. His style of driving was different to mine. He'd evolved it over ten years, right, and he'd evolved it with those race cars where I had evolved another style with my type of race cars, which was the IndyCar, which you drove very differently.

So that caught me out a little bit. That's why I say that in some ways I was following him a little bit too much."

But that's only human nature. Here's a man who's mastered it ...

"... absolutely ..."

... and you can plug in to what he's telling you ...

"... and I would try to adapt my style to that, and I couldn't, and that was a mistake. I should have done more of my own thing and I would have had I stayed another year. My results would have been 100 per cent different, I guarantee you. I think I could have won – well, maybe not with that team – but I could, would, have won races."

It's quite unthinkable that you can do so well in one and you can't translate it to the other.

"Right. It's all timing and my timing was all wrong."

You've only got to look at Mansell and what happened to him in his second year in IndyCars.

"Exactly. He'd been living off the development we did the year before [at the Newman/Haas team] and all of a sudden he didn't develop it any further and everybody else did and you saw what happened."

When you look back on Formula 1, what do you think?

"Sometimes your toughest years of life turn out to be your best years of life because you learn a lot. I think I learnt a lot, I grew up a lot, matured and in that way I wouldn't trade it for anything."

During this 1993 season Senna decided to join Williams for 1994, and Ron Dennis will be giving us the background to that by chapter's end. Before Senna left, however, he reminded the world of the fires which still burned. At the Japanese Grand Prix he was leading and lapped debutant Eddie Irvine (Jordan) but then found himself briefly unable to lap Damon Hill (Williams). Irvine therefore darted past Senna to unlap himself and thought no more about it until Senna came looking for him after the race. Irvine, in *Green Races Red* (with Maurice Hamilton/CollinsWillow) reasoned that this posed problems because Senna didn't know what he looked like. Senna found him, of course, and although Irvine had done nothing against the rules Senna felt, according to Irvine, "I had not shown him enough respect." For an instant Irvine thought no more of that either but Senna "wanted to leave me a reminder with his fist. The blow knocked me to the floor ..."

Trevor Foster, who works for Jordan, explains that "there was Senna, this very excited person, came down, was going to say whatever he had to say, then of course Irvine antagonised him by almost treating him with no respect: sort of *whadda ya talking about?* – a few flippant remarks, and that didn't help. Ayrton couldn't control that. With Schumacher it would have been quite a different scenario. Schumacher would have been cold, seeing his own side of the dispute certainly, but very rational and Ayrton was all, you know, drama. I remember standing outside thinking *what's going on in there?* and it was a bit of argy-bargy. I think talk of a fight has been overstated. It was a push."

Senna won his final race for McLaren, the Australian at Adelaide and the moments before the start were so charged with emotion that Senna and Jo Ramirez did not trust themselves to look at each other without breaking down.

Senna had come to McLaren as a 28-year-old who'd won six races. He left having won 35 more, and a mountain of pole positions, and three World Championships; left as one of the greatest drivers who has ever lived. To assess this, and the man who achieved it, I'm going to break with the convention of most sports books and offer you monologues helped along by a question here and there. *This* is the man and the achievement.

Hugh Moran captures the leaving. "One of the last times he turned up, he was going through the factory with Giorgio Ascanelli – Pavarotti! [Ascanelli was Italian and broadly built.] They were talking and they walked past the little bay where I was working. They walked on for another five yards then Senna stopped, excused himself from Giorgio, came over and said *oh, you're still working here*. He shook my hand then zapped off. He could be extremely pleasant, but I'm sure you had a Senna at the factory, you had a Senna at the home and you had a Senna at the circuit. At the circuit he had a job to do. Take a comparison with cricket: the next man to bat, you don't go and ask for an interview while he's waiting to go out. Same with Senna.

"One of the other guys I used to work with was telling me the story of how Prost was doing some test driving for McLaren a couple of years ago and he asked Prost how he rated his team-mates. Prost said *Arnoux, never got on with him, Lauda, got on well with him, Rosberg got on well* and he came to Senna. My friend thought *oh God, I'm going to get a good 'yak' here* but Prost said Senna was an amazing guy. While you were doing the de-briefs he held absolutely nothing back. Prost said you'd have thought Senna was his best mate, he'd relate everything to you and the thing Prost couldn't understand was once he got out of the de-brief Senna was a different bloke altogether, just wasn't interested in doing small talk. Prost said even in 1989, when they had the big falling out, in de-briefs he was still the best team-mate he ever had.

"There was nothing artificial about him, he would genuinely come up to people and say hello."

Tell me what and who you thought he was.

"The way I'd put it, he was very relaxed with himself. He didn't have to prove anything to anyone, never had to prove anything to any other human being. He was quite a religious guy. The feeling I got from him, he was doing it because he felt that was what he was stuck on this planet for – which is why, I repeat, he didn't have to prove it to another person. I think, as Ron Dennis rightly put it, if Senna wanted to go out and be the best ditch-digger in the world, he would have gone out and tried to be the best ditch-digger in the world. If he'd felt the calling towards ditch-digging that's where he would have gone. *That* was Senna."

All of this fits neatly, or awkwardly, into everything we've been talking about. The problem is to gauge the sheer, almost shocking, intensity of Senna before the maturing – and even the maturing involved search-and-find with E. Irvine, fire burning. Here is another example, this one of fire smouldering. It is provided by David Kennedy, former racer and now Irish television man, and it happened during the McLaren years.

"I got to know Senna when he was doing Formula 3. He was a customer of ours buying stuff from a motorsport shop we had in London, when I was driving for Mazda and he was driving for McLaren-Honda. I met him on several occasions going out to Japan and I remember one in particular. I was in Business Class, he was in First and he came down to talk to me. We were just talking motor racing and at the end I was completely indoctrinated into how Calvin Fish [in Formula Ford 2000 in *1982*] had once beaten him through having a better engine – well, a different engine. He spent the best part of *seven or eight hours* going through it.

"I'd seen the race. I was watching at Paddock and Senna would continually 'crawl' up behind Calvin at Paddock, Calvin would take the inside up to Druids and hold him off so, while I didn't see that many of Senna's junior races, I did see two significant ones – in Ireland, where he was marked out to be a very hot shoe, and the other where he lost to Fish" – the last round of the 2000 Championship when Senna returned from the Kalmar karting in that filthy mood.

"He wanted to explain to me in great detail why he lost. The fact was that he remembered every detail of it. You often hear about these people and you wonder if they really are like that. Well, I just happened to be the recipient of it. He remembered the story about his engine: where he'd got it, who'd built it, why Calvin's engine was better, who'd built that, how Calvin would continually pull away from him, how he couldn't get by because Calvin had taken the inside line."

What did you make of him?

"I thought he was over the top. His intensity was nearly pathological in the sense he was more than just describing that he had had a difficulty and lost a race, it was more like a personal slight that he could actually lose a race. It wasn't a terribly interesting conversation. In most instances it would have been painfully boring other than (1) I was a driver myself and (2) he was a driver of incredible skill: that gave him a certain licence to bore you for several hours while he explained why he lost."

But it must have been interesting boredom?

"No, not particularly. I suppose because of the unique nature of the individual I don't want to make it sound sacriligious and say *my God how could that be?* On another level, in the grand scheme of things, motor racing doesn't add up to much more than a hill of beans, you know. People add a certain sort of religious fever to these happenings but at the end of the day he's driving a racing car, you know, and it's no more than that – although he was incredibly skilful, unbelievably skilful. I mean, look at the statistics of his pole positions – extraordinary."

Since a theme of this book is accommodating contradiction, here now is a witness who will largely contradict everything we've heard so far. His name is Neil Austin, and he worked with Goodyear from 1985 to 1991 – his first race was Portugal, Senna's first win.

"He obviously had to be choosy about how many people he took on board because everybody wanted to be his friend. I loved him as a friend. I'd do anything for him and he'd do anything for me – if you were a friend he would. He was a bit of a joker in the Lotus days and I remember him making gas bombs at test sessions. He'd tape up cardboard boxes, fill them with gas – I don't know what kind it was – and put the battery charger on! He did it in the evenings when the mechanics were preparing the cars for next day and it was dark. You'd hear a great bang like a bomb going off. It was his way of having a laugh and a joke. Of course he didn't do it at the races, too many people around.

"Whilst he was working he was 110 per cent dedicated to what he was doing and everything around him didn't really matter, but when he wasn't motor racing he was such a fun guy to be with. He worked hard and played twice as hard but he wouldn't always let people see him doing it."

Why do you think that was?

"I don't know. It was just his way. There were always sides of him that were grey areas, if you like. He knew what he wanted, he knew what he was doing and there was always a reason for it. He would never be stern-faced unless there was a reason for that. The misconception of him was created because at any particular moment people didn't understand the reason why he was doing what he was doing. He couldn't mix his emotions to suit other things which were happening around him. It was *I am serious now and this is how it's going to be,* then, when we'd move on to something funny, he'd be laughing. He was not afraid to be unpopular, he didn't really care what other people thought about him.

"He wasn't lonely. He had his friends, he used to take his friends round the world with him and he'd have his brother with him at times, so no, he wasn't a lonely man at all."

What was it he had as a driver?

"Natural talent that you couldn't train for. I used to fly model aeroplanes with him and he had this special hand-to-eye co-ordination where his hands responded to what he saw – and it was an instantaneous thing. I flew model aeroplanes for four or five years, he learnt in two days!

"If you've ever seen photographs of him flying one at Silverstone that would have been my plane. He'd arrive in England, phone me up and say *Neil, I'm at Silverstone for a couple of days, are you bringing the planes?* Then he did the same in Brazil when we went testing in Rio. We'd fly off the start-finish straight after the testing had finished at five. I'd maybe send a plane from England and he brought his and we'd fly on that pit straight in the evening. Absolutely fantastic, clear blue skies – and he had the best planes!

"These models are delicate to fly, especially the take-offs and landings. You have to get it right and you don't usually get second chances but he was masterful, copybook stuff every time. And, as I say, his hand-to-eye co-ordination was brilliant. I couldn't get it like that and I'd flown for years. I see it as the same thing as driving a car, something just there. It wouldn't matter how much I practised to do that, he didn't have to. Once you'd shown him he'd say *ah, this is how* and he could do it. He didn't brag about it, he wasn't a bragger, almost kept it to himself: *I can just do it and if you can't that's your bad luck, isn't it?*

"Mind you, he did get the model planes up around the microlite boys" – who were flying over the Rio circuit – "and they probably didn't like it. If you're sat up there and a little plane is buzzing you, you're not too happy, are you? It was daring, you know what I mean?

"It was like when he went up with the Brazilian Air Force, an F17 or something, two-seater, and it came over the circuit and buzzed the pits. This, also, was in Rio. One plane came about 300 feet above us, the other one was about 150 feet and you don't have to ask which plane he was in. You know *go for it, let's go down.* I remember him telling me that the pilot asked *do you want to have a play?* and Ayrton said *yes!* He pulled the stick over and the plane rolled four or five times. He thought he'd done enough to take the plane round into a roll but with the speed that they were travelling it went over and over. He said it was frightening how quick the reaction of the plane was."

What would the pilot have thought?

"He'd have grabbed hold of the stick by then. I was asking Ayrton about the speed, 500 or 600 miles an hour, something like that. He said it doesn't really relate when you're up there because you have no landmarks to compare it to. Even at low altitude there's nothing going by you, no Armco, no 100-metre marker before a corner, so he said the speed wasn't really that exciting. It's why he buzzed the pits at 150 feet: *that's exciting.* He understood the mechanics of a plane, he knew what happens and he could fly his own jet although he didn't have a pilot's licence."

His pole positions – 65 – are a monument in themselves and his qualifying laps the stuff of legend.

"I used to be with him during qualifying. He'd go out and do his first lap, come in and sit with the monitor on his knee or I'd be holding it. He'd walk out into the pit lane and see what the weather – the sky – was like. Then he'd sit watching the pages on the monitor – he'd go to page 1 to see who was on the front of the grid, go to page 3 or whatever to see the fastest speeds down the straight. We'd discuss it. Sometimes he'd go off and talk about something else for five minutes then come back to the monitor. He'd point out a few things – *look at this, look at that, look at what he's done* – next thing he's pulling his overalls up from round his waist, helmet on, back in the car."

Why do you think he chose that particular moment?

"I don't know. He always left it to the last minute because I think he probably reasoned that nobody could do anything about it once he'd finished the lap – but he always watched the skies, he'd keep going outside and looking up to see what the temperature was going to be like. He was masterful at knowing how it was going to affect the tyres. If it was too hot, no point in going out because the tyres would go off half way round the lap and he wanted to make those tyres work for the full lap."

Was he difficult to speak to when he was concentrating?

"During the qualifying? No, he wasn't but you knew not to talk about the wrong thing, really. You didn't want to talk about what he was going to be doing that night half way through qualifying. You felt: we're only going to talk about motor racing now."

Peter Warr told me Senna could see the whole lap in his mind, predict the exact time he'd do.

"He'd sit in the car for those few seconds before he went out and he was almost *meditating* the lap, working out what he did the last time, going round the whole thing. *If I do this at such-and-such a point, that's where I'm going to get those tenths from.* Then he'd go out and do it. The car would be dancing and it was so, so good to watch. In the Lotus days he probably wasn't as clean as he could have been to get better times but it was so, so much good fun to watch. Anyone who was near a television screen, you could see the expressions on their faces. In later years at McLaren he did clean his driving up quite a bit. He was smoother and better times came with that and, of course, with his experience."

Watching him at close range must have been fascinating.

"He'd enter the pits after maybe a lap in the morning untimed session and on the way back in, even before he'd reached the garage, he'd be reeling off a dozen things that he wanted to do with that car prior to going out again. He didn't have to sit and think about it. He knew *we're going to do this and this* – ride heights, tyre pressures and so on. He didn't have to sit with an engineer, he could tell what he wanted and then he'd go straight back out again and, more often than not, he'd adjusted the car in the right direction.

"I socialised with a lot of the McLaren mechanics, and when he joined the team they were astounded at the way he could just know what he wanted at the end of one lap. He wouldn't be asking, he'd be telling them *this is what we'll do* – and if someone tells you what to do, and you do it, and he puts the car on pole you're not going to question him next time he tells you what to do."

When it's put like this there is no further mystery and the simple things do apply. But when you try to think things like this out in your own life, the mystery comes back very hard.

Nigel Stepney offers this shrewd assessment. "With Ayrton you went, and with Michael Schumacher you go, to the races because you have a chance to win. OK, you do your job anyway but in a sense that's beside the point of what I'm saying. For example, having worked with drivers like that, I could never join a team where you haven't got that possibility. You can't work with a driver who doesn't give you the maximum. I know that not every driver is the same in life but those drivers who have a chance to win pull the whole team along."

Anyway, at the end of '93, his face was carrying lines, and it could look like a sculpture, occasionally betraying exhaustion; a hewn face, what Frank Sinatra would have called *a lived in face*. He might have retired and exploited the other life he had been creating and cultivating, and several things might have drawn him towards that. He was in love. She was called Adriane, young, blonde and as captivated with him as he was with her. He already had the creature comforts which genuine wealth brings, not just his own jet and pilot but a superb house in Angra dos Reis some 200 kilometres from Rio, a farm in Tatui some 120 kilometres from Sao Paulo and a house in Faro on the southern tip of Portugal. He was actively building a business empire, importing quality products into Brazil. He had ideas about trying to alleviate the plight of stricken children – they're everywhere in Brazil – and had mentioned this to his sister, Viviane. To retire would have been no defeat and no surrender, but something mitigated against it. On the racing track he still had great truths to prove.

He went to Williams. (And thereby hangs a tantalising little tale. At the end of 1993 or beginning of 1994 Jordan, then running Hart engines, approached him to test their car to see what was wrong – and right! – with it. Brian Hart says: "Ayrton would have done it brilliantly in a short space of time and it would have been invaluable. He was interested, but then he felt there would be a contractual problem with Williams.")

Ron Dennis is the perfect man – arguably the only man – to conduct a proper review of Senna's six years at McLaren. "He drove for Lotus and, in driving for them, established a relationship with Honda. So there was that relationship and also a developing relationship between myself and him which produced a common desire for him to be in a McLaren – and ultimately he was. We'd had a mutual respect when we first met [in 1982] but there was certainly no legal commitment."

Did you think it was a risk partnering Senna with Prost?

"Not at all. They both had a commitment to win, both of them knew – Prost from first-hand experience, Senna through our reputation – that our philosophy was to provide both drivers with equal equipment and always run two front-runners. The competition within the team was fantastic for the team. Of course their personalities were very different and inevitably that led to the occasional bit of friction. If someone asks me what particular thing I am pleased with in my own career, and I've chosen the word *pleased* rather than proud, I'll say that I feel I did a pretty good job of managing two very strong personalities for over three years. Of course, because Ayrton was getting stronger and stronger and Alain was moving towards the latter part of his career, that process became more difficult. It fell off the rails a couple of times, but …"

Was that difficult for you personally?

"It was not from a business point of view, but it was from an emotional point of view. I am not a particularly emotional person but these guys gave everything. They'd always give 100 per cent in the car and out of the car. Therefore it draws you into their own personalities and when you see two people arguing – two people that I was very fond of and that I cared a lot about – then inevitably it gets to your emotions. You can see both sides and you can see that they were genuinely upset with each other over certain things. That wasn't comfortable but you got a satisfying feeling that, as and when these things manifested themselves, you were able to be part of the healing process: sort them out and then they'd go away and get on with their racing again."

Was there a moment when it really did break down?

"Alain had the opportunity to go to Ferrari for quite a bit of money but he was also fascinated by whether he could solve the problem: the traditional thing [take Ferrari to championships again]. Other drivers had tried and drivers today are trying. That was very interesting and very challenging for him, and he talked it through with me. I realised that, even though there was no decision taken, change was inevitable and in fact we executed the agreement with Gerhard prior to Alain actually taking the final decision. That was pre-emptive – but only because I knew Alain well enough to know that he would go to Ferrari, so it was better to be prepared. I was able to negotiate with Gerhard in an environment in which he – Gerhard – felt I had the option of continuing with Alain: possibly I did, but it would have been the wrong thing if I had talked Alain into staying."

I think it would have torn itself apart.

"Hmmm. I think I could have handled it, it would just have become more difficult."

At Toleman Senna had proved an outstanding prospect, at Lotus he'd proved a race winner, at McLaren he proved to be a World Champion.

"And continued to demonstrate it. Our relationship moved to a different level – to a level that was … well, it's wrong to say unique because maybe that's what Chapman and Clark had, but *that* level."

He once said the two of you got into negotiations and you both got so bored – the difference was three years at $500,000, ie $1.5 million – that a decision was made to do it on the toss of a coin and he lost.

"No, it wasn't quite like that. What happened was: it was clear even in the negotiations, the very first negotiations, that we were very strong-willed people. We arrived at a point which was just … deadlock. We couldn't resolve it, no matter what, and it was nothing to do with the money – it was to do with the principle of finding a way forward. I was happy to pay the money, the money wasn't the issue, it was the principle so I explained to him the value of leaving it to chance."

He stayed six years, which is a very long time. You're talking three championships, you're talking all those pole positions. Lots of people claim to have been close to him. How close did you get?

"To be honest, I don't want to comment on other people and it's not a question of putting my hand up and saying I was closer than anyone else. The people he was closest to were his family – hugely important to him, especially his sister and his mother. He was a gentle man as well as a gentleman but very determined. People sometimes misread his beliefs and his values. He knew through his parents what was right and wrong. He knew from his family how to conduct himself in life, and that came from all of his family. I suppose my relationship could be expressed as more towards a complex mix of brothers and father and son. I wasn't so much older than him that the relationship was father and son, I wasn't close enough in age for it to be brother and brother – but it definitely was a relationship where we talked about grand prix racing *and* everything in life. There were very difficult periods during his grand prix career that he really struggled with, nothing to do with competitiveness or lack of it but more to do with the politics of grand prix racing. The Balestre thing at Suzuka [refusing to move pole position] ..."

Did you realise the depths to which that had enraged Senna?

"For a time he had decided to retire. I never said *don't retire*. We talked it through, we did that on the basis of what the alternatives were and in the end his passion for grand prix racing over-ruled his dislike of that aspect of the sport. It was an aspect he always despised: the politics, the double-values and the double-standards."

Did you find Suzuka hard to take because there was abuse heaped on you as well as him?

"Yes. I think during that period other drivers were involved in other incidents and his view was: if other drivers can do things like that and there is no penalty, and that is the standard, then so be it – but he didn't like the standard. I felt that afterwards he regretted, very much regretted, lowering himself to drive in that way."

What do you consider his best race for you?

"The Brazilian Grand Prix in 1991. Honda had appointed a new technical leader to the programme, he was obviously inexperienced and that showed in the performance of the engine. So we started that race with significantly less horsepower than we'd finished the season before. We had made a better car and fortunately we were still competitive. Ayrton was excelling in difficult conditions which became even more difficult before the end of the race. Suddenly the whole gear mechanism locked and he was left with one gear. He actually drove quite a few laps with only that one gear but he managed to continue and won. It started to rain and Riccardo Patrese [in the Williams, catching Senna] backed off. He didn't realise the problem we had."

What about the leaving?

"Not at all difficult to understand. He was in some ways partially responsible for the lack of performance that we were getting from our car and engine – or the potential lack of performance – in the 1994 car. You have to remember that he won five races in 1993 and that year we made the best car we have ever made, with a very sophisticated active ride system. And even with the second-level Ford engine we won those five races. He realised that he had to move and there were two reasons.

"First, it was apparent that we were not going to have a very strong engine at that stage. In fact, we subsequently signed a contract with Peugeot and I think if we had done that early enough he might have stayed. But more importantly, and this has never really been recognised because I've never said it before, he always had tremendous financial demands. In satisfying those demands we effectively under-spent in various areas in the car so he inadvertently drained money out of the company as we met his very high retainer aspirations. In 1993, in fact, we were paying as we went and the final payment of his 1993 contract was paid in 1994.

"It was a very difficult period of time for us. That's when we made a policy change and decided to develop younger drivers and arrive at a situation which Williams had then, where they were making such superior cars that a variety of drivers could win in them. Those cars flattered some drivers. Several people, and I was certainly one of them, recognised all this, and so our attitude was *let's invest in the company, let's push harder to improve the resources within the organisation, then we can pick from several drivers and still win the races*. And that's what we've done. We knew we would go into a trough on the way and that it would take some time to work out of, but we did it the way we wanted to do it."

I know he was very emotional at leaving.

"He was on loan. That's the way I felt, that's the way he felt. There was no formal agreement but he would have come back. Therefore it wasn't difficult. It was better that we re-built the team and got some of the things sorted out, better that he went away, continued to win races and came back a different person. He wouldn't have retired. I think he would have stayed in grand prix racing a very long time and when he did finally retire he would have done it in a McLaren. Of that I am absolutely sure.

"I wasn't uncomfortable. I understood that he lived to win grand prix races and if we weren't in a position to deliver that to him then I completely understood if he was going to go somewhere which could. We just had to re-build the team to a point where he would come back to drive for us."

Then and now

The Neil Austin interview was conducted the day I went to Formula Palmer Audi *near Bedford. Austin happened to come by and Ms Taylor says here's a man you should talk to. She was right. Sometimes it goes like that – you get lucky. Austin sat and as he moved into memory his voice and his body tightened: he wasn't forcing his path through it, but nearly. He was also talking from a very personal place within himself.*

Imola? "*I wasn't there. I was at work in another job for Goodyear, at Wolverhampton in manufacturing, and I watched it live on TV. Straight away I thought this is not good. I watched it for a little bit longer and I thought this is definitely not good. It made me really ill. The company had their own internal hospital and I went there that afternoon because it really knocked me around. Death doesn't normally affect me at all, I've lost family and I think I've coped with it quite well, but Ayrton – I think I felt for all the other people who were feeling it as well.*"

The Martin Brundle interview took place at Monza during the 1998 Italian Grand Prix weekend. After retiring from Formula 1 he quickly established himself as a television commentator of confidence and wit.

The Ron Dennis interview took place partly in the immaculate factory at Woking, partly in his car. In the trophy room at the factory there's a vast placard bearing this legend:

   0–100kmh (62mph) 2.3 seconds

   0–200kmh (124mph) 5.0 seconds – David Coulthard, Canada. 1997

   Top 353kmh (220mph) – Mika Hakkinen, Monza, 1997.

   And you thought you were going to be a racing driver.

   Dennis is an extremely busy man who has mastered the art of handling five or six different situations simultaneously (and built a successful empire like that, now with more than 800 employees). Perhaps all leading personnel in Formula 1 have this capacity, not just drivers like Senna.

   Nearly Christmas 1998 and Dennis had to go from the factory to perform a small ceremony of thanks a couple of miles away. We did the interview in his car there and back, but when we did get back we sat very quietly as he outlined the naughty tales you'll be told in Chapter 9. Dennis is not, as he says, an emotional man but just this once his voice changed towards that. It meant more than a river of tears from another man.

Chapter 6

The fundamental things apply

THERE IS A FEELING which lingers over the Imola weekend of 1994: unfinished business. And a deeper feeling that it will always remain unfinished.

We have to start with images, strange images, haunting images, mysterious images. The first appeared in the prestigious French magazine *Paris Match* on 19 May 1994, a double-column colour photograph under the headline A MONTH AGO, HE SAW THE DANGER. The photograph showed three men standing against a wooded backdrop. Senna, wearing a blue cap, points at something with his left arm to a balding man in a suit. Another man, nearby, hands in pockets, seems to be listening.

The extended caption, translated here from the French, reads: "This image is drawn from a film taken a little more than a month ago at the circuit of Imola by an amateur film-maker and unconditional supporter of Ayrton Senna. Sunday 4 April, Alberto Castioni, camera in hand, followed his idol who had come to practise on what was to become, three weeks later, the tragic circuit. In this film, you see the [former] World Champion in a big discussion with Giorgio Poggi, the director of Imola. It is impossible to hear the conversation, but Senna's gestures are brusque. Several times he clearly points his finger towards the Tamburello curve, to the place where he will lose his life. We would know later that the [former] World Champion would show to the directors of the circuit a joining of tarmac on the ground which gave an unevenness of three or four centimetres. At 300kph they could provoke unexpected reactions, as much for the driver as for the car."

The photograph and caption seemed straightforward enough and because I wanted to include both in a previous book I contacted *Paris Match* who said it had been supplied by an Italian picture agency. I contacted them but the man who'd handled it was away, never did ring back and it became one of those Italian things which was clearly never going to happen. I let it go and in doing that didn't satisfy my curiosity, which had been stirred by two questions. April 4 had been a Monday, not a Sunday, and what did that do for the accuracy of the rest of the story? Imola testing had been from March 14 to 17, so what was Senna doing at Imola in early April, whether a Sunday or a Monday?

Part of the answer came from former Formula 1 driver Pierluigi Martini, who in 1994 was driving for the Italian team Minardi. Subsequently he said: "I was at Imola with Senna and others two weeks before the race, when we noticed a small bump in the Tamburello bend. The circuit officials were very efficient, and had the tarmac smoothed out, which was the only thing they could do. The cars still touched the ground and were disturbed, so you just had to hold your line.

"The repairs had only slightly improved the situation. Senna had complained to me three weeks before Imola at Aida that his car was nervous and the cockpit narrow. But Tamburello could only have created problems for a car that had problems. The people at Imola did everything they could to give us drivers what we asked for."

Explaining this today, Martini says: "There were in fact two FOCA [official] tests, one in March and the other in April, 14 or 15 days before the race. Senna and I together went to the director – Poggi – to explain that there was a 'jumping' at Tamburello. You can't say I thought of doing this or he thought of it: we did it together. We said the bump was a little bit high – but it was impossible to change the 'floor' of the track [completely] with the race so close. It was however better when they'd done what they could, although there was still a bump."

Poggi himself has retired and lives in Bologna. He has never spoken about Senna's death or the circumstances surrounding it because they were friends. Poggi was very upset by Senna's death and guards silence over – in the words of his daughter Simona, who was translating – "what happened with Senna previously or after the grand prix." He did say that he hadn't seen the photograph but he had seen some film. The same film? Silence again. I faxed Federico Bendinelli, managing director of the Imola circuit, asking him to clarify all this, but no reply came.

Strange. Haunting. Mysterious. I don't want to belabour such words but they do capture what really happened before, during and long after the San Marino Grand Prix at Imola on 1 May 1994. The before and during are the subject of this chapter, and the long after occupies the beginning of Part Two of the book. They are joined intimately, of course, but also separated by a great finality: the death of Senna.

Theoretically the reason for the public death of a celebrity (or anybody else) ought, with all the scientific techniques available, to be discovered speedily and conclusively – but the assassination of JFK refutes that absolutely, and how many aeroplane crashes remain unresolved, how many black boxes chart the last struggles of the crew but don't reveal *why?* It is important to remember this as we approach Imola and the delta of undercurrents, ideas, theories, testimonies, conflicting evidence, legal complexities, xenophobia and dark, dark suspicions which cannot be avoided.

I'm going to try to set it out objectively, even the outlandish suggestions, and, again, in chronological order. Perhaps that's even more important here because the *before* and *during* were enacted in the ordinary way as race meetings, as visual events, and only during *the long after* did the undercurrents surface.

Ayrton Senna joined Williams for the 1994 season. On 7 March, Owen O'Mahoney flew Senna and Senna's photographer Norio Koike from Faro in Portugal, where Senna had a home, to Bologna. On 11 March, O'Mahoney flew Senna from Bologna to Paris, where he caught a flight to Brazil.

On 27 March, from pole, Senna spun out of the Brazilian Grand Prix at Sao Paulo and Michael Schumacher won.

Emerson Fittipaldi remembers that. "You know, the last day I spoke to Ayrton in my life was at the Brazilian Grand Prix. I was very, very happy to see Ayrton. I really loved him, he was a really special person for me. I waited at the Williams garage after qualifying on the Saturday afternoon, and he was on pole, and I came up to Ayrton very excited. I say *Ayrton, you always dreamed of driving for Williams, this year is going to be your year.* But he was not very enthusiastic, not very happy, not smiling, and he says *Emerson, watch Schumacher. He is going to be my toughest competition, it's not going to be easy.* And Ayrton was right about Schumacher, of course – incredible talent – but I remember that day not for Schumacher but because I never saw Ayrton again."

On 4 April, O'Mahoney picked Senna up from Madrid – whence, presumably, he'd returned from Brazil – and took him to Jerez and the Williams testing there. On 6 April, O'Mahoney flew Senna from Jerez back to Faro.

On 10 April, O'Mahoney flew Senna from Faro to Heathrow, where he caught a flight to Japan for the Pacific Grand Prix. On 17 April, from pole, he crashed out at the first corner of the race and Michael Schumacher won.

Mechanic Nigel Stepney, watching events closely, understood the context. "When Senna went to Williams everybody thought none of the others would see him for dust but it is not as simple as that. The driver has to be part of the car, you can't just put him in it and expect miracles. The Press say *OK, you put Michael Schumacher in this car or that car and instantly it would be one second quicker.* It is not as simple as that, either. It takes time to adapt the car to the style of the driver, it must be done over time."

Time was what Ayrton Senna no longer had.

On 20 April, O'Mahoney collected Senna at Heathrow and flew him to Le Bourget in Paris, to kick off a friendly soccer match involving Brazilian players. On 21 April O'Mahoney flew him from Le Bourget to Faro. On 26 April, O'Mahoney flew him to Munich and, as O'Mahoney says, "that's when the whole thing started." Senna had business to do in the Bavarian city and more business to do in Italy before he arrived at Imola on Thursday, 28 April to prepare for the race weekend.

O'Mahoney is at a loss to know how, in the midst of all this, Senna would have gone to Imola, as Martini says, two weeks before. "There must be a chance, a slim chance, that if he went, he went in another driver's plane – perhaps Berger's." And the Williams testing schedule for that spring shows nothing at Imola for two weeks before the San Marino race. The schedule was Imola from 8–11 March, Jerez from 4–6 April, Nogaro from 25–26 April.

Senna came to Imola for the San Marino Grand Prix under obvious pressure. He had no points and Schumacher, nearly a decade his junior, a perfect 20. Suddenly it seemed that one era was ending as another was beginning. We can only speculate about the impact this exercised on Senna. If he'd been a Prost he'd have calculated that you win a championship over a whole season and 140 points remained available, no great hurry. But Senna was manifestly not Prost.

This Thursday, Senna rang Gugelmin – the last time they spoke. Gugelmin was now in the United States racing IndyCars. "I was in Miami. He was all pumped up because the car was going to have a new wing or something. He was coming to Canada for the grand prix pretty soon and Stella was pregnant with the twins so he was coming down to see where we were living and all that."

By now, Gugelmin says, Senna had altered the way he talked about his opponents. In the past, Prost was never referred to by name, only as "the Frenchman," Schumacher only as "the German." Gugelmin adds: "I'd never heard the word Schumacher from his mouth before, nor that of Prost." Now Gugelmin did. Was Senna softening? Was he reaching towards the final crossroads – where he could turn away from the obsessions of youth and early manhood?

What happened at Imola is well-recorded, maybe exhaustively so, and a *precis* will suffice. Rubens Barrichello, Brazilian and – some insisted – Senna's protégé, was injured after what seemed to be a horrific crash on the Friday. It reduced Senna to tears. Roland Ratzenberger, a rookie, was killed when his Simtek crashed on the Saturday. Senna commandeered an official car to take him to the scene of the accident (and was officially reprimanded for doing so). The impact of Ratzenberger's death is known on Senna. That night he rang Adriane, who had flown from Brazil to Portugal to await his return after the grand prix. He insisted he wouldn't race. Later he reconsidered. But he also made a decision he did not reconsider: something had to be done about safety. Professor Watkins, who'd informed him about Ratzenberger, told me that Senna had reached a point in his life where he was mature enough to take an overview and such matters were assuming an increasing importance to him.

At the drivers' briefing on race morning, according to Damon Hill in *Grand Prix Year,* "Gerhard Berger raised one seemingly insignificant but relevant point about safety, but what he did not reveal was that he had been put up to it by Senna. Ayrton didn't want to be the first to raise the point for fear of appearing to be the only person concerned about the problem, yet, typically, it was he who pressed it home." This, evidently, concerned the pace car which had been used at Aida to bring the cars round on the parade lap to the start. This pace car wasn't fast enough to allow the grand prix cars to warm their tyres properly, and cold tyres spell potential danger. According to Hill, when this subject was broached, the other drivers "backed Senna up" and the officials abandoned the idea. (The pace car would, however, continue to be available during the races to take the cars slowly round in case of accidents and/or incidents which did not merit stopping the race altogether.) One report says Senna was crying during this drivers' meeting, silent, private tears which, understandably, he tried to conceal.

As the clocks ticked towards 2.0, Senna nosed the Williams onto his pole position place at the front left of the grid, a couple of mechanics helping it with a shove. As the car came to rest he dipped his head in a tired motion, raised it and glanced first in the left-hand wing mirror, then in the right. Then he looked directly ahead and closed his eyes. Ordinarily you'd have thought he was locking into his process of absolute concentration, isolating himself, playing permutations of the start in his mind. Maybe he was – but he looked emptied. He'd take his helmet off, haul his balaclava off and sit barefaced. Photographers – scouring the grid, snapping anything and everything – took, cumulatively, a gallery of images of Senna. In each of these it is the same, a man who suddenly has a hewn look.

A roving camera captured the movement of this face – sombre, almost pained, craning and just once tightening as if he were near to tears. He closed his eyes and looked away, pursed his lips, opened his eyes, craned his head back to where it had been. He pressed his mane of dark hair against the headrest and closed his eyes a second time.

Because we know the background now, know the depths of Senna's mood, and know that we are less than 25 minutes from catastrophe, there is a temptation to see in the images what you want to see. I think the temptation is justified, even as the 34-year-old draws his balaclava back on, lifts his helmet and puts that on too, so that the expressions of his face are lost behind the helmet – for ever. I think it is justified because you cannot, absolutely cannot – even with hindsight – mistake a human being supressing such inner turmoil.

Only the day before, Professor Watkins had advised him not to race – advised him, in fact, to retire altogether.

Patrick Head made a joke (about the pace car, as it transpired) and Senna summoned a smile from a deep and troubled place.

They accelerated into the parade lap, Senna doing it so violently that his wheels left twin snakes of burnt rubber on the surface of the track. The old trick: lay the rubber, and then, when you've come round to the start, position the car's wheels on the twin snakes. Grip. As they accelerated into this parade lap, Michael Schumacher, on the front row and to Senna's right, was doing the same thing.

They came round, nosed to their places on the grid, settled. The noise of

25 engines rose from a snarl to a howl. Four red lights came on, in a row on the gantry stretched out over the track facing the grid. They blinked off and the row of four green lights below them blinked on. Senna was away fast, Schumacher too, Berger already probing his Ferrari into possible openings behind them.

Any grid, breaking up from its symmetry to the wild jostle for advantage, is a cascade of movement. For an instant the breaking up seemed quite normal. It wasn't. JJ Lehto, on the third row, stalled his Benetton. This is an instant of extreme danger because the cars behind, each coming at him with the gathering fury a Formula 1 engine delivers, had to miss him.

In succession, Heinz-Harald Frentzen flung his Sauber so violently that he pitched it full across into the other column of cars, Ukyo Katayama wrenched his Tyrrell hard left onto the black and white painted kerbing, and Gianni Morbidelli (Footwork) followed him there. Martin Brundle steered his McLaren rightwards into mid-track but that created a ripple effect forcing three or four cars from the other column – who themselves wanted to exploit this mid-track – to swerve back where they had come from. And so it went, all the way back to Pedro Lamy, on the eleventh row of the grid – and in the other column to Lehto.

"As we left the grid, the car I was behind – [Andrea] de Cesaris [Jordan] I think it was – dived to the right. I saw a space to the left and went for it. That's when I suddenly saw JJ and hit him. I had no chance to avoid him because up until that point I hadn't been able to see that there was a stationary car on the grid at all."

Lamy struck Lehto's Benetton a glancing blow but still powerful enough to pitch the Lotus onto the grass, scattering a swathe of debris as if a bomb had exploded. Bertrand Gachot (Pacific), who'd started at the very back, only just avoided it. Neither Lamy nor Lehto was hurt but the blow had been powerful enough to wrench two wheels off and hurl them – describing huge arcs – over the fencing into the crowd. There, one man fled as a wheel bounced behind him but three other people, including a policeman, were scythed down. They, too, were relatively unhurt.

It seemed that a terrible theme was being maintained: Barrichello who'd just escaped, Ratzenberger who hadn't, and now Lehto and Lamy who'd just escaped, four spectators who'd just escaped. It was as if, after Formula 1 had been safe for so long, all at once it looked dangerous *everywhere*.

Far away, round the imperious circuit of Imola, Senna stretched hard to build a lead, Schumacher tracking him, then Berger, then Hill and the rest. Suddenly the safety car – an Opel Turbo, dark coloured and with three revolving yellow lights on its roof – was out as workers struggled to clear the debris off the grid. Round the circuit marshals held out white boards with, in black, two letters on them, *SC* (Safety Car). To handle the situation this way, rather than stopping the race, remains controversial with so much debris who-knew-where?

The safety car circled holding the remaining 23 cars behind it in a crocodile, sometimes equidistant, sometimes closing up like an accordion.

They weaved to and fro to create friction to warm the tyres. Through Tamburello, such a gentle place at this speed, they weaved furiously and continued weaving along the straight past where Ratzenberger had been killed the day before, to Tosa. That was lap five. The safety car extinguished its lights, meaning *I will be going in, you can race*. On that fifth lap Senna deliberately hung back and let the safety car move away from him then surged towards it: another way of creating friction and generating heat.

The safety car slipped into the pit lane entrance, releasing the 23. Senna hit the power and threaded through the left–right onto the start finish straight, Schumacher two cars' length behind. The gap between them was 0.556 of a second. Berger, tardy, was a long way back and crossed the line at 2.586 seconds; then a similar gap – 5.535 seconds – to Hill, who was leading the bunch.

Into the Tamburello curve Schumacher clung to Senna and saw Senna's car 'bottoming.' Television cameras caught this too. The track surface was light tarmac although it had, here and there, geometrical dark bands across it where, presumably, work had been done. In the vicinity of Tamburello there were five such bands: one well before the approach, one at the approach, a narrow one a little further on, a broad one in the curve itself and, more or less on the exit, another narrow one.

As the Williams crossed the second broad band it churned molten yellow sparks from its underbelly, churned more about half way across the band and a cascade of them – for an instant they showered two or three metres into the air – as it crossed from the band back to the lighter tarmac.

There was a fleeting glimpse of low sparks as the car crossed the narrow band. It shed Tamburello and ran towards Tosa but on the way churned sparks on another narrow band of dark tarmac.

Schumacher closed up under braking for Tosa: quite normal because cars habitually do, and lose what they have gained on the exit because the car in front is always onto the power sooner *but* the closing up laid pressure-pressure-pressure on Senna. They moved through the left–right towards the start-finish straight and lap 7.

There were two computers on board Senna's car, one feeding the Williams team and another recording the engine management system for Renault. The latter had spare capacity and Williams were using that too, piggy-back style. The computer information was fired in bursts as the car passed the pits at the end of a lap; then the computers began recording very, very exact information about aspects of the car's performance again and these would be fired at the end of the next lap; and so on throughout the race.

This is the natural place for me to ask you to stop reading and find any timing device which records seconds – your wristwatch, a digital clock, the teletext service on your television, anything. Try to fix in your mind how brief each of those seconds really is. Now try to imagine a second divided into 50 parts. That is what the telemetry from Senna's car will be doing, and it means aspects of the sequence which follows, conveyed to you by the written word, may seem to be happening at a controllable pace – but in real time they were damn near instantaneous. Please remember, too, that Senna's car was carrying an on-board camera mounted behind, and to the left of, his head.

Crossing the line Senna had eked out a small gap and held that as they travelled across the white bays of the grid and rounded the gentle sweep before the thrust to Tamburello. That was into the parkland of Imola, grass verges to either side, tall trees beyond. He was forcing the Williams up, up, up towards covering 100 metres each second.

At **7.98** seconds from crossing the start-finish line he was travelling directly ahead and had covered 562 metres. The wall at Tamburello was some 930 metres from the line – 368 metres away. He had his foot full down on the accelerator: the car's speed touched 298kmh and was rising – at **8.00** seconds it was 300kmh. He was in sixth gear. Everything, it seemed, was normal: a man, a car, a track.

At **8.08** seconds he had covered 570 metres and turned slightly to the left. He was still at 300kmh.

At **8.50** seconds he had covered 606 metres – the wall 324 metres away. He still had his foot down, the speed up to 302kmh. In the spring sunlight the stooping trees on the left made beautiful silhouettes across the rim of the track, spreading like brittle fingers over to where the car rushed so urgently across them; and they were gone.

At **9.00** seconds he had covered 648 metres and the speed touched 305kmh. He could now see the mouth of Tamburello clearly up ahead, see it opening to him.

At **9.50** seconds he had covered 690 metres – the wall 240 metres away. His foot stayed down, the speed at 303kmh. He had almost reached the first band of dark tarmac, almost – but not quite – reached the car's absolute top speed. Everything, it seemed, was still normal. The G-force, the gravitational pull on him, was also normal, dancing from 0.29 at **7.98** seconds through a sequence of small variations to 0.25 at this **9.50** seconds.

At **9.56** seconds he reached the first band of dark tarmac. By now he was bringing the Williams over from the right-hand side of the track to the inside: the trajectory of Tamburello was an arc and the fastest way through was the shortest way through – the inside line, over near the kerbing on the left. The band of tarmac was around 16 metres deep and he was doing 307kmh.

He passed from the band at **9.76** seconds.

At **10.26** seconds he had covered 755 metres and reached the second, narrower band of dark tarmac. He was tight to the inside of Tamburello's arc now, nicely placed to go round quite normally. As he crossed onto the band the car 'bottomed' again, flinging back a stab-like flurry of sparks. The band was ten metres deep and he passed from it at **10.38** seconds, speed 307kmh.

He ran towards the third dark band 62 metres away. During those 62 metres he kept his foot down, the car doing a constant 306kmh and the revs steady even when, it appears, he ran over a small bump. That did not affect the car's speed but was sufficient to cause a little distortion to the on-board camera.

At **11.04** seconds he had covered 817 metres, he was doing the 307kmh and the wall was 113 metres away. The track surface was uneven because the camera picture distorted again and worsened at **11.10** seconds as he crossed onto the third dark band. The speed snapped up to 309kmh, the picture heavily distorted.

Did all those years of intuitive understanding tell him NOW that something was wrong? Was it NOW that the process of reacting to it began?

At **11.16** seconds the picture was further distorted by a big bump. At **11.18** he still had his foot full on the accelerator but he must have known by now that something *was* wrong.

Did – maybe – the steering feel light to his touch? Did he think – maybe – he had a puncture? Did – maybe – he think he had understeer?

By **11.20** he had covered 834 metres and he *was* reacting, foot coming off the accelerator. The wall was 96 metres away. The car ran over a small bump. At **11.22** seconds his foot had come much further off the accelerator.

At **11.24** seconds the picture on the camera was almost clean, his foot still coming hard off the accelerator and the car virtually at the biggest bump.

At **11.26** seconds his foot had come almost half way off the accelerator. This bump must have disturbed the posture of the car because it bottomed, grinding sparks from the tarmac.

At **11.28** seconds the car was steering left but at **11.30** slightly to the right.

Was that because the steering felt light and he was adjusting the wheel to pick up the steering load again? Good drivers do this on the limit all the time: you're turning in, turning in, it goes light and you bring it back until it picks up again. Did the power steering read this adjustment as the prelude to a change of direction and, trying to help him by anticipating it, take the car that slight bit to the right?

At **11.34** seconds he had covered 844 metres and the wall was 86 metres away. He ran over a small bump. At **11.36** seconds he was clear of this bump but at **11.38** ran over another.

At **11.40** seconds he had covered 852 metres, the picture clean again and he was steering slightly to the left; at **11.42** further to the left and at **11.44** further still.

Did he – NOW – understand the extent of his plight? Did he see it clearly: I am not going to catch this car.

His helmet moved into the camera's view because, as it would seem, he was on the brakes. The G-force on a car going forward is expressed in ordinary numerals. The G-force on a car slowing is expressed by a minus sign. At **11.42** the G-force had been 0.01, at **11.44** it was –0.42, at **11.46** it was –0.93.

At **11.50** seconds he had covered 860 metres – the wall was 70 metres away. He had his foot completely off the throttle and although the G-force had dipped fractionally it would increase again almost instantly. He had the speed down to 303kmh. His helmet dipped fractionally, as if he might have been trying to look at something.

He was fighting for his life.

At **11.54** he steered slightly to the left and the brakes locked – fleetingly – the rear wheels.

At **11.56** his helmet dipped again, the speed about to drop to 299kmh and the G-force now –1.09.

At **11.62** seconds his helmet dipped a third time, the speed at 299kmh but he must have come partially off the brakes because the G-force flicked from –1.04 to –0.61. Perhaps he eased off the brakes a fraction in response to the wheel-locking of 11.54.

At **11.64** seconds he began braking desperately and as the brakes bit the G-force rose like hammer blows: –0.73, –1.30, –1.83. The speed was down to 291kmh and at **11.72** he had his foot hard on the brake, the G-force –3.10.

At **11.78** seconds he entered the fourth band of dark tarmac, at **11.80** the brakes bit a chunk out of the speed – from 291kmh to 274 – as he ran over a small bump. His helmet dipped a fourth time, again as if it might have been trying to look at something – or perhaps forced there by the braking.

At **11.82** seconds, the brakes bit harder and harder, the G-force had vaulted to –3.75 then –4.34.

At this point the camera was switched off by the FOCA director – a decision taken some ten seconds earlier because, then, everything had seemed normal and more interesting action lay elsewhere. A fuller explanation of this is in the next chapter – but it meant that somehow, from here on, Ayrton Senna was alone, the movements of steering wheel and helmet unseen. He was now seeing it entirely by himself. As the picture from the camera melted at this **11.84**, he became a solitary man confronting his destiny.

At **11.90** the brakes bit a second chunk out of the speed, from 274kmh to 260. The car passed from the dark band and 'bottomed' again – a lick of sparks, no more – then veered to the right so fast it completely vanished from Schumacher's on-board camera. Schumacher's camera was, like Senna's, mounted on the left-hand side of the cockpit and Schumacher had his Benetton placed on the inside going round Tamburello: both camera and car were pointing away from Senna but the vanishing was trapped in a terrible suddenness of speed.

At **11.92** seconds the G-force was around –4.30.

From **12.00** seconds, the brakes bit and bit, everything began to slow – but not by much.

At **12.08** seconds he ran over another bump because sparks were churned from the bottom of the car. The G-force was –4.70.

At **12.10** seconds he had the speed down to 243kmh and he touched the throttle but only gently – trying to straighten the car?

From **12.18** seconds to **12.20** he left the circuit – at **12.18** the left rear wheel was still on the track, the rest of the car on the grass beyond. The wall was 38.5 metres away. That's 42 yards. His foot began moving on the clutch – trying to straighten the car? As the car was leaving the circuit its front wheels rose and when they came down they left tyre tracks. The revs dipped below 10,000. That was 912 metres and he had the speed down to 229kmh.

At **12.36** seconds he touched the throttle and was still working the clutch – trying to straighten the car again? The change in surface from tarmac to grass seems to have pitched the car slightly to the right. That was **12.38.**

At **12.48** seconds the car was on the concrete run-off area in front of the wall. The change of surface pitched the car a second time: left and right. On the concrete the brakes gripped better than on the grass but it was too late, far, far too late.

At **12.60** seconds he must have braced himself for impact. His foot was back on the throttle – again gently and he still worked the clutch. As the car screamed towards it, the wall must have loomed at him, vast, inescapable, impenetrable: deep as a static sea.

At **12.78** seconds he had covered 928 metres – the wall two metres away. His foot dipped into the throttle – a reflex action?

It was **12.80.** He had covered the 930 metres.

The dispassionate precision of the telemetry – the millimetres of travel, the percentages of usage, the lbs per square inch, the lateral and longitudinal G-forces, the steering pressure, the steering target, the steering strain, the steering pressure difference – was meaningless now.

Senna's car struck the wall hard enough to gouge the concrete.

The images began then, images which haven't gone away and won't be going away. Each person guards his own.

Perry McCarthy had known Senna as so many others had known him, from somewhere in the middle distance and, just like so many others, McCarthy was not at Imola. He was moving into a new house near the town of Brentwood just beyond the fringes of Outer London. To him, the race was important, because if you're a driver all races are important, but really just another round of the 16 in 1994. That was how it seemed. "It was while we were putting our stuff into the house that our next door neighbour, who knew who I was … suddenly he's come running out of his house and he said to me *Perry* – and he was pretty sombre about it – *Perry, Ayrton Senna's had a big accident*. So I said *oh, is he OK?* He said he wasn't sure. I went in to his house because he had his TV set on – we didn't even have ours plugged in – and then I saw Ayrton laying by the side of the car. I knew there and then. I could see the blood. I was stunned. I had to leave my wife to put everything together and I just sat down … thinking."

Mauricio Gugelmin watched the race from Miami. He knew Senna was in terrible trouble "when the car came to rest." Senna's head made a small convulsive movement – "he just shook a little bit, his head went down, that was it" – and didn't move any more. "Then I had to play things down because Stella was really shocked. She was seven months pregnant with the twins. We closed the house up and we went for a walk. I'd watched until they put him in the helicopter and when I saw the way the ground was I knew. After that was just hell."

Peter Warr was in Hampshire, sponsoring a golf match. He'd worked with Jim Clark in the 1960s and, when he heard about Imola, he felt the same shock and pain as he had on Sunday 7 April 1968 when told what had happened in a Formula 2 race at Hockenheim.

Adriane Galisteu, who was planning to spend the summer with Senna in Europe, had gone to the home of his long-time friend Antonio Braga near Lisbon to watch the race on television. She was due to fly to his house at Faro in the south – he ought to have been home by evening. Reportedly she had no money on her at all and Braga paid for her return flight to Sao Paulo.

Emerson Fittipaldi was testing with the Penske team at Michigan. "It was the first time ever in my career a team manager called me in on the radio. I was doing a long run, a full-tanks run on the new Mercedes engine that was going to Indy [the Indy 500 race at Indianapolis]. He called me and said *Emerson, come in.* I asked why? He said *just come in.* And then I come in and he says *your wife's on the phone and she wants to talk to you.* I was shocked. I thought maybe one of my kids had a problem. She just says *it's Ayrton.* I had no words."

I suppose my image was of a distant day at Spa in 1988 when I was interviewing Dennis Rushen. Rushen was sitting in one of the old pits on the descent to Eau Rouge and he was merry about his memories of the Formula 2000 days. Then, without any particular warning, he said: "He means a lot to us. I want to see him quit before he kills himself. That's always a fear I have – that he'll kill himself. You can want it too much on just that one lap and you know it happens, doesn't it?" Rushen must have been preoccupied by this because speaking to him in 1995 he said, again without any particular warning: "I did feel quite strongly at the end of the McLaren era he should have quit."

Why?

"Ummm. Yes, that's a very good question. I don't know. I just felt it. Ummm. By that stage, he'd made his point, he'd done enough and he had enough other things in his life. It wasn't worth just to keep doing it and doing it and doing it."

But he did.

Gerhard Berger went to the Maggiore Hospital and saw that Senna was still clinically alive – "I want that to be known" – and then went to Bologna Airport, where he had left his plane.

Significant sections of the Formula 1 fraternity had left the circuit as they normally did, as soon after the race as possible. They arrived at the airport for their evening flights home with nothing but rumours about Senna's condition to go on. Brian Hart was among them. Then Berger came and said *it's over* "and word of that spread through the airport. We knew." Hart went to the bar and reached for a drink. He was not alone.

Then and now

Owen O'Mahoney still flies Senna's plane for the family and has trained a couple of Brazilian pilots to help. He still feels, I sense, a strong attachment to the family as well as a duty to them. He also flew Michael Schumacher around for a while. O'Mahoney is in demand, he swears, because "people like to have a dash of white hair in the cockpit ..."

Mauricio Gugelmin did not go to the funeral "because I just couldn't." Stella had the twins: Bernardo at 11.58pm on 13 July, Giuliano at 12.25am on 14 July. That was Stella's birthday.

Martin Zustak, who has been such an invaluable help in this chapter – he recorded, charted and sent me all the telemetry unbidden – is a Czech working for an American company in Galway, Ireland. We've never met but we speak on the telephone. One time I engage in a little banter: "Before the Berlin Wall came down, you couldn't get a visa to come here, now you show up with a Visa card!" He explains that it took him about three years to adjust from the command communist economy to roving capitalism but his parents haven't and probably never will. Too much time gone by.

Part Two

TIME GOING BY

(2 May 1994–1 May 1999)

Chapter 7

No matter what
the future brings

THERE HAD TO BE an investigation and a trial, because Italian law demands it following an unnatural death. This was represented in the British media as either a strange foreign foible or a gross interference in the sanctity of motor racing, as if the laws of a country applied to every facet of life *except* motor racing. (The fact that the same was not done for Ratzenberger weakened the Italian argument suggesting, as it did, that the scale of Senna couldn't be withstood but the fate of an Austrian rookie could – and was [see note at the end of this chapter].) Many millions of people wanted to know why Senna had died. An investigation and trial seemed the best, and probably only, chance to answer the question.

Stefano Galli of the firm Studio Legale Calzolari-McCracken explains how the legal system works in the case of Senna, and it is (mercifully) simple. "The Italian penal procedure is made of different steps. **1.** There must be a complaint of a crime to the police. **2.** There is then a preliminary investigation, led by a State Prosecutor in collaboration with the police. He can summon technical experts and ordinary people and question them. **3.** After a maximum of 18 months he must decide whether to send the case to trial or dismiss it. **4.** If it goes to trial, the leading figure is the Judge. He looks at the evidence given by the State Prosecutor, looks at the evidence brought by the defence, listens to witnesses and if necessary can summon experts. **5.** After this, the State Prosecutor and the defence express their final conclusions. **6.** The Judge closes the hearing and decides whether to convict or not."

The crash's immediate aftermath caused turmoil inside grand prix racing – the rush to safety and the implications of that are discussed elsewhere. If the previous chapter was largely about the most intense chronological order – at fiftieths of a second – to describe the sequence of events up to the Tamburello wall, this one is an exploration of the possible reasons. It centres on the trial, and many witnesses will be called.

The car was impounded, initially at the track.

In Bologna, the nearest big town, the investigation was ordered and a man called Maurizio Passarini appointed as State Prosecutor. Step 2 – the preliminary investigation – was under way. Passarini, aged 39, was described as a small, shy man who wore glasses and kept a couple of pipes on his desk (although nobody has ever seen him smoke).

Passarini would marshal the evidence, employing and deploying whatever experts he felt could get at what had happened. He enlisted help from the University of Bologna, where there was plenty of expertise: Enrico Lorenzini, their Professor of Engineering, and another Professor, Alberto Bucchi, a specialist in road construction systems.

Passarini broadened the scope. He enlisted Mauro Forghieri, formerly of Ferrari; Emanuele Pirro, former grand prix driver; Tommaso Carletti, an ex-Ferrari race engineer; Francesco Bomparola, a representative of state road contractors; Roberto Nosetto, ex-President of the Imola circuit; and Antonio dal Monte, a professor of sports science and an ex-Ferrari team manager. When they had completed their report they would hand it to Passarini, and he'd decide the next step.

Far from being a foible this was being handled with civilised care.

Passarini brought in a company called CINECA, based near Bologna, and they worked quietly and methodically in the background.

A skilled technician, Antonella Guidazzoli, explains that CINECA is "a consortium of universities and the main idea is that they are united in order to use computing power. Our centre is the most powerful computing centre in Italy." She works in the visual information technology lab whose aim is "to help scientific associations in image processing in order to understand the data from certain situations. That's what we try to do. An example. For bio medicine, we can create some neurosurgery [on the screen] – show a surgeon what the surgery would be like. We can reconstruct ancient worlds, and even archaeology can benefit from image processing." Ms. Guidazzoli conjures an image onto her computer, a simulation of a bird hitting the windscreen of a helicopter. "We can control the speed of impact and the idea is to design the windscreen better without sending a human being up in a helicopter to look for a flock of birds!"

To her fell the task of co-ordinating the visual evidence of the crash at Tamburello. She is "not a fan of motorsport, just a working electronic engineer and to me it could have been helicopters and birds, or a roman temple. It just happened to be Senna. We don't specialise in F1 here! Passarini telephoned and said *we want to explore everything in the data images that we have about the Senna incident in order to understand better.* This is our work. It was not because the film stops" – as we have seen, the camera was switched off by the FOCA director at **11.84** seconds because everything seemed normal and the director would move to more interesting action elsewhere. (She estimates "we lose about 30, 40 frames before he hits the wall.")

Anyway,"Passarini gave us the videos – *this* from Schumacher's car, *this* from Senna's car, and *this* from our national TV company, *RAI,* from their fixed camera. Three views. And *here* was the curve.

"What we did was to synchronise the telemetry which the University of Bologna gave us – there were many researchers involved at the University – and in the trial there was a discussion because there was another black box [of the Williams team, which reportedly had not survived – witnesses will be testifying to this. CINECA were using the Renault black box]. You had lateral acceleration, steering strain, number of revs and so on. The task was to try to synchronise all this information. The telemetry was synchronised by Mauro Forghieri. He came here. We used only the telemetry from Senna's car. We are experts in images, we can synchronise images but we are not experts in mechanical problems. That was what Forghieri did." (An example of the telemetry is on page 171.)

Ms. Guidazzoli used dark tarmac strips – lying like bands across the track – on the entrance to Tamburello as fixed points to co-ordinate the Senna and Schumacher on-board videos.

I went to CINECA in autumn 1998 so that Ms. Guidazzoli could recreate her method of working and take me through it.

Imagine that she is manipulating her computer with easy dexterity, clicking away so that image follows image.

"It's a different colour road. This little band you can see easily."

From Schumacher's on-board camera, Senna's car bottoms very briefly.

"We have synchronised these two sequences with the sparks – they are a temporary event which happened very quickly. You can see the sparks here and here."

They last for two frames.

"One frame is one-fiftieth of a second because in one second you have 50 different images on a video. Here you are going frame-by-frame, which means one-fiftieth of a second."

Ms. Guidazzoli found another fixed point, this one entirely from the camera on Senna's car, positioned over his left shoulder. It afforded a view of around the top left-hand third of the cockpit, with a portion of the steering wheel in the bottom right-hand corner.

"You must have a look at this yellow button. It is on the steering wheel and its behaviour runs round a circle: that means you can follow the way the wheel is being turned."

The button is one of the controls on the steering wheel. The wheel has three main spokes, one vertical from the bottom joining the other two which stretch across the middle. Together they form a T-shape. Above this, three smaller truncated spokes – a bit like shorn horns – splay out, one at an angle to the left, one (stubby) upright and one at an angle to the right. The left and right 'horns' form a V-shape. The yellow button is at the tip of the 'horn' to the left, 83mm from the centre of the wheel.

Ms. Guidazzoli did not know the function of the button. That was completely unimportant to her. What was important was that she had an exact point of reference for what the steering wheel was doing – and by inference exactly what Senna was making it do. It was utterly simple geometrical law. If the button dipped to the left he was turning the wheel to the left, if it rose to the right he was turning the wheel to the right – and "if the button makes strange movements, it means the steering wheel wasn't fixed."

At this point Ms. Guidazzoli introduced something else. "Here is another 'history,' because in the beginning they gave us a VHS videotape and VHS means about 200 or 300 lines of resolution. Then during the trial, I don't remember when, suddenly a Betacam videotape appeared. It had the same content but a different resolution because Betacam is the standard which normal television uses and it's 500 lines. That's a big difference. I can say for sure that we have seen something strange, even on the VHS. For me it was clear, but it was difficult to show."

When you say something strange, what do you mean?

"The behaviour of this button."

Ms. Guidazzoli backtracked to the film of the previous lap, to when the safety car pulled off. She was then able to chart the movement of the steering wheel on that lap and superimpose it on the next – fatal – lap, frame by frame. She superimposed it using small green crosses. The rim of the cockpit provided another fixed point: you could see what the yellow button was doing in relation to it. She then superimposed red crosses in a V-shape and "here you have a distance of about 4 centimetres between the yellow button and the V, which is in the centre of the steering wheel."

Ms. Guidazzoli moves the video sequence on towards its end.

"This is Senna's glove. You see, even just looking at the image, in my opinion this behaviour is very strange. You know, *down, disappeared from the picture*. It's translating up and down, not rotating. Here you can see the behaviour of the button during the last seconds …"

… the button is jumping everywhere.

"Coulthard in the court room said it was normal. I'm not an expert but I think it's not normal."

Alberto Nico, a spokesman for CINECA, sums up: "We processed only the telemetry from **7.98** seconds to **11.98** because that was all the State Prosecutor asked of us. It is what we showed during the trial. Once we had done the synchronisations between the different video sources, Mr. Forghieri synchronised the pictures with the telemetry data. The yellow button showed the most movement at **10.56** seconds, when it fell below the red line, 55mm below its normal position. It is also important to notice that the button's movement started at about **8.0** seconds and went on until the peak time of **10.56**. This is all we can affirm thanks to the scientific visualisation."

Inevitably, as is the nature of these things, the investigation proceeded discreetly and silently all down that long summer from 1 May 1994.

Inevitably, too, the discretion and silence opened the way for rumours in any newspapers and magazines who cared to indulge themselves. Several did.

British newspapers carried a story attributed to Interpol vice president Romeu Tuma saying that mechanical failure had been the cause of the accident. When contacted, Interpol – whose job it is to track people down – said they didn't know where Mr. Tuma, *their own vice president,* was. Williams said they knew nothing about Mr. Tuma at all.

As Ernest Hemingway once remarked, never confuse movement with action.

By early August two French newspapers, *L'Equipe* and *Info-Matin,* carried stories which, they claimed, came from a source inside the University. In sum: experts concluded that Senna's Williams suffered a steering failure as it entered Tamburello. Extensive tests had been carried out on June 28 and the conclusion, evidently, was that the failure might have been one of quality control or possibly in a layer of the metal. *Info-Matin* reported Williams chief designer, Adrian Newey, as saying that the steering column had been modified at Senna's request so he could see the cockpit controls.

The Williams team said the stories were "unfounded" speculation, but whatever their validity – or lack of it – a shape was emerging grouped around a central reference point: the steering column. The speculation was sharpened because at least one Press photograph, taken when Senna was out of the mauled car and lain down, showed the steering wheel out of the car too, with part of the steering column still attached to it. Steering wheels are detachable, which is how drivers get in and out of the cramped cockpits. Anyone who has been around Formula 1 for even a few days becomes accustomed to the ritual of the drivers putting them on and taking them off. It's almost reflex action – like pulling on your driving gloves.

The question now loomed. *Why was even part of the column still attached to the wheel?*

With its civilised care, the investigation proceeded but Williams's lawyer, Roberto Causo, claimed there was "strong evidence" that the steering was working "at the point of impact. Two weeks ago I was at an aeronautical centre which has conducted tests on the steering column and they cannot say that the column was broken prior to the impact. We have traces which show that it was working. Experts investigating the case at the University of Bologna did not accept our telemetry at first and asked Renault to supply theirs. It showed the same."

The investigation carried an inherent possibility that Frank Williams, Patrick Head and other members of the team might be charged, depending on what was found. Causo declined to say what the charges might be but did add: "The Judge is under strong pressure to do something because of the hysterical reactions of TV commentators in Italy, which led to bad public opinion."

The report of the investigation was due in mid-October but that passed in silence. There were suggestions in January 1995 that the report would be submitted "within a week" amid further suggestions that, if it found the steering column had failed, Frank Williams and Head might be charged with manslaughter.

In early February, Head was quoted as saying; "We have a copy of what is supposedly the experts' report going to the magistrate. I hesitate to make too much comment, but I cannot actually believe that the technical people who I am aware were involved had any influence on it. It does not appear to have anything like the structure of somebody with a technically-trained mind. We gave a comprehensive report on the telemetry from the steering and did a lot of tests here [in England] which we recorded on video. We presented documentation within a month of the accident which pretty much showed that we couldn't get any of the data that was recorded without the wheel being attached to the column."

Head revealed he had paid "a couple of visits" to Italy but been granted only five or 10 minutes access to the car and added that a second report had been prepared by Williams because "we thought it was important to give an opinion on what we did think happened." He explained that although it had been couched in "layman's terms" the investigators said it was still too technical to be understood.

FIA President Max Mosley said in London: "I expect the report will give an explanation for the causes of the accident and say that the steering column was broken. It will also probably mention the bumps on the track, which we all know about, but not much more." Mosley added that he felt Frank Williams wouldn't be going to prison. "I have to be very careful, but it could make us look at where we race and the circumstances under which we race. It's possible that we might want a special law to protect the teams from civil action. The teams are looking at these things."

Two weeks after that, the 500-page report was handed to Passarini and he decided to interview Frank Williams and other members of the team. Seventeen people were under formal investigation.

In April, Passarini said he was not yet ready to announce his findings. He was speaking at the time of the 1995 San Marino Grand Prix, when there had been fears that Frank Williams and Newey might be arrested. They were not. Passarini suggested he might need another six months – cynics pointed out this meant October, and therefore after the Italian Grand Prix at Monza. Otherwise, Formula 1 teams might boycott the race because of possible action against them if there was an accident.

October came and went.

In March 1996, Head responded to suggestions that the steering column had broken. "We haven't had the opportunity to look at any of the parts properly but [the conclusion] certainly would not tie in with the data we have from the car. The report [by the Bologna investigators] states in black and white that the data on the car indicates the steering was working correctly at the time of impact. And then at the end it says the car must have gone off the track because the driver couldn't steer. It doesn't try to say how the data does not tie in with their judgement."

He added the report said there was 'fatigue cracking' in the steering column and clarified rumours that it had been modified on the eve of the race. "After Senna was hit by Nicola Larini at the start of the Pacific Grand Prix, the steering column was subjected to very careful fatigue crack detection in the factory. There were no cracks and it was straight." The team concluded the column had not been subjected to any unusual load in the impact, so it was put back on the car.

In June, the London *Evening Standard* carried this headline:
RACING CHIEF CHARGED OVER SENNA'S DEATH
The story underneath said Passarini was pressing for Frank Williams, Head, four English mechanics, members of the company which owned the circuit and the track's director [Federico Bendinelli] to be charged with negligent manslaughter, which carried a penalty of up to seven years in prison. [Roland Bruynseraede, the race director and an employee of FISA, would be included, and Giorgio Poggi, the circuit manager.]

The story said Senna's steering column "had been modified to make his driving position more comfortable but, it is alleged, the work was done badly, with the wrong materials, and the shaft did not stand up to the strain." It added: "After the crash, the car's 'black box' was taken immediately to London by technicians from Williams and when it was returned to the investigating authorities in Italy it was said to be 'useless'."

It was step 4.

The trial was supposedly due to begin in November 1996.

Frank Williams responded by pointing out that there was "no official release yet" from the State Prosecutor's office "but this time I would think the volcano would erupt. I would think it's going to be out in a few days and they will be asking for a prosecution. It will be tomorrow, the next day or perhaps it will be in six months' time."

November came and went but in December a date of 20 February 1997 was set. The trial was to be in Imola. Williams's lawyer Causo said his clients would be denying the charges "absolutely", adding that the chances of Frank Williams, Head or Newey going to prison were "not even one in a thousand."

According to *Autosport,* who'd obtained a copy of the summons, Senna had "found the steering wheel to be sited too low in the car and asked Williams to raise it." The prosecutor would "allege that Williams did not adequately evaluate the force to which the modifications would be subjected. The joint between the sections was of inadequate radius. The material used in the smaller piece was different and inferior to the original. Tool marks were left on the modified piece, reducing the resistance to stress. The piece of reduced diameter was at the point subjected to the greatest stresses."

A nightmare stretched into the far, far distance. *If* the Williams trio were found guilty when the trial had run its course they could go to the court of appeal in Bologna – which might last two more years – and *if* they lost there they could go to the Italian Supreme Court.

Under Italian law, the defendants did not have to be present at the Imola trial but, in early January, Frank Williams said: "I will be there and I will be defending my company and myself. Why should I not go? I know one is not obliged to but I think it is correct to represent the company. It is my job."

Four days before it began, the London *Sunday Times* published a photo taken by French photographer Paul-Henri Cahier, who was at Tamburello. Captioned *Imola '94. Lap 7,* it showed Senna's Williams approaching what seemed to be a small piece of blue-green debris on the track directly ahead. The colour of the debris suggested that it *could* have come from a Benetton: by inference and deduction, from Lehto's Benetton following the start-line crash.

In April, the magazine *F1 Racing* carried the next photograph in the sequence, under a headline
THE EVIDENCE THEY ALL MISSED
The photograph showed Schumacher's Benetton approaching the debris and was captioned: *Imola '94. Lap 7. Senna has just passed. Debris has moved and is flattened.* The text of the accompanying article was understandably cautious, pointing out that "the relevant distances have been foreshortened by a long camera lens and that, given the radius of the corner and the angle of photography, it is not possible to make any firm judgement about Senna's line. We can, however, surmise that the debris would at the very least have disturbed the Williams: and at this point, remember, its tyre pressures were down and its tyre surface temperatures low."

The photographs, however, were of the left-handed curve just beyond the grid – and therefore around 700 metres from Tamburello: too far away to have any direct influence unless the Williams suffered a slow puncture, something generally discounted because it would have become *visible* at some point (and, I'm told by a former Goodyear employee, there was never any suggestion of that).

The *Sunday Times* feature had been written by Peter Windsor, journalist and former employee of Williams, who now had to defend himself against accusations that the article was 'placed' by the Williams team to help their defence. That was absurd – and so was the 'revelation' in his *Sunday Times* article that sometimes Senna held his breath for the opening lap of a race to heighten his senses. I am sure Windsor didn't believe this for a moment and was only recording what he'd heard.

In another development, Bendinelli said that "Senna's death was due exclusively to the fact that part of the suspension block on one of the wheels snapped off and broke through the visor, hitting his forehead. It was like a bullet. If it were not for this he could have walked away from the accident."

And so to the trial, presided over by Judge Antonio Costanzo.

One report said of the first day that "the makeshift court in Imola may have been besieged by journalists and expectations of shock revelations high, but the proceedings were remarkably mundane." It's the way the world is.

Because of the scale and the number of people involved the trial was held on the first floor of a retired people's social club in Imola. You went through a broad, deep ground floor room where, ordinarily, the elderly locals drank their coffee and read the papers and chatted and argued. You went up linoleum-clad stairs to another broad, deep room where, ordinarily, meetings could be held and plays staged. It was more Gilbert and Sullivan than manslaughter. However the room was now decorated to resemble, as much as possible, a real courtroom. Bendinelli attended and so did a lawyer representing the Senna family, acting as an observer.

(Alberto Antonini of *Autosprint* says: "The real court room was being refurbished but the court had to sit at Imola. The actual room chosen for the trial was a dance hall – a ballroom, something like this – right in the town centre. Essentially it was a club for retired people and actually the biggest room available in downtown Imola. That's why they chose it for the job. It was quite funny because the lights – the coloured bulbs – had to be removed so that the place looked like a court.")

And in place of the shock revelations, the trial was adjourned until 28 February to consider the defence's claim that two of the accused – Bruynseraede and Newey – were not properly informed of the investigation in progress against them; but not before Costanzo had ordered the besieging media out of the hall. He allowed two fixed cameras to remain but instructed that they could not film any defendants who might object.

When the trial resumed Costanzo rejected the defence claims about Bruynseraede and Newey and adjourned until 5 March. The prosecution would put its case then. (Antonini says: "At first the trial was attended by lots of people but after that it was quite deserted: just a few journalists and very, very few other people".)

On 5 March, Passarini told the court that faulty engineering and a defect in the track were responsible for Senna's death. He said the modification to the steering column had been "poorly executed causing it to break. The steering column had been cut and a new element – which was not of the same metal or of the same diameter, being 18mm instead of 22mm – was welded in, and it was where the new element had been welded in that the column broke. When Senna had a steering wheel dangling in his hands he was doing 192mph [308kmh]. He braked and hit the wall at 130–136mph [210–218kmh]. If the track had been completely flat he would have been more able to brake and his speed could have been reduced to 105mph [168kmh]. Senna paid the price of these circumstances."

The trackside was at an angle to the track itself.

On 12 March, former grand prix driver Pierluigi Martini gave evidence, saying that "a driver like Senna didn't go off at that point unless there was a problem," adding he had no idea what the problem might have been. There was a "small bump in the middle of the track which disturbed the cars" but this "bump effect" was normal to all racing tracks.

A week later, Michele Alboreto – former Ferrari driver who had been in a Minardi during the San Marino Grand Prix – said that the "way the Williams swerved to the right makes me think of a mechanical failure. There was nothing exceptional about Imola. We raced in a lot worse places."

The trial would be centred on this but reach into other areas too – like the black boxes. The Williams box recorded data from the gearbox and the chassis, the Renault box recorded data from the engine but, as we have seen, Williams were 'piggy-backing' on the spare capacity in the Renault box. Charlie Whiting, the FIA technical delegate, said he had been unable to download data from the Williams box because its download port was damaged in the crash. An electronics expert, Marco Spiga, contradicted this by saying the port could be used, although at impact the battery had failed – most of the data would have been lost.

Whiting explained that he had given permission for the Williams black box to be removed from the wrecked car and handed to the team – something evidently against FIA regulations – because it was vital to see if any data indicated a problem for Senna's team-mate Damon Hill, who faced the re-start of the race. However the data could not be read.

Bernard Duffort, a Renault engine electronics expert, confirmed the Williams box had been damaged and contained no data, adding that the Renault box's data had been transferred onto a computer disk on the day after the crash and given to the Italian authorities.

In a sense, however potentially important, the tale of the black boxes was a sub-plot. What was important was the missing data and what that might have told, not how it came to be missing.

Always the trial would return to its central theme, the action not the movement.

On 15 April, Forghieri said: "I believe Ayrton Senna turned his steering wheel firmly to the left shortly before the crash. If he had not done so he would have crashed immediately. Senna would have realised the steering on his Williams-Renault was functioning abnormally and, after twice easing off the accelerator, he began to brake."

Two Williams engineers claimed that as Senna passed over a bump he had oversteer, twisting the car to the inside of Tamburello. To correct that he steered right but the car passed over another bump taking it nine degrees off the racing line. They said at this point Senna decided to maintain the line he was on and hit the brakes.

Here was the theme again. The prosecution claimed the steering column had broken, leaving Senna helpless, the defence claimed the track's bumps had pitched the car out of Senna's control despite his efforts at correction.

Then, on 15 May, another sub-plot. Passarini accused FOCA of withholding evidence – the on-car video footage ending at **11.84** seconds but the impact not until **12.80.** Passarini claimed footage up to the impact existed. Outside the courtroom he said: "I am certain that the pictures supplied by FOCA are incomplete. Several details show this to be the case and I shall say so in the hearing."

However Alan Woolard, directing the Imola television coverage, insisted the decision to switch from Senna's car had been taken on entirely legitimate grounds: Senna in the lead, an empty track ahead and no way of knowing a terrible accident was to come. The decision had been taken some ten seconds before, placing it shortly after Senna crossed the line to begin the lap, but it was not implemented until the ten seconds had elapsed because the three-man FOCA crew had to make sure *RAI* were not showing Senna's on-board pictures. If they were, and FOCA switched, presumably television screens all over the world would go blank.

Conspiracy theorists saw suspicion here – they saw it everywhere – but the start, or re-start, of any race is the time of maximum action, and following a leader whose on-board camera hoovers just such an empty track is not what a producer would be doing when so much might be happening further back. The decision was taken to switch to Ukyo Katayama's Tyrrell, towards the front of the main pack, but mistakenly it went to Berger's Ferrari which resulted in 14 seconds of slightly blurred images.

FOCA threatened to sue Passarini on the grounds that he lacked evidence for what they felt were defamatory statements.

On 2 June, Damon Hill gave evidence for three and a half hours. Passarini questioned him about when the steering columns on his car and Senna's had been modified. "I don't remember the exact date," Hill said, "but I seem to remember it was before the start of the World Championship. I seem to remember it being done before we ran the car. In other words, before it went to a race track."

Video of Senna's on-board camera was played and Hill proved reluctant to be specific but he did say "there are two distinct times when the car looks to be over-steering and the steering wheel is exactly the way I would expect to see it to correct oversteer." Asked whether the oversteer had been produced by low tyre pressure or the bumps on the track he said "you cannot separate the two. My idea looking at it is that the car seems to oversteer when it crosses the place on the circuit where there are some marks. The steering always moves up and down with the car, and it may move sideways, but only by a very small amount."

He said that Head had told him to switch off the power steering, which could be done from the cockpit, for the re-start. "It was obvious that they wanted to be sure things were all right in the car. I didn't ask for a reason. I just did what I was told."

Hill described attending a meeting called by Williams afterwards when the team attempted to reconstruct the crash. "We examined every possibility – the steering column, the suspension, the aerodynamics, the underside of the car hitting the asphalt, everything." He was convinced the steering failure theory was "not valid. There was no proof that it was the cause of the accident. There had to be something else."

On 4 July, Williams engineer Gary Woodward explained that after each race the team's cars were subjected to a 'crack test'. Penetrating liquids were employed to pinpoint any fractures in the suspension or steering column and the tests made on Senna's car after the Pacific Grand Prix showed no defects.

Simon Scoins, a Williams electronic engineer responsible for downloading telemetry, said: "I was shocked when I lifted the cover from Senna's car. The Williams data recorder [black box] was above the gearbox, 180cm from its natural position. Three of the four connectors were disconnected or damaged. I carried it to the garage where I attempted to connect it. It was useless."

Next day, Passarini introduced the Beta video images which had been prepared by CINECA. Thereafter the court went into summer recess.

In September, Alboreto responded to written comments by F1 driver David Coulthard – who'd said the amount of 'play' on Senna's steering wheel, judged by the on-board camera, was normal. Alboreto said: "It's crazy to think that if a wheel moves that much it's normal. A movement like that means something is broken. You don't go off that bend unless there is a mechanical failure. It was not the driver's mistake or a sudden medical problem." ("No steering wheel moves a few centimetres," he added.)

In late October, Head and Newey appeared but opted not to answer questions. Instead they would submit written statements later on. Then Frank Williams arrived, so frail and so strong, a man with an aura about him, and a man come to defend what he had spent his life building – his team – and damn near died building it too; came with that wan, drawn smile, came with his precise eloquence which instinctively strips away action from movement.

Passarini cross-examined him for over three hours and Williams reiterated what Head had said so long before: the team conducted an investigation and "we were looking at as much fact as possible. We were anxious to see as much television footage as we could." He felt the accident might well have been caused by low tyre pressure through having to follow the safety car. "After the examination of the telemetry, we as a company formed the opinion that the steering column did not break." He didn't contest the fact that the steering column showed evidence of metal fatigue but in a perceptive comparison offered this thought: "I'm certain that the aeroplane in which I arrived yesterday had cracks in it".

Outside the court Williams spoke in his quiet, measured tones. "I doubt if we will ever get to the truth. It has been three and a half years – a long time – and no-one has come up with a guaranteed answer. It is not to say it's wrong to have a trial but I don't think it is the place where you find out the truth."

In November, Passarini summed up. He suggested that charges against Frank Williams, Bruynseraede, Bendinelli and Poggi be dropped – Williams had no direct control over work done to the steering column and the other three had committed no crimes. However, he argued that Head and Newey were negligent because they "did not check how the plan [to modify the steering] was executed" and recommended one-year suspended prison sentences.

Newey's defence argued he had played no part except agreeing for the modification to be done and, when Williams conducted their internal investigation, was not even asked to attend. Head's defence argued that "Passarini's reconstruction of the incident which cost the life of Ayrton Senna has no basis in proof, it is unfounded and those accused must be cleared."

In mid-December, Judge Costanzo acquitted all six defendants and the defence was lost in an eruption of delight. They punched the air, which would have been quite something in a British court. None of the Williams team was present for the verdict but their lawyer, Peter Goodman, was and he said "we had a good hearing, all the facts came out and I'm sure the right verdict was reached at the end."

And yet it seemed, as Frank Williams had intonated, that no conclusive, incontrovertible truth had been established. It was a feeling compounded by the fact that the Judge did not have to give his reasons for 90 days. Moreover, Passarini could appeal against the decision and said it was "very likely" he would, although he'd have to wait for the Judge's reasoning to be published.

Costanzo did publish in June and said in his report that a steering failure was the most likely cause of the accident. He had acquitted Head and Newey because there was "no evidence to suggest that their role with the team could involve legal liability, so they had to be acquitted. The verdict is that what they did is not a crime."

The report – exhaustive and, at points, dauntingly technical – tightened the central reference point to fractions of time. All views were summarised but it made chilling, frightening reading with no escape – and more chilling because at a certain point in time (there was a measure of disagreement about exactly when) something desperate was happening to Ayrton Senna. There was, though, broad agreement that for whatever reason he was trying to make corrections to his direction.

The report recorded that Forghieri had explained Senna carried out a correction because the car was veering towards the left after he lost grip going round the corner. Forghieri said: "Before taking the curve, at a certain moment Senna carried out this corrective movement" and added the telemetry "proves there was a correction towards the left."

The telemetry recorded strain on the steering and, Forghieri said, "before **10.5** seconds there was no unusual phenomenon – at least that we can read. If we look at the readings after 10.5, we see lateral acceleration begins to drop until it reaches 2.01 G and that's at a time of **10.80** seconds. Simultaneously we can see that a fraction of time before, **10.78**, the steering strain is significantly less. This means that the car is steering left, because there is less acceleration and less steering strain. At this point the driver corrects this movement, increasing almost simultaneously his strength on the steering wheel. That's **11.18** seconds." According to Forghieri, while Senna was correcting his steering movement to the left he noticed something abnormal happening with the steering wheel – "this was just when he was reaching maximum lateral acceleration and at that moment he exerts maximum force on the steering wheel."

Professor Vittorio Giavotto, an expert in air and car crashes, worked with Forghieri. Discussing the movement in the steering wheel, Giavotto said "it's highly probable that Senna felt ... not necessarily a breakage but he could have felt a change in torsional rigidity." It would explain Senna's response in moving the steering wheel. "Perhaps that didn't cause anything to break but Senna may have thought that something serious had happened."

Forghieri expanded on that: "It's also possible the driver made a brusque steering movement at the start of the accident because he felt that the car wasn't responding in a normal way." Senna might have been trying to cope with two factors simultaneously: this lack of normal response from the car *and* less response from the steering. This remained speculation, however. "The reason it's very difficult to make an educated judgement on the reasons for Senna's movements is because we don't know the degree that the steering wheel was turned. The only information we have is the steering strain measurement."

On behalf of Head and Williams, Giorgio Stirano – an engineer – said that at **11.10** seconds Senna's car touched the ground. There were a series of three bumps and that corresponded to the third bump. "Therefore there is interference which is also registered on the car's camera." The car could have left the ground, and even doing that slightly would explain instability at the front of it.

To answer the question *why did Senna change direction?* the Judge said the marks left on the track were examined by the road police and, "taking into account the telemetry data and television images, the Public Prosecutor's consultants come to the conclusion that at a certain point, when Senna's car abandoned the curve and went off at a tangent, it was about 9 degrees from the normal line. From around **11.20** seconds he started this, basically from going round the curve to going in a straight line. The car stayed on the track for 83 metres lasting about one second, then from the edge of the track for another 38 metres, so in total he had driven about 121 metres in 1.6 seconds. At **12.80** seconds the car crashed against the wall at an angle of 22 degrees. The variation in his trajectory is shown in the telemetry readings by a gradual decrease in acceleration which is registered from **11.20** seconds – which is the same time he starts going straight ahead."

In trying to establish when the car changed direction, opinions differed.

The prosecution: Senna stopped accelerating at **11.20** seconds because at **11.18** the accelerator pedal was being used 100.60 per cent but at **11.20** that was down to 99.40 per cent and then fell to 83.90 per cent at **11.22**, then 63.50 per cent at **11.24**. This lift-off was when Senna realised there was a problem, and in particular when he realised there was a problem with the steering. Forghieri said Senna lifted "his foot off the accelerator, let the wheel turn slowly back to its initial position and, immediately the wheel is virtually straight, he starts braking."

The defence: At **11.20** seconds Senna lifted off and started turning the steering wheel – opposite locking – to the right to counterbalance the oversteer he had had at **11.10**. He changed direction because the car 'bottomed' between **11.24** and **11.26.**

The report said that before Senna left the track he tried 'energetic' braking, and that was the last movement he made before impact. Opinions differed about this braking too.

The prosecution: Senna decided to brake when he lifted off the accelerator completely, between **11.46** and **11.48**. At 11.46 he was using 34.40 per cent, at 11.48 that was 10.60 per cent and at 11.50 zero.

The defence: Senna started braking at **11.68** and he continued to at least **11.74**. He decided to brake at **11.44** or **11.48** – at 11.48 he realised the car was out of control after having driven for about 2/10 of a second with his foot only half on the accelerator.

The Judge made an interpretation: "Also, at 11.44 he drove over another bump. It is a further factor which makes me think that to go ahead and take the curve just through steering would not have been successful. There is a lapse in time between his decision and execution of braking. We must bear in mind that at 11.68 he is already 4/10ths of a second off his trajectory – quite a lot of metres. Therefore he is off the racing line and in an area of the track completely unknown to him. That's why at this particular moment his reaction time is a little slower than the norm, which for Senna was between 0.10 to 0.15 of a second. This is backed up by the fact that we know at 11.44 Senna still had his foot half on the accelerator: he decides from there to take his foot off completely and to start braking."

The report described an analysis of Senna's head movements, using the on-board camera footage. "From **11.42** seconds we can see the lateral movement of the driver's head. His helmet is in the frame from right to left. This corresponds to the moment when he abandoned the racing line. You can see the yellow button quivering and shaking a split second before Senna's head comes into frame. Normally when you take these bends you create about 2 to 4 G. Drivers' muscles are tightened to react to this immense force but it's relatively low at this particular bend – although still two and a half times the weight of his head. On a bend, a driver's head will have a tendency to be pushed towards the outside – but if suddenly the trajectory changes and becomes a straight line, the centrifugal force disappears and the neck muscles force the head inwards. That's what we see a few moments before we see the yellow button on the screen. Between **11.10** seconds and **11.50** he lost the racing line. His trajectory becomes straight ahead before 11.50."

The report discussed the attempt to establish Senna's speed at impact. One estimate was 188kmh, another between 210kmh and 220. These conclusions were reached working backwards through the last 38 metres using data like the speed at the moment he left the track and his braking speed. The figures do not seem of over-riding importance either way but, since this chapter is an attempt to set down as much fact as possible, I've included them.

The report said that some particular pieces of information should not be forgotten: at the point of impact the driver remained in the cockpit held in place by safety belts. The first people to come close to the car were medical and one of the first things they did was take off his crash helmet. To remove Senna from the cockpit it was *not* [author's emphasis] necessary to remove the steering wheel, which is usual in such accidents. Nobody intervened with mechanical help to cut away the cockpit or the steering wheel.

After the accident one thing is clear, the report continued: the steering column was in two parts, broken at about 20cm from the steering wheel. The steering wheel was found outside the cockpit, hanging but still held on by a cable. This can be seen by enlarging a colour photograph which was produced by the public prosecutor – the photographer was behind the barrier.

(Martin Zustak wonders if the fact that Williams were able to record all the power steering data was via this cable.)

Once out of the car, Senna was surrounded by medical staff and safety marshals. The steering wheel and cable are on the ground.

The trial sought to establish that the accident was not due to driver error and, from the start, it was considered highly improbable that a mistake by Senna's movement of the steering wheel could be a possible explanation: first because Tamburello is not difficult for Formula 1 drivers and normally it is driven at very high speed in top gear as though a straight line; second because none of the accidents there in the past were through driver error; and lastly because Senna was highly experienced and knew the circuit well.

The explanation that it could have been a medical problem was also excluded. The macroscopic examinations by medical staff showed he was in perfect health – what would be expected from a man aged only 34. Drug tests came up absolutely negative, showing no traces in his body. Sudden illness was also excluded because, on the first lap after the safety car pulled off, he led and recorded an excellent time. During the accident he showed his reactions were still extremely fast and, right up until the last moment, he was trying to reduce speed as best he could by braking.

The report stressed that a main objective had been detailed analysis of the steering column's condition. It was already broken when the first wave of officials reached the car, so it was obvious it had nothing to do with these officials or the marshals.

Forghieri explained the reason for the breakage. "When the car left the racing line the column would already have suffered extensive strain. There were already signs of it suffering from excessive flexibility. All of this is a design problem in the part." Some aspects, Forghieri said, were known for certain: just before Senna went straight ahead he carried out a corrective movement to the left at **11.10** seconds. The car crossed the first bump but contact with the ground didn't produce any sparks from 'bottoming.' Senna tried to avoid some kind of problem a little later, while he was steering left. Therefore, Forghieri added, Senna moved the steering wheel "quite energetically and applied greater strength than would normally be necessary at Tamburello." The timing of this was between **11.19** seconds and **11.20**: during it, the column was wearing out and there was undue stress on it. After the steering to the left ended, and Senna abandoned the racing line, there were no further corrective movements.

The steering wheel's movement – which could be seen on the camera images – does not correspond to normal handling and is not compatible with the direction in which the car is going.

Then the Judge's conclusion.

On the basis of all the data, he said he preferred the prosecution's theory but there was no proof that Head and Newey had any hand in planning or designing the steering column, and no proof that they gave their design office any detailed information: for example, what the column should be made of or its dimensions. They were not responsible so "I had to absolve them of this charge". However the Judge did say that, as technical co-ordinators, Head and Newey were responsible for guaranteeing certain safety standards and they had not lived up to those. On the other hand Frank Williams was completely absolved of all charges because he had no technical responsibility.

The Judge could not conclude that the steering column modifications were badly planned or badly conceived.

Ms. Guidazzoli agrees with the reason the State Prosecutor gave for the accident, "but nobody was guilty. It was a sort of fatality. For the Judge there were problems about the steering." She points out that the famous yellow button should be in its normal position if the car is going straight ahead – which it was at **8.0** seconds. "This is an important point: for these drivers this kind of curve is not a real curve. Next we go *here* and at **11.34** seconds the button has disappeared. If the car was going straight ahead we should be able to see the button. That was the point of the prosecutor. The fact is you can't see the button: the car is going straight ahead but Senna had turned the wheel to go round. His helmet is leaning as if to go left. Passarini was able to use all this and our work wasn't contested."

Alberto Nico, the CINECA spokesman, says "we saw Coulthard in a museum [at Williams] and it was very funny [peculiar] because we saw a strong man trying to reproduce this movement" – the steering wheel going up and down.

Ms. Guidazzoli added "even if I drive my car the steering wheel only moves one centimetre up or down. For the Judge it was enough."

Who first noticed the yellow button?

"I really don't remember but we were looking at everything."

In October, Passarini gave notice of his intention to appeal. The whole thing would have to be gone through again taking it, as someone remarked, into the new Millenium.

Antonini of *Autosprint* observed the trial closely. "There was a lot of discussion on that particular corner about the tarmac, the camber, the run-off areas and the way it had been reshaped. In the Judge's final report, the track was not directly concerned with the accident. The fact is that Ayrton went off the track and, whatever happened after that, he was killed by a bit of suspension which went through the helmet. I'd say the track lay-out is not relevant – it was proved in court that most drivers were actually happy with the way it had been laid out. We at *Autosprint* carried pages from the past of crashes at Tamburello. All were caused by technical failures on the car and all the drivers were able to walk away. Well, Berger's car caught fire but he wasn't hurt except for bruises and burns and that sort of thing. On the other hand, with Senna most of the discussion focused on the car and the steering column."

Did you feel it was a fair trial?

"Yes. There wasn't any particular pressure – political or even public – because every trial tries to avoid that, especially a trial like this. Apart from the early reaction to the accident I don't think there was a movement to find some culprit, to blame it on someone. The discussion was long and, in a way, fruitful. I listened to all the points of view and all the expert reports – I'm not pretending that I understood more than 40 per cent of what was actually said in the technical part – but what everyone there, not just the journalists but the people, agreed was that the Williams line of defence proved to be very weak. As you know, in the case of an accident it's not up to the defendant to prove he's innocent, it's just the other way around – the same as in England. You have to prove somebody guilty.

"They did have an explanation for what happened on the car. What they used was a sort of computer simulation system called ADAMS and it was very well carried out but the problem with any computer simulation is that it has to rely on information taken from the real world. The data they used was mostly taken from other cars. In the case of tyre pressure and temperature, because the car had been running behind the safety car for five laps, the tyre pressure had to be built up again.

"These were all factors which Williams defined as relevant to the accident itself because they said the car 'bottomed' too strongly and this was the reason the driver lost control but most of the data was taken from Martin Brundle's McLaren when he went back to the pits after the accident. I don't know why, or if, they were taken only on Martin's car but what the Williams experts relied upon for their simulation of the accident was that. I'm not saying this data doesn't show anything but, in a court case, I can't see why and how you can be discussing it on the basis of data collected from any other car.

"I don't think it's relevant. It could be misleading. You can't feed a computer with the survival instinct but the driver definitely has that. What the prosecution tried to do was use points of reference because if the camera is fixed on the outside of the car – as it was – you may expect some vibration so you have to be very, very careful to determine what is happening; but the button on the steering wheel is moving independently. CINECA drew the red line and the green line and you could *see* the cockpit was not moving.

"I am trying to be as unbiased as I can, but my point of view has been the same from the beginning: it must have been a failure, a failure must have occurred, because first of all no-one severed the steering column and after the accident it was lying near the driver. I talked to several people who'd been in Formula 1 for years and nobody had ever seen anything like that. And no-one of the rescue team could remember having taken the steering wheel off.

"As we found out later on, the steering column had been cut *like this* [GESTURES] and a new piece of metal inserted in order to accommodate the driver in the cockpit. What's more interesting from my point of view, the steel of the steering column was examined by several people, by at least three parties: one from the prosecutor's side, one from the defendant's side and an independent one – a military institution. All these parties agreed on the fact that, even before the crash, where the steering column had been welded showed some signs of fatigue or stress, some cracks had developed in it. The only difference from that and what was being said in the court was the extent to which those signs of stress would have affected the steering capacity. The prosecutor's point was crucial: that the driver could not control the car any more.

"If you demonstrate there were cracks – and everyone agrees there were cracks on the steering column – I'd be eager to know if after a normal mileage any Formula 1 car has signs of stress. I don't think it's normal."

Under Italian law there had to be this court case, didn't there?

"It had to be. Whenever you have a case of death [like this] there has to be. No case was offered about Ratzenberger and that, too, was a matter of discussion and controversy. Was the driver taken away to hospital just to prove that the death occurred outside the track itself? The track would have been impounded by the authorities [if Ratzenberger had died within its confines]. All I can say is I spoke to one member of the rescue team and he told me he'd tried to give artificial respiration – mouth to mouth – to Roland but he was bleeding massively from his mouth. He said he tried everything in the book to rescue him. You can't possibly say anyone pretended the man wasn't dead at the time. Human beings do not even think like that. Technically Ratzenberger did not die at the circuit: his heart stopped beating on the way to the hospital. And, of course, Senna did not die at the circuit, he died some four hours later."

So why was there a Senna trial and not a Ratzenberger trial?

"Well, it's not up to me to give explanations." [See also the note at the end of this chapter.]

Can you clear up one mini-mystery. In Britain we assumed that the report of the investigation would be published. We waited but never seemed to see it.

"Well, they did issue a report – actually several reports on the different functions of the car, tyres, electronics, chassis. The monocoque was inspected as well. All the data and all the information collected by the experts was discussed by the court."

And one final mini-mystery, the whereabouts of the car?

"It was held in the garage of a police station in Bologna. I don't know whether it's there any longer [autumn 1998] but I suppose it still is. They won't let you have sight of it. As far as I know about its condition, it's pretty bad. When I talked to Patrick Head I remember him complaining some of the car's components were so rusted that there was no way you could use them in a proper investigation. He said some of the parts were covered with rust. I haven't seen the car myself but I have seen pictures. I don't know who took them."

This leads to a further mini-mystery. A member of the *Autosprint* editorial team – not Antonini – either knows, or has a shrewd idea, how a photograph was taken surreptitiously and smuggled out. Beyond that he would say not one word. Instead he just looked conspiratorial.

Then and now

The Autosprint *office is in a small town just outside Bologna. It's a square, modern building with the editorial department on the second floor. You walk down a corridor to it and, on the walls on either side, are 13 pictures of Senna – no-one else, only Senna. Of the 13 mostly they're Formula 1; also, he is pictured with a dog. The first picture you see is of him standing on the rocks, a classic study taken in Portugal by* Autosprint's *Angelo Orsi. It's from the Lotus days, he has black and gold overalls on, is clasping his helmet in both hands to his chest and, with a slightly pained look on his face, is gazing into eternity.*

The offices of the Comune di Imola, where the Judge's summary of the trial is kept, are exactly like a living museum. It's a heavy, ornate building full of imperial staircases, marble floors which echo to footfalls across them, and statues in corners. It dates from the 1200s.

While some documents are being prepared, Vinicio Dall'ara, the Press Officer, takes me out for a coffee. The centre of Imola is a living museum, too – it dates from 200BC. Beside the Commune's offices are two squares, a large one and a small one. This small one is the original forum and, Dall'ara explains, "people have always met here since Roman times." As we move towards the coffee shop, here they still are, dozens of them arguing and gesticulating and talking – and, just this once, time doesn't seem to be going by.

CINECA is in a modern building in a business park. If you're into these things, you can see the fruits of their labour at http://www.cineca.it/visit/ SENNA/processing.html

Speaking of the internet, there's a site called The S Files with no further clues about who is putting the words on it. The S Files remain a handy reference point for the trial, set out on a daily basis. I E-mailed and a lady who would only say her name was Angela rang me. This is the story she told:

Her husband followed Formula 1 and in 1988 they were watching a race on television together. She asked who was in the red and white car and he said "a bloody Brazilian." That's when it started. She became a "fan, not a fanatic" and after Senna's death "felt a need" to know – and transmit – what was happening in the court case. This is on http://www.ayrton-senna.com/s-files

Nicola Santoro – who has published a whole book on the crash (La Curva Dei Silenzi, The Corner of Silence) – says: "You must remember that when the preliminary investigation starts, the State Prosecutor can analyse facts with the police. There was a brief investigation into the Ratzenberger–Simtek crash. They found a piece of the car's front wing, which was considered enough to demonstrate that what had happened was a normal motor racing crash due to driver error (he climbed onto a curb)."

Alberto Nico of CINECA points out: "We processed the video of Ratzenberger's death and Passarini presented it at the beginning of the [Senna] trial. Since the judge considered the dynamics of Ratzenberger's crash clear, the case was soon put into the archives."

Chapter 8

Never
out of date

"MANY PLANS HAVE BEEN on my mind for quite some time, but I still haven't found a way to put them into practice. And all these plans become a dream. As I watch them grow larger and develop I can see other people becoming happy because of these plans."

Senna's words, from 1993, have led to an extraordinary, touching and important crusade far beyond the remit of a sportsperson: to help the impoverished to help themselves. That he did not live to see any of it remains a shocking sadness but in no sense dilutes the dream.

Some two months before his death, Senna confided to his sister Viviane that he wanted to "develop a social improvement project" and would finance it through part of the proceeds of his children's comic *Senninha* (Little Senna) – a small, lively publication which showed its readership the sort of virtues he had embraced as a young man, but not in any overbearing way.

After his death the family decided to form the *Ayrton Senna Foundation* in London and the *Instituto Ayrton Senna* in Sao Paulo. These were established in July 1994 to raise money from the use of Senna's name and image. Viviane said: "The aim is to avoid simple charity but rather to help with projects which will have long-lasting benefits to both community and country and will act as an inspiration for others to follow." This was not publicity-speak. It has happened.

The launch was on 21 March 1995 in Sao Paulo. An actor, Antonio Fagundes, was master of ceremonies and both the mayor of Sao Paulo and the State governor attended. A singer and choir brought the launch to an "emotional climax" and "the audience was profoundly moved by the performance."

"We want to create new outlets, to be a hope factory, because we are trying to mass-produce hope with a name and a child's face." These are the words of Caio Fabio d'Araujo, President of the wonderfully named *Hope Factory* in Rio de Janeiro – an organisation supported by the *Instituto*.

A promotional video, issued to the media towards the end of 1995, hacks out image after image of what destitution really means. The sonorous voice of the commentator states: "In north east Brazil 70 per cent of the children are undernourished." We see a tiny child in his mother's arms, his legs so thin that the knee-bones seem bulbous. The camera continues to the withered little arms, the fingers of each hand hanging like a cluster of hooks; and by now you can see the face, the mouth hidden behind a blue dummy. His eyes gaze at you, mute, from some kind of hell.

A moment later a mother holding another child says: "Every time she went to the hospital, thinner and thinner, they said she was going to die. Even the doctor said she wouldn't live." Then another image, of a baby being weighed whose body is so thin that the skin looks wizened. This is the *Institute for the Prevention of Malnutrition and Retardation* at Fortaleza, a coastal town 3,000 kilometres from Sao Paulo – and it is supported by the *Instituto*.

"The moment you provide proper food, better hygienic care and above all a family offering a path in life, we can be sure the child will have the same potential as the rest of us. It's a joy to see a life that could have been lost for lack of help, lack of opportunity, totally recuperated. All this is the miracle of life," the *Institute*'s President, Ana Maria Teles, says.

There's more: the plight of children living rough on the streets of Brazil's major cities. It is an underworld: little bodies sleeping beneath footbridges. The kids complain of being woken and beaten by the police at night. One says with a terrible inevitability that his mother died and so he ended up here under this blanket, as if, when your mother dies, there is no other place you could possibly go. The talk is of violence and sniffing glue and drugs; and you don't have to speak Portuguese to recognise the word *crack* in the middle of a sentence. The voice of the speaker sounds about nine. The image shows three lads crouched near the corner of a street and one of them has proferred what might be marijuana to another, who inhales in a long draw and turns away.

At the end of the video Viviane speaks, with a photograph of her brother smiling on the wall behind her. The whole effort, she says, "is a tiny seed that must still grow and develop into a great and beautiful tree." Then a list of the programmes being supported scrolls up: *Nutrir Project,* Sao Paulo; *Nutricentro Project,* Curitiba; the *Fortaleza Institute*; *Sports and Talent Project,* Sao Paulo; *Santo Amaro Project,* Recife; *House of the Working Child,* Natal; *Sao Joao School,* Campinas; *The Hope Factory,* Rio de Janeiro; *Street Children Reintegration Project,* Curitiba; *Juvenile Specialised Attention Center,* Brasilia.

The statistics which the *Instituto* relays are painful. Malnutrition affects a third of all Brazilian children, rising to 70 per cent in the poorer north east. Truancy is endemic: only 39 per cent of children finish elementary school. Some 45 million Brazilians live in poverty and 16 million in great need.

Some 20 per cent of children live in *favelas*. Some seven million children live on the streets – equivalent to the entire population of Austria. Part of the *Instituto's* task is the most basic one of all, to feed starving children. In Sao Paulo it set out initially to supply 13,000 of them per day with "concentrated and enriched soup." The target area: "very low-income regions in the metropolitan region of Sao Paulo." Then there were the 23,000 "seriously undernourished" youngsters in the state of Ceara, the computer courses and the street children in the city of Campinas, work to be done in the Acari *favela* in Rio …

When Senna joined Lotus the team's main sponsors, John Player, hosted a dinner at an imposing hotel in Cascais before the Portuguese Grand Prix at Estoril. By chance I sat next to him and during the course of the conversation I wondered how he could live surrounded by the poverty of Brazil. He did what a good man would do and defended his country – especially, no doubt since he was abroad and I was a foreigner. He defended it so vehemently that a third party intervened to diffuse this potentially undiplomatic incident.

From then on I never doubted Senna's patriotism and whenever he spoke of his love for Brazil, and how he felt a kind of homesickness when he was not in Brazil, I never doubted that either. What I didn't suspect, that opulent evening at Cascais – while the wine waiter hovered and Senna put a hand over his glass and murmured *water only, please* – was that he felt anything more than the ordinary but helpless regret that we all feel when confronted by kids under blankets under pedestrian walkways.

The population of Brazil is 160 million spread over 8,511,965 sq km – the fifth largest country in the world. Its average annual income is about one-fifth of that in Britain, its infant mortality more than seven times higher.

As Senna grew in stature the question of Brazilian – and by definition, world – poverty preoccupied him more and more. This culminated in one of his most perceptive statements expressed, as was his way, in piercingly plain language: "We can no longer go on living on an island of prosperity in a sea of poverty."

November 1998. At the University of Sao Paulo, which is backing the *Instituto,* the aim is to "stimulate the sporting abilities of underprivileged children" and provide them with "medical and dental treatment, psychological help, family counselling, transport and meals. In return, the children are expected to try hard at school." Beyond enriched soup to stay alive, it doesn't get much more fundamental than this.

As it happens, Senna did a lot of his fitness training at the University running track and, somewhere, there's film of him padding round, pushing himself, wearing a body strap round his chest, presumably to monitor his heart rate. The track is a curious thing now because it looks exhausted: the dark tarmac surface has been worn away revealing a bright pink substance underneath.

Over there, nestled into the trees, is the metal tubing platform where he used to limber up before running. On the running track this afternoon a huddle of kids are sitting, legs folded or sprawling, while a young woman – stern in the schoolmarm way – lectures them on the ethics and tactics of football. The kids are maybe nine, ten, eleven at most and each wears a white Senna tee-shirt with his face smiling out. These tee-shirts alone must be priceless if you have nothing. The kids' eyes are glistening at the prospect of the football, and they're fidgeting the way impatient kids do – but they don't move.

The goals are traffic cones and the match (boys and girls; one of the girls a promising midfield orchestrator, as the football reporters used to say) gets under way. It's an ordinary match, with all the enthusiasm and kick-and-rush you'd expect – but no shouting, no histrionics. They're running and dribbling and passing and getting their breath back, hands on hips, and they're loving it. They are loving it within obeying the disciplines of the game.

About 200 children a morning are sampling the University's facilities, another 200 in the afternoon and the *Instituto* officials there – some volunteers – are a happy bunch, full of laughter and optimism in the lovely, toothy, open, easy Brazilian way. One of them says maybe what they are doing will show the government what can be done, and the government will flex its big muscles and really do something.

Well, maybe.

The football match stops because one little lad has committed some infringement. He stands immobile as the young woman is extremely stern with him, wagging a finger to admonish him like any proper referee. Maybe the trouble she is taking with him here shows she cares, in a way he's not experienced before? Maybe it is the very first step to giving him human dignity.

This is a broad campus. The playing fields, the running track and the makeshift pitch are part of a landscape marked by rows of trees and, over there, a curved football grandstand and, further over, the flat rooftops of the University. A lot of people are around, walking, jogging, reading, lost in thought, arguing, couples holding hands furtively: any university's eternal air of subdued activity.

Most of the people will have a promising future, some of them a big future. The little lad standing there, perhaps a bit defiant, getting his wigging has come from hell, but here he is on the same campus as they; and what he's got now is a chance.

The man in whose memory this chance has been created was a lot of things to a lot of strangers over his decade of fame and fortune, but surely never more precious than near the traffic cone goals, a few paces from the track where he used to run.

Ayrton Senna is getting bigger all the time.

Chapter 9

Hearts full of passion

EACH FORMULA 1 DRIVER has two lives, the public and the private. In this sense he is the same as other celebrities, but with differences of nuance. The driver competes 16 times a year at ring-fenced circuits and within ring-fenced paddocks which teem with people making demands on him. Because the sponsors pay the big bills, and are in it for publicity, obligations fall on each driver to be presentable, polite, informative and at certain times available.

There are compensations, but it's not that easy.

The media has a hunger for information, an insatiable appetite, and the driver can use that – manipulate it, if you like – to settle scores, bid for drives with another team, explain why crashes weren't his fault, criticise his own team (using thinly veiled code language), psyche an opponent and so on. The skilled operator understands the hunger among the media assembled before him 16 times a year and he can become almost like a lover in this single aspect, withdrawing his favours as well as bestowing them. Every journalist discovers this, many to their cost.

The more famous a driver becomes, the more the demands on his time increase until they become a constant that he cannot escape except inside the twin sanctuaries of the team's motorhome and the racing car itself. Even the pits get full of people. A young driver in a little team at the back of the grid can wander the paddock largely unnoticed and certainly unmolested. Ayrton Senna could barely take a single step before a crowd closed on him and he vanished within it, sometimes shoved and jostled under the press of people. From the early 1980s, and with gathering intensity, all the leading drivers – Mansell, Prost and Schumacher as well as Senna – have been confronted with this and found it harder and harder to control.

Senna was a master manipulator and a consummate communicator – when he chose to be. He could be disarmingly candid or impossibly remote. He might bare his soul or ignore you altogether. He didn't forget that fans who could never meet him in person were longing to know about who he was and what he thought, and the media were a conduit between him and those mute millions. He felt a certain responsibility to make his public face available, or at least as available as it was sanely possible to do. He could not give a hundred interviews a day because that would have precluded him from driving the car at all, so he struck a careful balance.

From 1981 to 1983 he was interviewed occasionally and it was easy then. The hunger had not begun, single-seater racing in the lesser formulae was cosy (in the sense of no great external pressures) and Senna was an approachable chap anyway.

Simon Arron was "an avid – avid, avid, avid – follower of national racing. Obviously I followed grand prix racing as well, but I used to go to Oulton Park and Mallory Park as often as I could. I'd seen Senna racing in Formula Ford 1600. A friend, Phil, and I went whenever we could find a compliant mother to lend us a Renault 5, Mini or whatever. We were hugely impressed by him then because he was a bit win-or-bust, very entertaining to watch, spectacular, and he did win a lot of races.

"We were also familiar with the notion of Brazilian kids coming over, and by and large they only ever came over if they were fast. It was the career-minded ones who came. You did get the odd one who wasn't much good but amongst the whole ocean of talented Brazilians who washed over us he was obviously one of the better ones. I did stuff for the local papers and for *Motoring News,* although I was still at university. Mind you, I was in awe of the sport as a whole and I thought anybody in a racing car was bloody marvellous!

"I reported Formula Ford 2000 races for *Motoring News* and some Formula 3 races. You'd try and grab a quick word with the winner but you were covering all ten races so quite often you did a report without any quotes in it. You'd write, say, 40 words on the race and that would be that – and it was name-check city, you got as many names in as you could. All very hit-and-miss. I was a cub and I hadn't had any training or anything.

"By 1983 it was a little bit more structured and the job of interviewing Senna came to me in a freelance capacity. A magazine called *Automobile Sport* approached me. They had a series called *A week in the life of* and asked if I could do Senna for them. The interview happened at Oulton Park in September. It was something I arranged on the day because access to Formula 3 drivers wasn't much of a problem. The fields were small – even though there was a lot of quality at the top end with Senna and Brundle – so talking to all of them wasn't much of an issue. Senna was one of the more difficult ones to get hold of just because his de-briefs were longer, even then. He spent time looking at data and facts and figures, lap times and temperatures and all the rest of it.

"I walked up to him, shook his hand, said hello and told him what I'd like to do. He agreed immediately and I asked when would be convenient. We fixed on a time, I think between qualifying and the race, which were both on a Saturday. I met him at the West Surrey Racing truck and we sat, the two of us, on stools with my tape recorder under his nose. We chatted about his life in Britain, his general routine and his schedule between races.

"A typical week wasn't all racing but it was related to race preparation, like his diet, the gymnasium and so on. We were talking about an Ayrton Senna generic week, not one specific week, between March and October. There was nothing which was going to make the front page of the *News of the World,* certainly. It was all very standard stuff. Most of the drivers were still at that stage of their careers where the Press was useful to them so by and large they were all fairly accommodating. Senna was different because by then he did have a reputation: he was going to be the next great thing, supposedly.

"There was an element of nationalistic conflict because it was him versus Brundle in a battle for the title: friction around. I didn't have a problem with Senna at all. At that stage he could be slightly enigmatic but engaging. I do remember very clearly that we were chatting about the general situation because there had been a lot of protests and counter protests. He said he thought that certain people weren't – well, weren't exactly out to get him but that there were elements of national favouritism in certain areas. At one point he looked at me and smiled and assumed a conspiratorial air. He leant across, put his hand towards me and pressed the red Stop button on my tape recorder. He said *they're complete bastards!* and ranted about them for a little while – but he was laughing as he did it. Then he switched the tape recorder back on. We chatted for 15 or 20 minutes."

In general, Arron found that "for a rarified sportsman, I thought Senna was OK. He was someone I saw and spoke to at weekends but he made, on a regular basis, that bit of my job very straightforward. He wasn't a problem to deal with. We could all see how good he was in a racing car but we couldn't predict quite what a global icon he was to become. The fact that I spent those 15 or 20 minutes in the back of a truck chatting to him at my favourite racing circuit is something I will treasure.

"I did meet him subsequently. During the first year he was with Lotus – 1985 – I saw him a few times in the paddock, and I saw him a couple of times in hotels. He always came over and shook my hand and said *how are you?* The last time I saw him was in 1992 or 1993, I think 1993. It was a Boss* dinner at Heidelberg and we were standing having cocktails, just a group of journalists. There was this tap on my shoulder and I turned round

---

* *Boss, a McLaren sponsor, hosted this dinner for journalists on the Saturday before the German Grand Prix. (One year I was seated next to a ravishing tri-lingual blonde who turned out to be Senna's girlfriend.) In 1989 Senna and Prost both attended, were placed far apart by the seating plan – nothing sinister, they were doing the corporate hospitality thing to as many guests as possible – and had to leave early to get a good night's sleep before race day. This was four months after the Imola debacle and the cries of betrayal. As they rose and threaded through the tables they traced separate routes to the exit and took exquisite care that their eyes did not meet: blind people dancing a minuet.*

and it was Senna. I did not expect it at all. He said *hi. Are you well?* Then we shook hands. He hadn't forgotten me, and it must have been at least four or five years since the previous time we'd shaken hands."

When Senna's Formula 1 career began in 1984, the hunger was only beginning to grow and it was still possible to chat to drivers socially, even during grand prix weekends. His relationship with the media reflected what the hunger did as it grew; it also revealed a great deal about Senna himself, his creeds and the depth of his sometimes curious sensibilities.

To introduce this, here are the recollections of Maurice Hamilton who, in 1985, was working hard to establish himself as a motorsport writer, specialising in Formula 1. Hamilton is a methodical, careful man – and, perhaps because he's from Ulster, highly attuned to the nuances of human inter-relationships (or the lack of them). He is also a man of integrity. This is the story he tells about securing an interview with Senna for a magazine feature, and the disastrous aftermath.

"I organised the interview myself. It was at the final race of '85, the Australian Grand Prix at Adelaide and he'd been to a Press Conference. The Press Room was originally way over at the far side of the track and it was a long walk back to the paddock. This tells you a lot: later on there were mini-buses but in '85 they did it on foot like everybody else! Anyway, he was walking, I caught up with him and I said *listen, I've been asked to write a feature about you for* Life *magazine. Can I come and see you for an interview?* He said *sure, no problem at all.* I said *well, what's the best thing to do?* He asked where I lived and I told him. *I live in Esher,* he said, *why don't you give me a call and come up?* I was quite pleased about that and I said *sure.*

"So I'd arranged it, and I duly called him and he said *come up* again. It was about six o'clock in the evening and he gave me directions to this place in Esher. I arrived and found – Esher is a very smart suburb of London, very smart – a cul-de-sac which had been built recently at that time. It had about five or six expensive detached properties. It was quite in keeping with the area if you were going to build something new: only five or six. I wouldn't like to hazard a guess at the price, but expensive.

"I went to this particular one, whatever number it was, and here in this big house you had Ayrton Senna, Mauricio Gugelmin and his wife Stella. And that was it. They had no real worldly goods: an empty big house, and clearly it had been sold with carpets included. The décor was modest, pastel walls and pastel-shaded carpets. We sat in the kitchen because I don't think there was any furniture anywhere else! I could certainly see, as I walked past the lounge – the door was slightly ajar – a light powder-blue carpet and model aeroplanes parked against the wall.

"We sat at a pine table, one of those with bench seats like you'd buy in Habitat. It was quite a nice kitchen but fairly basic, not de luxe by any standards. Actually, the four of us sat round the table while I did the interview because that was the way they were. Mauricio and Stella joined in occasionally and that helped, kept it chatty. My transcript of the interview runs to ten pages so that tells you that he was very co-operative, very friendly. I came away pleased, thinking: well, I've got the material I need for the interview and I've also got to know him a bit better – because he was obviously a man of the future."

The interview moved into two dimensions. Obviously there were the orthodox motor-racing matters.

So the fact that you knew the car was capable if only you had the reliability, sustained you?

"'Exactly. We just kept pressing on that side because we knew the car could do it. It was a matter of having the things together.'"

Almost unconsciously the interview broadened. Here is an extract.

You understand the English sense of humour quite well.
"After being here five years, you should have some idea."
The Lotus mechanics are famous for little jokes.
"They never stop. They are really hard."
But you appreciate that, if they do that, they really quite like you.
"Oh yes, of course. The humour … when people are working so much, it's good to have a sense of humour."
Did they do the cream bun with you?
"Yes … yes … they were a bit shame of me to make the big one. [The meaning of this is unclear, but a liberal interpretation is that the mechanics caught Senna with a cream bun which was pressed into his face.] But, first time I came to Lotus last year, they jack my car up with some pieces of wood, just inside the rear wheels. The wheels were just *that* much off the ground. They waited for me to go inside. When I got close to the car it seemed a bit funny. Then I look and I could see the wood there so they didn't quite catch me on that. It was 50–50 [in practical jokes won and lost]."
I understand you got them with some sweets.
"Ah, in Brazil I got Bobby [Bob Dance, experienced team manager]. Bobby is the responsible one. He is the worst one. He is nice and so on and it is never him but he is the one who gets people to [do it] … he is the one, the head. So I got him in Brazil with the sweet. He was all blue. That was in the morning. It was the last day of testing. Later in the day he went to the hotel to have a shower and go to the airport. They were all in the same room because they had to check out. So he went to the toilet and suddenly he shouted out *it's all blue!* because he was passing blue. So I got him nice." Well not passing blue, but only one letter away from passing.

The sweets were Brazil's equivalent of boiled sweets and they were full of blue dye, which made its way from the mouth to being expelled in the natural way, but to the complete consternation of Bob Dance. I cannot resist a further quotation from the interview, but on a more serious matter: qualifying.

Gerard Ducarouge says that you have the ability to translate what the car is doing as you go through a corner: as it turns in, whatever. Is that automatically going through your mind? Does that come easy?

"Normally, yes. Only one place where it didn't happen like that, where I couldn't recall, was Adelaide. That was the only lap from the whole year in qualifying that I couldn't remember."

Why not?

"I don't know. I just couldn't. Normally, when you do your first run, you know your warm-up lap, which pace you took, which power, brakes, turbo, tyres, how they were feeling, corner by corner; when you start the lap how much power you put [on]; sometimes you might not finish the lap if you put too much power [on] to start with. It's a lot of things together. If you manage to put everything together in the right place with the right touch, then you make the thing. Normally, I can recall everything: when I stop after the first run I know exactly what I did, good or not. I am able to understand where has been good, where has been not so good and where has been the area to improve for the next run. Then, when you go to the second run, what you did right you do automatically again, and where you didn't do you know how it is supposed to be and how you can do. Normally, is a big step. At Adelaide I couldn't. I thought about my first run and then I did my second but I don't remember what I did. Then I did my third run behind Mansell and it's OK, I remember. But the quick lap I don't remember."

This was second qualifying, and as an historical footnote here are the times:

First run	Second run	Third run
1m: 34.412s	1m: 36.112s	1m: 20.946s
1m: 21.750s	1m: 19.843s	1m: 20.912s
1m: 21.348s		
1m: 43.097s		
1m: 21.053s		

They are revealing. Disregarding all the 'out' and 'in' laps, which don't really count, Senna drove six fast laps in Brazil, six in Portugal, 13 at Imola, 23 at Monaco, 18 in Canada, six in Detroit, four in France, ten in Britain, seven in Germany, six in Austria, two in Holland, four at Monza, nine in Belgium, five in the European Grand Prix at Brands Hatch, six in South Africa and 12 at Adelaide where he took pole with that unremembered 1m:19.843s on his second run. Hamilton remembered the lap as looking "very untidy" by Senna's standards and Senna confessed the only way to wring a fast lap from the circuit was to attack it head on, use "as much road as you could" and ride the kerbs – and by implication ride them ferociously.

Perhaps this is the key to the missing lap. For once in his life he was so preoccupied with the necessity and mechanisms of the attack that he became more like other drivers than he had been before or would be again: the lap fled past him and, breathless, he wrestled it into submission rather than see it in a slow-motion film clicking evenly along frame by frame. The fact that he had driven a total of 137 hot laps across the season and could remember the other 136 in daunting detail only lends a sense of incredulity to the 1m: 19.843s which hadn't registered.

Anyway, "in the intervening period between the interview and it appearing," Hamilton says, "I dropped round to him a calendar and a diary from *Autocourse,* because I was the editor of *Autocourse* then. I wrote the feature, which was published in a supplement to *Life* magazine worldwide. The supplement was produced by a little company in London. They were sub-contracted and they were the people who had hired me. There was a long lead-in time and of course I was also, being a freelance, doing bits and pieces here and there. One of them was *Old Mo's Almanac* in *Autosport.*"

This was a light-hearted and satirical look back over the previous season, month by month, highlighting the various events. Hamilton had been writing it for some years.

"At that time Ayrton was big news because he was going to do his second season with Lotus and he had barred Derek Warwick. That did make big news. *Motoring News* had run a headline across their front page, rather cheekily, saying DEREK WARWICK: JUST TOO FAST FOR SENNA."

It appeared in their 29 January 1986 issue with a sub-heading*: Dumfries finally confirmed as Team Lotus acquiesces to its number one.* The text included this: "It is clear that Senna felt, quite simply, that Warwick was potentially too fast a team-mate ..."

Motoring News then retraced the history of the story. "As the weeks went by, perhaps mindful of the personal tension which developed between him and the courteous Elio de Angelis last season, Senna's attitude hardened. Eventually he became quite specific. At Rio testing the week before last, he reiterated the statement that he did not want Warwick in the team. What's more, he made it crystal clear that he *would* leave the team if Warwick was signed, as had been rumoured."

The headline was too much for Senna.

Hamilton recounts how "Gugelmin told me later – many years later – that when Senna saw that he went into orbit. He went absolutely ballistic. You can imagine how he took it: that would really upset him. So he's not very keen on *Motoring News* and I do my Almanac – and *Motoring News* do theirs. And theirs made bald and pretty blunt reference to: Senna is running Lotus. That was in fact the theme of both our Almanacs, but *Motoring News* took theirs a stage further. They brought in Senna's mother, they said Ayrton Senna did this or that – the Senna family had taken over Lotus. I saw theirs, thought no more about it, wrote mine and thought no more of that either."

The *Motoring News* Almanac appeared at the bottom of a page, with a label rather than a headline, and was a series of chronological and self-contained paragraphs. It was unsigned and, although it reached far and wide,

Senna flowed through in the guise of a dictator controlling everything. Here are all the references to him and you can be sure that, as he read it, his eye fell upon them to the exclusion of all else the Almanac contained.

"**January 28:** Ayrton Senna accepts post of team manager at Lotus.

"**February 12:** Ayrton Senna starts design work on Lotus 99T.

"**March 11:** Ayrton Senna calls press conference in Paris to finalise 1986 GP calendar.

"**April 5:** Ayrton Senna takes over as chief tyre technician for Goodyear.

"**May 17:** Ayrton Senna completes revisions to electronic management system on latest Renault engine.

"**June 25:** Ayrton Senna stands for US President, shortly after becoming Member of Parliament for Esher.

"**August 25:** President Senna gets his mother the number two seat at Lotus for the balance of the year.

"**September 6:** Senna becomes the first US President to take over as head of FIFA.

"**October 12:** Brands Hatch hosts its sixth GP of the season. Monsieur le President, President Senna mops up, prior to dominating Bald Tyres Kart Challenge at Burgess Park. Awarded freedom of South London.

"**November 15:** Barnsley GP* dominated by Monsieur le President etc etc. Becomes first US President to win World Championship. Releases first single 'If I Ruled the World.' Number one within three weeks – but number two still undecided.

"**December 18:** The new King of Brazil, HRH Monsieur le President, President Senna da Silva Esq signs as number one driver for every F1 team in 1987."

The tenor can hardly have delighted him, and we may assume that stoical self-mocking English humour was remote from him, but it seems that the reference to his mother sent him into orbit again.

"First race of the 1986 season in Brazil, I thought I'd go and say hello to him and he blanked me," Hamilton says. "This surprised me a bit, but I thought: *oh well, this is the race where he is the centre of attention, it's Brazil, photographers everywhere. Never mind.*

"Time passed and I don't get to see him, but the feature is published and now I thought I'd take him a cutting of it. This was Paul Ricard [for the French Grand Prix in July] and I'd had no contact with him. In those days the drivers got changed in the back of the trucks and there he was in the back of the Lotus preparing for the first day of practice. Before I could even say *here is the article* he launched into me verbally. I can't remember his exact words but the gist of it was *I trusted you, you abused my hospitality, made jokes about my family – this is not right, you don't make jokes about*

---

* *The Almanac was full of references to the controversial miners' union leader Arthur Scargill, who came from Barnsley, a no-nonsense working town in the north of England. The union had been in bitter dispute with Margaret Thatcher's government over pit closures.*

families. You come in to my house and make jokes about my family, you write terrible things. I said *I'm sorry, I don't know what you're talking about. I haven't written those things.* He said *you have* – and he was pointing his finger. He was very angry. I left the magazine and went, because he had to go and practice. As I was leaving I said it again: *I'm sorry, I don't know what you are talking about.* He said *you do, you do, you look, you look, you go and see, you look.* It was clearly bugging him so much that later that day I was standing beside the JPS motorhome talking to Annie Bradshaw [a PR lady] and he came up behind me on his way to the motorhome. As he came by he said *you look, you look.*

"I was wracking my brain thinking about all the things where I had mentioned him. I looked up all my various columns and stuff and it was mild. Then I remembered the Almanac. This is now several months after it appeared. I read mine and thought *no harm in that, a bit near the knuckle perhaps but nothing about family.*"

The Almanac was spread over two pages, the first of them bearing a photograph of Senna. The words of the Almanac had, again like a theme flowing through, the notion that every team wanted Senna and, month by month, the teams were making him offers into the more and more remote future.

APRIL

"Senna rejects McLaren bid for Lotus."

Other themes ran through – about the unreliability of the Lotus car, for instance, culminating in

AUGUST

"Senna and Lotus join 'AA Relay.'"

Senna was the main target for this fun but plenty of others had to take their medicine too: James Hunt, Princess Michael of Kent's Great Aunt, Esther Rantzen, Ron Dennis, Richard Branson, an unnamed tea lady at McLaren and inevitably the President of FISA, the governing body – Jean-Marie Balestre. It was that type of column.

Once Hamilton had finished reading it "I remembered *Motoring News,* dug it out and there it was. I thought: what do I do now? He's mistaken me for *Motoring News.*"

And, remember, the *Motoring News* Almanac was unsigned.

Hamilton found that *Motoring News* had been "blunt, not subtle. I thought: I don't want to make him look stupid, I don't want to embarrass him too much – so what I did was, I photocopied my Almanac and sent it with a covering letter saying *I think this was what you were referring to* – because he had tried to refer to it, but he didn't know its name. *I have read it several times and I can find nothing in it which, in my view, should cause offence and certainly no reference to your family. However, as we are from different cultures, if inadvertently I have said something in here which has caused you offence I apologise unreservedly. Yours sincerely.*

"I did not send him *Motoring News:* I'd let him work that out. Time passes – Hockenheim, so he's had two races and just before practice started

I was drifting about in the paddock. He came walking by, stopped, said *you were right, you were right, it wasn't you that I was thinking of – but what you said was still not very nice and you abused my hospitality after I invited you to my house*. And that was it. He walked away, obviously upset that he had made a mistake. He would accept so much of his being wrong, but he had to have the caveat *but what you did say wasn't very nice*. And that I'm afraid was it. I was blacked. He never forgave me for having abused his hospitality.

"I was talking to my wife Diane about it. She'd worked in Brazil for a couple of years and we were trying to understand what he was thinking. I showed her the *Motoring News* Almanac and immediately she saw the reference to the mother. She said *that's it, because in Brazil the family is everything, absolutely everything*. She explained that any reference to the family is hurtful and insulting. Now if that had been Derek Warwick he'd have burst out laughing. He'd have said *they've got my mum doing the contracts at Lotus!!!*

"But it wasn't Derek Warwick. Offence had been caused in Senna's mind and it wasn't me necessarily but – again in his mind – I was associated with it. He never spoke to me again. Sometimes, you know, you meet – say, in the paddock, when you can't avoid it and then there'd be a nod but he wouldn't look at me eye-to-eye, just a nod. There'd be recognition but only the minimum recognition.

"Apparently another journalist did something far more heinous than I'd done. He went to the family home in Sao Paulo and then betrayed him – probably in a minor way but he did something, because Senna did make reference over the years to learning about life, and life's lessons, and one of these was that you trust people and then they betray you. *I've had journalists in my home* and I'd think *oh God, he means me again*.

"So anyway it was irreparable and I had a go at him over the years – on the 1990 incident at Suzuka, for example, but I didn't write anything which I didn't think was fair and I didn't write anything I would not have been happy for him to read. Senna never ever took issue with me over anything like that.

"In 1994 I was writing a book with Damon Hill. I've got Damon's confidence and Ayrton joins the team in 1994. I thought *this'll be interesting because it won't be a chance meeting in the paddock once a season, I am going to be there at Williams, I am going to be part of the furniture, I'm going to be hanging about, he's bound to see me and I'm not going to go away. There'll be a moment surely when I'm waiting to speak to Damon and Senna will turn up and then there'll just be the two of us. I'll say 'Ayrton, please, I do regret what happened and if I was writing an Almanac now I wouldn't write it but in those days I was trying to make a name for myself and it was a chance to do so. Now I don't need to and on reflection I regret it.'* I wanted to say to him: *'look, sorry. Can't we just forget it and start again?'*

"The first time that he realised I wasn't going to go away was Aida [the Pacific Grand Prix, second race of the season, remember]. He retired early,

Damon had retired and I had to go and see Damon. Williams had a huge Portakabin and the race had just finished, the podium presentation was taking place. The whole team was sitting round a massive table, Frank, Patrick, engineers, Ayrton, all sorts. Damon beckoned me in and there was a chair beside him. As I sat down Damon whispered *welcome to the party!* – because they were watching Schumacher [who'd won] on the television screen. In fact they were all watching this, stone faced.

"Ayrton was suddenly aware that somebody had come into the room, he turned round and saw it was me then did a double take – he'd registered that I was with Damon. I thought *right, we're on our way.* Then we went to Imola. I was walking through the paddock and he was walking the other way. I was with Georgie Hill, chatting, hands in pockets, just passing the time. He looked across, nodded – and smiled. I thought *that's the first time since 1985.* And that was race morning at Imola ..."

For your interest, Francesco Longanesi of the FIA estimates that by Imola 1994 the media hunger had grown to between 450 and 500 journalists (TV, radio, newspapers, magazines) at a typical grand prix and 100 photographers. By 1998 it was up to 600 journalists and 120 to 150 photograhers "and this represents a ratio of about 3:1 applications to acceptances."

Whether Senna trusted or mistrusted the British media after the Warwick debacle is unclear and probably always will be. But it's important to consider this: the British media is the most numerous and – for historical reasons as well as sheer weight of numbers – wields the most influence. Only four teams (Ferrari, Minardi, Sauber and Prost) are *not* based in Britain. English is the language of Formula 1. The three most important figures in Formula 1 – Bernie Ecclestone, Max Mosley and Professor Sid Watkins – are all English; and so it goes.

Senna lived in England from 1981 to around 1987 when he took an apartment in Monaco, which must mean that between those years he was more exposed to the British media than any other – in the sense that he was constantly in British newspapers and magazines and on British television. He could see what journalists were writing about him. A direct consequence was that he went into orbit over DEREK WARWICK: JUST TOO FAST FOR SENNA and remained in orbit over the two Almanacs. He was able to see these things for himself. If they'd appeared in, say, West Germany he would almost certainly have been unaware of them unless someone bothered to point them out to him and then bothered to translate them. Ordinarily, life's too short. *Motoring News* and *Autosport,* however, he could have delivered to his doorstep in Esher every week.

All this may explain the 1990 interview which a Canadian, Gerald Donaldson, obtained. This interview contained passages which remain so striking, so personal and deep that the background to the interview itself becomes relevant.

"It was at the test at Imola and I'd never had a one-to-one with him before," Donaldson says. "You know the way he was. He'd size you up and there'd be an interval before he'd even agree to it. I was waiting and he watched me literally for two days – talking to other people, hanging around – because he didn't know who I was. Then it was raining during the test so he had an interval. He was sitting with Berger in a road car laughing and joking. Finally he got out, came over and said *right, let's talk.* The more we talked, the more we got into it, the more he opened up and he seemed happy to be able to unburden himself – because at that time, as you might recall, he had strained relations with the English-speaking press. He was very forthcoming."

It was almost a baring of the soul?

"I tried to understand him, which I think a lot of my colleagues had failed to do at that point. He was using me perhaps as a conduit to explain how he'd been treated by the British press – misinterpreted, misunderstood – but it was very emotional. In fact by the end he actually had tears in his eyes. There was an incident during the interview – I think I mentioned it in *Grand Prix People* [MRP, 1990] – where we were talking and we were sitting under the canopy of the motorhome. There was a whole crowd of Senna fans out there and somebody brought a cake which this guy's wife had baked and that brought out a lot of emotion. People made pottery for him, all these gifts, and the cake, and that's when he started talking about how we can't understand the depth of feeling we provoke in the fans, and how we become part of their hopes and dreams.

"I began covering the sport in 1977, so that's 21 years, and I'd rate that interview as one of the highlights of the ones I've done. One aspect of it was that most drivers don't talk like that because they don't think like that, but it was very rewarding for both of us because we both went away feeling that we had accomplished something. As you know it happens rarely that a driver will unburden himself and you need these quiet moments: you can't do it on a grand prix weekend."

This is how Senna revealed his experience of going beyond the limit. "Monte Carlo, '88, the last qualifying session. I was already on pole and going faster and faster. One lap after the other, quicker, and quicker, and quicker. I was at one stage just on pole, then by half a second, and then one second … and I kept going. Suddenly, I was nearly two seconds faster than anybody else, including my team-mate [Prost] with the same car. And I suddenly realised I was no longer driving the car consciously.

"I was kind of driving it by instinct, only I was in a different dimension. It was like I was in a tunnel, not only the tunnel under the hotel, but the whole circuit for me was a tunnel. I was just going, going – more, and more, and more, and more. I was way over the limit, but still able to find even more. Then, suddenly, something just kicked me. I kind of woke up and I realised that I was in a different atmosphere than you normally are. Immediately my reaction was to back off, slow down. I drove back slowly to the pits and I didn't want to go out any more that day.

"It frightened me because I realised I was well beyond my conscious understanding."

And, later in the interview, as Donaldson describes, "a fan broke through the circle of onlookers which perpetually surrounds him. The man shyly presented the superstar with several gifts, among them a piece of ceramic sculpture with Senna's name on it."

This was the moment when tears welled in his eyes and he said: "I have never seen the guy before and he comes with a piece of art, something that he made himself. And his wife has baked a cake for me. It ... it makes me feel embarrassed and humble."

The relationship between the leading driver and the media from his own country is more intense and that subjects it to special strains because here the hunger, on a daily and sometimes hourly basis, is much, much stronger. The journalists *need* to know – their jobs may depend on it. Wagner Gonzalez, a long-time reporter of Formula 1, explains that there were 12 Brazilian journalists full-time – TV, radio and newspapers. The system worked like this: Senna recognised their need as well as his own obligation to tell Brazilians what was happening, and would speak to them every day. He always honoured that and to satisfy – or attempt to control – the hunger he employed a Press Relations lady called Betise Assumpcao.

She'd corner him after, say, a qualifying session and get his thoughts on it, then emerge from the motorhome (or wherever) and read the thoughts out to the little, expectant coterie of waiting journalists. It had several virtues. It satisfied the need and took the pressure off him. Betise also acted as a filter for interview requests and was a lively, combative person in her own right.

"Obviously some journalists were closer than others but he didn't shun any of them," Gonzalez says. "He'd do it Friday, Saturday and Sunday and never missed although, understandably, if things had gone badly he was more reluctant to talk than if things had gone well." Protected from the swirl of a jostling crowd whenever he took one step from the motorhome towards the pits, this necessary ritual with Betise took place. It was part duty, part just the way it was: a dance round the central flame.

Everybody danced to these same steps but in different halls. The Brits tracked and hung on every word Mansell murmured, the French did the same with Prost, the Dutch got themselves worked up over any transient Dutch driver *because he was Dutch* and so on, right through all the nationalities. Senna, of course, had become something far beyond any of these constrictions. However competently he satisfied the hunger of the 12 Brazilian full-timers, he'd now gone global.

Once upon a time the written word *was* the power of communication. When Senna began in 1984 that was already tilting towards television and much more so by the 1990s. Thus he became a living presence in every corner of any place which had a set, which was just about everywhere. (When he died, letters of condolence came from places as remote from Formula 1 as Afghanistan and mainland China.)

This is no place to debate the tilt towards the small screen, but it did make television access to the leading drivers an imperative. Fortunately for the BBC, they had an honourable tradition of covering motorsport for decades and in Murray Walker a man who had an honourable tradition of commentating for decades. Walker knew the drivers and the drivers knew Walker. Here, then, is his experience with Senna.

"He was punctilious, correct and utterly reliable as far as I was concerned, because I knew that if I asked *can I interview you?* and he said *yes, after qualifying* he would always be there, even though I might have to wait a long time. I waited once six hours for him. He was inside the Marlboro motorhome on the top deck, I was outside it and I had a funny sort of feeling that he was sitting up there behind the smoked glass looking out at me and saying to himself *let's see how long it takes before he loses heart and goes!* But I didn't go and I did get the interview.

"There was another occasion at Monaco when he was racing with Prost in the McLaren team and they weren't the best of friends, of course. I waited four and a half hours and they had been de-briefing. When they finally came out I was at the steps of the motorhome. Prost came out first and I said *Alain, for God's sake what have you been talking about in there for four hours?* Prost paused and said *Oh, sometimes zis and sometimes zat but I do not like to be ze first to leave.* I knew why – because if he had left, Senna would have said *I almost forgot, blow the rear tyres up another couple of pounds.*"

(This anecdote is interesting because it stands in direct contrast to what we have already heard of Prost's feelings about team-mates.)

"I rate Senna as highly on interviewing as I would rate him on everything else. He was the most astonishingly deep thinker: deliberate, sincere, analytical. I'd ask him a question and he'd sit there saying nothing and initially I'd think *this Brazilian dolt doesn't understand what I'm talking about!* Then all of a sudden out would come the most comprehensive, clear and concise answer to the question I had given him. I felt ashamed of myself – and full of wonder and admiration – at his thinking processes and his ability to communicate with me in what was to him a foreign language."

Progress was not always so smooth for Walker, however.

"I've forgotten which season it was but it was a World Champion season for Senna. The BBC and Mark Wilkin [a producer experienced in motorsport] wanted to do an end-of-season interview with Senna."

They arranged it through the official McLaren channels but Walker nurses a strong suspicion that, for whatever reason, the official channels didn't arrange it with Senna.

"So we went down to the factory at Woking. You know the showroom area where they had the cars and the leather couches [next to the reception desk]? We said *let's make this as easy as possible for him, we'll set the camera up and get the seating positions right so that all he's got to do when he arrives is sit down and we're off into it.* About ten o'clock he turned up, and we had been there some time. He walked in through the doors and he saw the camera and he saw me. I said *hello, Ayrton,* he said *hello* and walked straight past. We waited all morning and we were told *he's coming, he's coming, he's coming.* We had lunch at the next table to him and he took no notice of me. In the end we went without doing the interview and I have always thought – rightly or wrongly – that it was because he thought that we had presumed upon him to do it without checking with him: he judged that we were being impolite or inconsiderate. That was the only interview I never got with him."

Reginaldo Leme worked for the Brazilian channel *TV Globo* throughout Senna's career. "I was commentating together with Galvao Bueno. I did the analysis. In Brazil it's different to England: we call a commentator the analyst, and you call the commentator the person who tells you what is happening. Bueno did that and I was the analyst.

"Galvao was the very best friend of Senna and, it's an incredible coincidence, but that moment of the crash at Imola – at that exact moment – Galvao was not watching the monitor. The old commentary booth at Imola was very small, we couldn't see the cars and the pits, and Galvao was trying to see something in the pits. I pushed him very strongly to pay attention to the monitor. When he turned and saw the monitor it was terrible. His face changed.

"Senna crashed, crashed hard and Galvao was quite silent. During the next 15, 20, 30 minutes probably I had to speak and the pictures were getting worse and worse and worse. Normally he speaks and I am waiting for my turn. He couldn't speak. He touched me and said *you speak*. I had to speak, I had to speak. I didn't think Senna was dead but I had a feeling that he was very, very bad and I had the precise feeling of what Brazilian people were feeling in those moments. I felt it was necessary to say *I don't know exactly what the situation is but I do know it is critical*. I could not say he would probably die. Nobody knew – and it was specially important because it was *TV Globo* and all his family and friends would be watching."

Senna's brother Leonardo, however, was at Imola and in a commentary booth. Leme saw Leonardo's face and "Leonardo immediately left the booth." One of Senna's business partners was in there too, but he stayed. Leme looked at him and he looked at Leme. "We were in trouble but we did not speak one word – we knew it was trouble." Nor did the broadcast dissolve into emotional abandon, with hysteria coming back down the line from Brazil to Leme. The people handling it were experienced and, as Leme recounts it, properly professional. It is invariably so: you do your job and shed your tears afterwards, privately.

Long before, Leme had had a problem with Senna, and such is the way of Formula 1 that this problem became both common knowledge and a discussion point.

"I can say I had been one of Senna's best friends, not only as a journalist but actually as a friend from 1981. He knew that. When he started in Formula 1 he asked me to tell him what he was doing wrong. *Please, tell me everything*. Not on the track, of course, but relationships with the other drivers, autographs, and I told him a lot. I remember one day we got onto a plane at Rio and it had come from Buenos Aires. Inside the plane were Riccardo Patrese, Elio de Angelis, maybe one or two other drivers, and

Senna was going to his own seat to sit down. I said *they are in your country, please go to each one and say hello.* And he did it. There were a lot of things like that in '84 and '85 and '86 and '87 and '88. Even in '88 – one time when a kid went to him in Rio to ask for his autograph, he was absolutely upset with some problems with the car, and he gave one autograph. A small girl asked *please, another for my sister.* He said *no, I stop.* I went to him and I said *you're crazy.* I was still trying to tell him what he was doing wrong. He didn't take it well. He didn't accept what I was telling him. I said *ok, it's finished, I won't tell you again.*

"We began to have problems at the end of 1988 before the Japanese Grand Prix, before his first World Championship. We spent all 1989 without any problems but it began again at the end of 1990. It was told to a mutual friend – another journalist – that he would not speak to me at the Japanese Grand Prix. I did not know about this, so I went to Japan. On Friday, after first practice, I went to him to make the interview. He said *no, I don't speak to you ever again.* I felt incredible. And next day, well, anything that happens in the paddock, everyone knows. Next day Alain Prost came to me to ask *is it true that story about Senna?* I told him *yeah. I'm sorry, I'm very sorry, but it's true.* So after this *Globo* made different arrangements for the 1991 season. I left my career as a reporter, I became an analyst and *Globo* sent another reporter to every race.

"I felt Senna had changed a lot during all this time – not because he was great, not because he was the best but because of the people 'living' around him. I remember he spoke to me a lot of times and he said *it is very important that I know how to separate the people who want to be my friends from the people who need me.* He was never confident in knowing what kind of people were 'living' around him and he forgot some friends. I could not understand why he thought me, and some other friends, were around him only because he was the best. That's crazy. That's absolutely crazy.

"As we say in Brazil, his feet were no longer on the ground. He'd lost that. I can tell you after all these problems, which lasted from 1990 to half way through 1993, he started to talk to me in a completely different way. He was almost asking me for pardon. During that 1993 season he was – this is very important – he was feeling free from his family. I'm not saying that his family is bad, not at all, but his family was very concentrated on him."

You were going all round the world to tell Brazilian people about the most famous Brazilian, you needed to talk to him and he wouldn't talk to you.

"I felt bad, I felt very, very bad. It was some of the worst moments of my life. He was so great for Brazil that *TV Globo* was undecided. They didn't say *Reginaldo is our commentator* and I felt I was in trouble, really in trouble. Today, everyone who meets me on the street talks about Senna. Everyone knows this story – but everyone knows I did not do bad things to Senna."

So why did it happen?

"How can I say this? It was Senna and Piquet. Senna was very jealous about me and other journalists who had a relationship with Piquet. Senna spoke to me, Senna spoke to me about … about the relationship with Piquet. It was strange, very strange, very, very, very strange."

Tell me who Senna was.

"Senna was one person before 1989, another person between then and 1993, and in 1993 he became the person he had been before: the real Senna. The problem was the people around him, who made him feel good, and there were so many of them he lost, as I have said, his feet on the ground. That's the story. I never felt he was happy between 1989 and 1993, never, never, never."

Why?

"I don't know. It was not a problem of money or glory. He felt like he was in a prison. He had to know what people were really doing, whether they were his friend or not. He didn't know about you, me and other people. So he was not happy. The last time I saw him really happy was when we were in the same room in the *Club Med* in Mauritius after the Australian Grand Prix in 1985. In *1985,* yes [as Gerard Ducarouge has already described]. He was joking a lot. No, this is not correct: I saw him the same in the *Club Med* in 1987. He was really happy, not much pressure.

"The next time he felt well was when he met the girl [Adriane]. I cannot judge the girl. He spent four or five months with her and it doesn't matter, it's normal, but she was really the first woman – woman, not girl – in his life. She was 22 years old, a child but not a child – a woman. He was really involved and his family felt this: really involved. At that moment he was moving towards staying the whole year in Portugal. That would have been the first time, because every time he came to Brazil – every 15, 20 days – he stayed with his family.

"After the Brazilian Grand Prix of 1993, which he won, we went to a nightclub – separately, of course – and about one o'clock in the morning another friend, Jayme [Brito] said to Ayrton *look who's over there, it's Reginaldo.* At the end he was dancing with Adriane, the same night that he had first met her, he left her and came to me. I told him: *That was the best win you have had in your life* and we did – how can I say it? – a *cheers,* a glass of champagne, me and him.

"Two months later he came again to me at a race track in Europe – I don't remember which one it was – and we started to talk again. That's why I said to you he was trying to ask for pardon, to apologise. He never said this, but you knew Senna, and coming up to talk was the apology. I remember sitting at the McLaren motorhome and he sat and wanted to talk about things other than racing: about life. It was a very different Senna but probably the same one before 1989. I was saved because someone at *Globo* did some research and decided my name was important to the Formula 1 coverage even if Senna didn't speak to me."

My own experience was quite different from all these because in 1989 I decided to write a book about him. There is no law which prevents an author from writing any biography he chooses (and the subject of the biography is often surprised and disconcerted to discover that they do not have an exclusive right to themselves). When you tell people you intend to write a book about them, you get all the mixed reactions you can imagine. Senna's reaction was interesting. It was neutral.

Each year at the German Grand Prix, Boss held that Press/drivers dinner at an expensive hotel in Heidelberg, the historic town just down the autobahn from the circuit – the dinner at which, years later, Senna tapped Simon Arron on the shoulder.

As hinted earlier, it was habitually an evening of some style – champagne in the garden, a delicious meal, good wine and plump cigars – and the team's two drivers (Senna, Prost) moving around. During the aperitifs Senna was chatting to long-time journalist and aviator Jeff Hutchinson – I suspect that Hutchinson was trying to get Senna to buy a plane or hire Hutchinson to fly him to the races in the little plane Hutchinson owned, because that was what Hutchinson did.

Memory is so curious. I remember *exactly* where Senna was standing, in a corner to the right of Hutchinson, when I approached him and said, out of courtesy, that I was going to write the book and that I was also going to try to set his career into a broader context than motor racing. I mentioned that I'd try and compare him to the Brazilian football legend Pele. He smiled at that. Otherwise he betrayed nothing: neither pleasure nor displeasure, and certainly not hostility. I did say, since it was his life, I'd appreciate him reading the manuscript and he nodded. Then he resumed chatting to Hutchinson.

A bit of context here. I'd been covering Formula 1 for the *Daily Express* since 1982 and in 1983 I'd taken to ringing Senna to hear about his exploits in Formula 3. That season his struggle with Brundle had reached the point where the national tabloid newspapers were showing a proper interest – something which had never happened before to Formula 3 and I don't think has happened since. Ordinarily, any newspaper's· space is so tight that packing in the major sports is challenge enough, never mind a junior event in what was still then a minority sport – but I covered the decisive race at Thruxton and so did Derick Allsop, then of the *Daily Mail*.

After that, of course, Senna was into Formula 1 and rapidly becoming very famous indeed. I was neither close to him nor unduly far away: I inhabited that no-man's land familiar to many journalists who are doing their best as fairly as they can to cover a lot of unusual people in a constantly pressured atmosphere. He was a leading member of the cast but there were plenty of others in that cast too.

So I researched and wrote the book, which was to appear under the title *AYRTON SENNA: The Hard Edge of Genius* (PSL). Courtesy of Peter Stayner of McLaren International a copy of the manuscript was duly delivered to Senna in Brazil, where he had retreated to enjoy himself in the close-season (as he invariably did). There were two or three controversial passages – Dallas with Toleman, the messy leaving of Toleman, the 'arrangement' with Prost at Imola – which, in a covering letter, I asked him to comment on because I felt it important to have his side. I also asked him to read the whole manuscript for accuracy and write on it any comments he wished.

I had no way of knowing if he'd do this. Formula 1 drivers can have short attention spans (let us say) if they are reading book-length manuscripts in a foreign language, even if they speak it well – especially if they are surrounded by family and friends, on a beach, their *own* beach, and the jet skis beckon. And, believe me, Formula 1 drivers soon recover from the novelty of people writing about them. I had no way of knowing if he would pick the manuscript up at all, let alone read it. I was quite prepared for Stayner to ring me a couple of months later and say *Ayrton says no problem* or perhaps *Ayrton won't say anything about it* – code for he hasn't read it and he isn't going to read it. Instead Stayner rang and said *the manuscript's back and he's done a hell of a good job for you.*

I had completely misjudged him, and the extent of it still makes me feel rather ashamed. He read every word. I know because at least once he corrected a spelling mistake I'd made. He added and subtracted wherever necessary in crisp but small pencil, all of it clearly legible. He did this to such an extent, and in such a way, that something else emerged altogether: a portrait of himself, what was important to him and what was not, and through it all a sort of burning insistence on having it told as he really believed it was. He also revealed his sense of humour, thus:

"Senna now shared a house with Mr and Mrs Gugelmin not far from London," I wrote because someone had told me the tale. "Of an evening he would sit watching television, his right hand moving endlessly along the arm of the armchair in precise, rhythmical motions. It was not a nervous mannerism, nothing like that at all. He was practising changing gear to the point where it became absolutely subconscious."

Under this paragraph he wrote

I honestly don't remember that?

I could hear him laughing as he wrote.

Conversely, certain things irritated him and one of them had clearly irritated him since the World Karting Championships in Estoril – in 1979. The rules had been changed in a most complicated way which, in recreating the championships, I'd not properly understood. He had, though (*the explanation correct is in previous page about the results of semi-finals*). Down the side of the page he scrawled *changed the rules!* like a cry from the heart. Across the top of the page he wrote: *Previously in the case of same points after the 3 finals you would count the two best ones and if the points were the same you would then count the result of the third final and declare the winner the one who finishes ahead of the other. This year they decided to use the result of the semi-finals to decide.*

At the time, when Senna realised that the rules made him second in the championship, he broke down in bitter, convulsive tears. He believed he had been beaten by the rules which weren't fair dealing. That violated

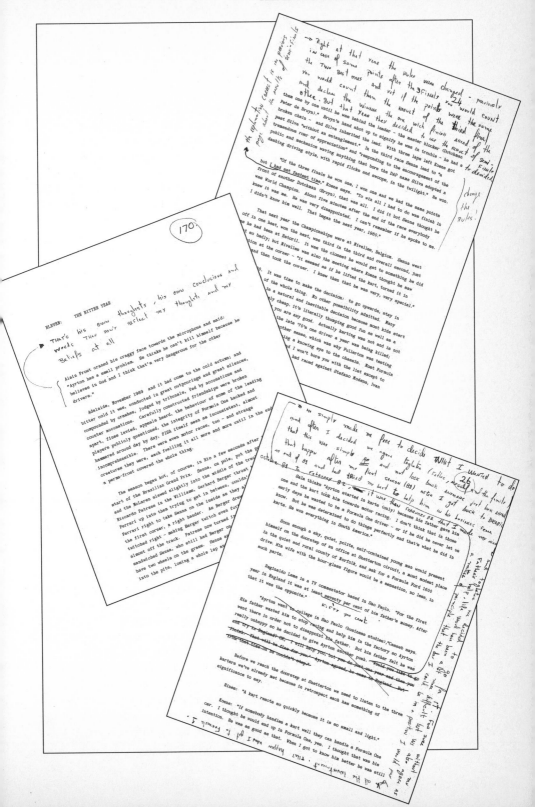

something deep within him – that and the fact that he hadn't won.

He could not tolerate his integrity being challenged or his trust betrayed. Mauricio Gugelmin puts it succinctly: "If he thought you had done that, you were a dead man."

I survived somehow. I'd quoted Chris Witty, a Toleman employee, as saying that at Senna's first grand prix – in Rio – "he'd asked for something ridiculous like 35 passes" to get friends and family into the pits. *No, no, no, Senna said, I just had two like everybody else and we organised a system of handing them from family-member to family-member so everyone got a chance.*

Of the Prost detonations, he was almost circumspect, although he put his point of view firmly enough. I'd quoted Prost as saying "I had the possibility to say no to Senna joining the team [McLaren] but I thought the team would have need of his worth when I stopped."

Senna underlined all this and wrote in the margin: *Correction: One year earlier than McLaren having Honda – 1988 – both Ron (Dennis) and Prost even went to Japan specially to convince Honda to come to McLaren and yet Honda came to Lotus. As for '88 I initiated the work towards Honda, and Prost wouldn't have Honda in '88 if Senna was not part of the team!!! OK.* He was, however, at some pains to explain why he had apologised to Ron Dennis about overtaking Prost at Tosa to create the first detonation. *The apology was only made to help bring things to a possible working relationship.* It doesn't come much straighter than that.

Of a crash at the start of the 1989 Brazilian Grand Prix, he'd been quoted as saying "Patrese and Berger trapped me and I lost the nose section. That's all there is to it." He could easily have let this go but instead he crossed it out and wrote: *Today my honest view of that incident is that 3 cars tried to do the same corner at the same time and there was only room for 1.* He did underline the figure but didn't say which 1. Anyway, it doesn't come much straighter than that either.

And so it went. The book was, I hope, honest enough to confront the controversies of his career head on and he seemed to appreciate that. After Imola '94 it was extensively used for reference (and much pirated) but that didn't trouble me so much. Because he had read it hard in manuscript form, and all his corrections had been incorporated, whatever it was or wasn't, it *was* accurate. After Imola I had a strange feeling: did he foresee that one day an authentic reference point for his career would be needed, and that's why he took such care over each word? Maybe. More likely his attention to detail drove him to be meticulous over this as everything else. He was incapable of carelessness – especially over his mortality, incidentally.

The other thing was that, at his fundamental level, he was a courteous man. That will make many people guffaw but they ought to ask those who were genuinely close to him. So if someone had shown the courtesy of sending him a manuscript about himself, he was incapable of doing anything but returning the courtesy by responding. Mind you there were complications, and I offer you this to demonstrate how he understood nuances. At Imola during testing I wanted to speak to him but he spent a long time huddled with two French journalists and occasionally they'd point towards where I was lurking. To try and be obtrusive (*I'm waiting here to talk to you*) and at the same time unobtrusive (*whatever it is, it can't be my fault*) is not easy. I failed, never did get to talk to him. The problem? On the cover of the French edition of the book was a statement that it was his official story. Well it was and it wasn't, and he could have let that go. Instead he wanted the record straight.

That's the way I remember him.   •

To balance this up, I must mention another book (*Gerhard Berger: The human face of Formula 1/PSL*) because it amplifies any portrait of Senna. He and Berger were genuine friends. Typically, talking to *F1 Racing* magazine, Berger reduced it to simple, direct emotions. "Yes, very good friends. We were similar ages, too, and we respected each other. You know, sometimes you have people you get on well with; sometimes you have people you don't get on well with. And he was somebody I got on well with." (Berger also said, intriguingly: "Actually, his driving style didn't exist … he tailored his driving style to the problems of his car.")

Berger had spent the whole of his life as a diabolical and dangerous practical joker and the seemingly austere façade of McLaren – and Senna – must have seemed a delicious challenge. The amplification is that Senna was more than able to defend himself. I originally approached Betise Assumpcao to ask Senna if he'd talk about Berger for the book. She was sceptical, pointing out that Senna had a natural reluctance to talk about *any* other driver because whatever he said could be lifted out of context and fashioned into howling headlines. A couple of weeks later, however, came the message: he'll do it. I assume this decision was governed by his affection for Berger, his shrewdness that no book on Berger could be complete without at least some Senna thoughts, and – perhaps – the fact that *The Hard Edge of Genius* was at least honest. Howling headlines there would not be.

I faxed off various questions, including *what is the worst thing Berger has pulled on you?* and *what is the worst thing you have pulled on Berger?*

Senna clearly relished answering them. ·

1) En route by helicopter to Monza, Berger tried to throw Senna's briefcase into Lake Como but was restrained by Ron Dennis's wife Lisa. Berger did manage to grab and throw it when the helicopter was about 300 feet from the ground. It was an expensive briefcase (containing Senna's credit cards and passport) and cost a fortune to repair. Berger's riposte: *get a cheap one like mine and then you won't care!*

Game drawn.

2) Both ended up struggling on the hard shoulder of an autostrada at night to get control of the ignition key for Berger's Ferrari. Why is not explained, nor who won, therefore:

Game drawn.

3) Berger inserted a picture of a naked lady where the title page in

Senna's diplomatic passport ought to have been. Senna flew home from the Australian Grand Prix via Buenos Aires. A steward said that if he waited in the VIP lounge, Argentinian passport formalities would be taken care of for him. Senna sat for a long time in that VIP lounge before the official returned, chastened, opened the passport to reveal two large, black breasts and murmured the equivalent of *Mr. Senna, they don't think it's you.*

Advantage, Berger.

4) Senna and cousin were strolling past Berger and his girlfriend's hotel room in Adelaide and noticed the maid was making the room up. Senna entered, pretended the room was his and absconded with the key. Later, Senna and cousin return and put clothing in the bath, put clothing in the ceiling fan and turn it on, open Berger's Filofax and scatter the pages everywhere.

Advantage, Senna.

Next day round the pool Senna anticipated Berger would berate him. Berger and girlfriend sunbathed, saying not one word. Senna, unable to contain himself any longer, asked *everything OK with your room, Gerhard?* To which Berger said *yup* and kept on sunbathing. (Ron Dennis will be explaining the unwritten rules of the game, which dictated that Berger must remain silent.) Therefore:

Advantage, Berger.

5) Also in Australia, Ron's wife Lisa and Berger hired two locals to catch frogs and they caught 26, which were then hidden in Senna's bedroom. Senna found 16, found Berger and exploded. Berger took that calmly, pointing out that *there are another ten frogs up there and did I mention the snakes?*

Advantage, Berger.

6) This story came from Jo Ramirez of McLaren. "I remember going into a carpark in Belgium on a very windy day. Ron got Ayrton's address book, took all the pages out and threw them into the air. Gerhard [for once the peacemaker] had to go round trying to pick them up."

Advantage, Senna.

7) This story came from Mark Blundell, then the McLaren test driver. The team were staying at a chateau near Magny-Cours and Berger whispered to Blundell to help him carry a statue up and put it in Senna's bed. There, it was partially covered and looked, at first glance, like a corpse. When Senna went to bed, he damn near screamed.

Advantage, Berger.

Berger wins 4–2.

Ron Dennis once accepted that whilst McLaren may have a cold image from the outside, it's warm inside. Many people have said this is correct and you do not create what Dennis has created without understanding *all* the currents of management, including fun. What he has to say about the game, set and match above is particularly revealing, and touching.

"It was mostly instigated by me! Humour is a great tension breaker and it lightens people up. The problem was that with Gerhard there is no limit and therefore the whole thing escalated to very, very significant heights. Being the quite competitive person that I am, I was part of this escalation and there was no question the most detailed and complex practical jokes, that sometimes took days to put into motion, were so effective that even now – despite the fact he's not around to defend himself – I think *my gosh, that embarrassed Ayrton!* I must add *or Gerhard.* I have to say a couple of times I was caught out too …"

Talcum powder in the briefcase?

"Oh, all sorts of things."

Frogs and snakes in bedrooms?

"Oh … the whole twist was, no-one would ever admit to being *got.* It didn't matter what happened, you didn't admit it."

This explains why Senna wrecked Berger's hotel room, round the pool next day and …

"… no reaction. We never ever, ever acknowledged the joke having happened and gave the other person the satisfaction. Of course the other two would always talk about it – namely what had been inflicted on the third party. Sometimes of course the best thing was to actually do something and tell them about it during the race!"

You didn't do that, did you?

"Oh yes. There was no limit."

But during the race?

"Might have been the slowing-down lap or something like that. It was done at a time when it didn't influence the race but there were no holds barred. It brings people together and I think the other thing that was really great about it was – yes, there are a few bits and pieces that people hear, but to their credit, and it's the way I am too, no-one really knows what we did. Gerhard, myself, a little bit my wife Lisa – who was involved in some of the jokes being implemented – well, no-one spoke about them. And that's what makes it special. That part of the relationship between the three of us – Ayrton, Gerhard, myself – is that much more special because it's still not talked about. Bits are. You've touched on things, but …"

… but the passport in Argentina, the black breasts …

"Oh yes. The funny thing was the authorities actually held him there for a day and of course we" – the other two! – "were in raptures that they physically held him all day and he couldn't get out. It's a perverse pleasure, but it was good fun. But you knew he'd be working on hitting back and that used to raise the anticipation. And that was … just … the good fun bit."

This may all seem no more than jolly japes and in a sense it is, especially when you know the perpetrators were highly intelligent, extremely worldly and rich men. That is what makes it so delightful: that it was possible to be little-boy naughty in such a grim grown-up world, to be as dedicated as any other people on the planet about the important aspects of their professional careers, but *still* make time to be plain silly. As Ron Dennis murmured to me, you put it all together and it's called life.

Anyway, the Berger book was finished and printed by February of 1994 so that I was able to take it to Estoril, where Senna was preparing to drive the Williams for the first time. Just before a little Press Conference for the British journalists, Betise gave him the copy and he patted it, smiled. I have no way of knowing if he read a single word – or all of it. Nor ever will now.

The idea of Hollywood filming Senna's life may seem an obvious move by some studio or other, but think about that for a moment. Grand prix racing had become a stranger to the United States – the last race there was in 1991 (Phoenix) – and the drivers were now strangers too. Senna was instantly recognisable just about everywhere on the planet *except* there, so a film about him faced forbidding obstacles: the first – would Americans pay hard cash to see the story of a stranger? (The domestic audience is the financial bedrock which makes American films viable.) How much of the film would, of necessity, be spent explaining who he was, who the other drivers were and what Formula 1 meant? How would that play across the rest of the planet, where everybody already knew? And, at another level altogether, how elusive would Senna be to any scriptwriter?

This did not deter a man called Jeremy Lew of *New Line Cinema*, based in Los Angeles, and owned by Warner Brothers Studios. Lew was a scriptwriter of experience – he had worked extensively in American television on series like *Simon & Simon, Moonlighting* and *Hunter*. He then went to work for the famed producing team of Don Simpson and Jerry Bruckheimer, whose credits included *Flashdance, Top Gun, Beverly Hills Cop, Days of Thunder* and *Armaggedon*.

Lew had in mind doing a biographical study of Senna. "I had been a huge fan of his since he joined the McLaren team with Honda in 1988, but he was killed and I dropped the idea of a bio-pic." Lew ruminated, and wondered about a full-blown Hollywood drama of Senna's life – and the obstacles became challenges. He began to put something together, at first with Renny Harlin as director. Harlin, a Finn – and therefore no stranger to Formula 1 – had handled several major action films, including *A Nightmare on Elm Street 4, Die Hard 2, Cliffhanger, Cutthroat Island* and *The Long Kiss Goodnight*.

Lew set about researching the subject and did so to an amazing degree. He contacted all the right people, talked to them, befriended them, flew to races at places like Monaco (where Berger regaled him and offered to help but only if the film was X-rated!) and Montreal. He spent hours gaining insights from Adriane and became something of an expert on Senna. His enthusiasm stirred reciprocal enthusiasm from McLaren, for example, and his sincerity encouraged people to speak candidly to him, sometimes through their tears.

Lew describes it himself. "As an independent producer and writer, I decided to approach the Senna family in the summer of 1996 with the hope of gaining their co-operation in doing a Hollywood film about their son. Spanish film star Antonio Banderas, who had expressed interest to me in the project, was in Argentina shooting *Evita* so I arranged for him to meet the

Senna family in Brazil. Unfortunately, my association with Banderas fell apart over creative differences and I elected to proceed with the project on my own at *New Line Cinema* with Renny to direct. Thanks to the help of Brazilian Formula 1 and CART driver Emerson Fittipaldi I was able to meet and spend considerable time in Miami and Brazil with Senna's last girlfriend Adriane Galisteu and (Antonio) Braga, a personal confidant of Senna's. Though I met with considerable resistance early on, many of Senna's friends and colleagues eventually opened up to me and spoke very candidly about their relationship with him – but only after I had spent considerable time explaining to them how I was approaching the film."

That represented the hub of the whole thing, because Lew was wise enough to realise from the outset that to make the Senna story into yet another crash-and-bash motor racing melodrama would be a betrayal of the man – the films which had taken that basic approach (*Grand Prix* with an international star cast, *Le Mans* with Steve McQueen, and *Days of Thunder* with Tom Cruise) tended to be one-dimensional and with contrived endings. Lew intended to portray Senna as authentically as he could.

He described to me how he had had to take some "dramatic and creative licence" in the initial script, but that was unavoidable given the nature of film, any biographical film. It happens everywhere all the time, and the question is always one of degree. Lew handled this licence with sensitivity and I'd like to demonstrate that by reproducing, with his kind permission, how he opened the film in his initial script. Even this brief extract will show his method of approach, his depth of knowledge and give an insight into how a film is written.

1 EXT. BRAZILIAN COUNTRYSIDE – DAY (1970)
    TITLES OVER. SEPIA TONES. A working cattle farm nestled alongside a man-made lake surrounded by lush, rolling hills. A narrow, dirt road divides a vast open plain. In the distance, a cloud of dust. A Jeep truck clears the rise. Approaches the farm at a good clip. Grazing cows scatter.

2 EXT. FARMHOUSE – DAY
    4-year-old LEONARDO "LEO" SENNA DA SILVA peddles around on a tricycle. His skinny 10-year-old brother AYRTON "BECO" [Senna's nickname] perched on a rail surrounding a pig pen. Fidgety, filled with coiled anticipation. A stocky farmhand, LUCA, ushers the pigs towards the feed bin. At the sound of the approaching truck, the two brothers turn their heads.
    LEO
    Papa!
    Leo peddles towards the motorcourt to meet the Jeep. Beco rises to his feet. His eyes already betray an inner strength seen in those destined for greatness.
    Senhor MILTON DA SILVA, 40, lowers the rear door to the Jeep. He is

tall, imperious; emotions don't surface easily on this man's face. A dusty tarp [tarpaulin] covers the payload. Pulls it away revealing a Tche go-kart, all chrome and polished.

Beco stares, eyes rapt. Milton comes up behind him, squeezes his shoulder.

MILTON

Just win

Beco looks at his father. The alternative is not a choice.

There was constant speculation, of course, over who would play Senna, ranging from Val Kilmer and Tom Cruise to Banderas. There was, too, long in-house searching about which parts of Senna's career to highlight – the era against Prost, for example – and how to portray Adriane. These must have been delicate, difficult hours.

In the background, Sylvester Stallone was rumoured to be making his own grand prix film and had allied himself with Bernie Ecclestone. That perhaps increased Lew's obstacles but as I write these words he is still in there, enthusiasm undiminished. With hindsight, it was always going to be like life itself: a long haul.*

Then and now

Maurice Hamilton has a pleasant, well-organised office over a bakery in a quaint Surrey village. He is wise in the ways of motorsport and, I suspect, accepted long ago that the falling out with Senna was, well, one of those things.

It's early October 1998 but still warm enough that we can eat outside the café next door. As we eat I switch my tape recorder on and he modulates his voice from polite conversation to giving a serious interview. I'm struck by how much detail he can remember – colour, carpets, furniture – about an evening in a house in Esher in November 1985. Maybe the mind records some things for ever.

In 1939 Christopher Isherwood wrote in his novel Goodbye to Berlin: *"I am a camera with its shutter open, quite passive, recording, not thinking … Some day, all this will have to be developed, carefully printed, fixed."*

Both Gerald Donaldson and Murray Walker were happy to talk in the Press Room at Monza, 1998. This Press Room, a broad, spotless place

---

* Here I declare an interest. Lew has bought the film rights to The Hard Edge of Genius *as well as* The Second Coming *and* The Legend Grows *(1994/1995, PSL). More than that, I have helped him wherever I can and stand to gain financially if and when the film is made. That said, I trust that what I have described has been done dispassionately and accurately.*

intimately connected to the rest of the planet by just about every form of instant communication you can imagine, itself charts progress.

When Senna first raced here in 1985 (and finished third behind Prost and Piquet) the Press Room was in what was surely an abandoned house. If you needed to connect with the rest of the planet a wonderful Italian comic opera awaited you. To make a phone call involved writing your name and the number you wanted on a piece of paper and giving it to a harassed lady behind a counter who already had plenty, as did the lady next to her and the lady third along. And they all tried to connect with the great Italian telephone system ...

Donaldson is a gently-spoken Canadian who works unobtrusively but sees, amid the push-and-shove of Formula 1, what is important and what is not. Walker, at 75, represents a sort of life force although he wonders how long he ought to keep on delivering 100mph race commentaries on television. He doesn't, he insists, want to linger until he's an echo of what he was.

Simon Arron, now a respected senior journalist on Motoring News, *can't remember the first time he met Senna – "it's a long time ago" – and paradoxically the magazine for which he wrote* A week in the life of *folded before the article ever appeared. So nobody's seen it, and never will now – the tape long gone, the carbon copy (typed on yellow* Motoring News *paper) long gone too.*

Chapter 10

A fight for
love and glory

IN LATE OCTOBER 1998, before the decisive Japanese Grand Prix at Suzuka from which either Mika Hakkinen or Michael Schumacher would emerge as World Champion, a "revolutionary extractable seat" was announced. It had been a joint effort by engineers at the Lear Corporation, one of the world's largest automotive suppliers, Alan Jenkins, then Technical Director of Stewart Grand Prix, and the FIA in the persons of Professor Sid Watkins and Charlie Whiting, the technical delegate.

Watkins said: "Formula 1 has taken several huge steps in safety during the last five years, particularly since the death of Ayrton Senna. I think this seat is the next enormous step in terms of something that's directly applied to the driver rather than the car. It's going to be 100 per cent better than moving somebody in the cockpit and putting a spinal splint on, and it's going to be a lot quicker. It will significantly enhance our efforts towards fine-honing the medical response."

The Stewart team said: "The seat is intended to be used in case of an accident which renders the driver incapacitated. Its design provides a means for securing the driver, immobilising his head and body, and allows for extraction of the driver while still in his seat. The seats can also be used to keep the driver immobilised while being transported to either the infield or local hospital."

Jackie Stewart himself said: "It has been some time now since there's been an opportunity to provide this kind of protection for the driver – and offer this kind of benefit to medical and safety crews. Professor Watkins has been a staunch advocate of improved safety and he was one of the first to see the potential of this seat. I think this is going to be marked down as a significant arrival for the sport."

The seats would become mandatory on all Formula 1 cars by the start of the 1999 season.

The fallout from Tamburello remained a spectre but acted like a living, breathing imperative upon the body of Formula 1. That was true from 2.18 on 1 May 1994, and was powerfully strong in the hours and days immediately after: there was near panic, and a rush towards whatever anybody thought might be increased safety.

The shock was in part because Formula 1 had seemed so safe for so long. Riccardo Paletti was the last driver to be killed in a grand prix, and that was 12 years before. Elio de Angelis was the last man to be killed in a Formula 1 car, testing, in 1986. Suddenly, Formula 1 found itself confronted by Barrichello's resurrection on the Friday, Ratzenberger's finality on the Saturday, and then Senna's fate on the Sunday. This was a disaster of almost Biblical awfulness. A plague.

Moreover, since Paletti and de Angelis had died, a whole generation of media people had arrived to whom death on a race track was a complete stranger, something the older people reminisced about with a shiver: *the bad old days*. But the danger had never really gone away. Today's commentators were now facing bad days of their own. Just out of view of the Media Centre on the first floor – Tamburello was too far away to be seen by the naked eye – a man everybody knew was dying *now*, and they were all watching him die, and any moment *now* they would have to produce their words about his death. It added another layer to the intrinsic shock of the thing. In the old days drivers died and barely made news bulletins never mind global grieving.

2.18 changed everything. The world wasn't the same and the perception of death wasn't the same, either.

Part of Senna's legacy has been that his death has concentrated a lot of minds on safety. Examining safety became an absolute necessity, and measures put in place have and will save lives. There is no irony in death bringing life, because it happens in many spheres of human activity, but it is poignant here because of all the circumstances surrounding the tragedy at Tamburello.

Nor is there irony in near-death bringing life. This is where it all began – not with Senna but a long, long time before. We must travel to Spa on the afternoon of 12 June 1966 and see 15 cars lined up on the grid to contest the Belgian Grand Prix. This grid, in 3–2–3 formation, was not where it is now: it was on the slope down towards *Eau Rouge*. Nor was Spa as it is now: the track stretched 14.10 kilometres through the Ardennes countryside – farms, fields, trees, stone walls – and essentially offered the drivers no protection from these natural hazards. Spa was a very, very frightening place. Even such an experienced (and perhaps hardened) reporter as Pat Mennem of the London *Daily Mirror* once confessed to me that he dreaded covering the grands prix there because you always wondered what terrible thing the race would bring.

This afternoon in 1966 John Surtees (Ferrari) had pole, Jochen Rindt (Cooper) alongside and Jackie Stewart (BRM) on the right of this front row. Heavy folds of cloud hung over the circuit but it wasn't raining yet. It would rain about a minute after the 15 cars left the grid, all over the back of the circuit: hard rain. The 15 set off down into *Eau Rouge,* then out into the countryside.

The place was called Burnenville, a 150mph right-hander, and as the cars went over the brow of the hill to reach it they ran full into a wall of water. Four cars slithered off and one came to rest suspended over a farm wall. Then, further on at the kink in the Masta Straight – again fast – Graham Hill (BRM) spun round and went backwards. He came to rest against a straw bale and saw Stewart's BRM on the other side of a ditch. Stewart's car was damaged, Stewart was trapped and petrol from the tank seeped over him. Hill ran there and switched the controls off to staunch the petrol flow.

He tried to haul Stewart out but couldn't because the steering wheel was in the way. He'd need tools to do that and sprinted off to "ask a marshal to find a toolbox" (*Life At The Limit,* William Kimber, 1969). Hill and the marshal did remove the steering wheel and they helped Stewart, who had been trapped for perhaps 30 minutes, to "a small farm building nearby. I took all his clothes off because they were smothered in fuel. No assistance had arrived so I ran to the marshal's post again and telephoned from there for an ambulance."

Memories would distort what happened next. Stewart remembered three nuns appearing and trying to put his clothes back on. Hill remembered getting back from the marshal's post as the ambulance arrived and seeing the nurses trying to dress Stewart. It is more or less certain that the ambulance had once been a bus. Stewart was laid on the floor. It is absolutely certain that, on the way to the hospital at Verviers, the ambulance driver lost his way.

Jackie Stewart decided that the whole question of safety must be addressed and fundamental changes made.

His wife Helen once told me: "In the beginning I was very naïve, as Jackie was. It was a shock not to have people you knew around any more." She equated it to having a dinner party for friends and only Jackie came because he was the only one still alive. "When Jackie began to campaign for safety he got called *chicken, chicken* but he got the job done. When he crashed at Spa I couldn't eat, I lost 14lb in weight. After Spa, I couldn't get food down my throat."

Stewart's concerns about safety provided an undercurrent to a 1990 interview he did with Senna for the television channel *Nine Network Australia.* The interview was at Adelaide, last race of the season and the one after the Japanese Grand Prix. Since both the combatants were eloquent enough, I'll simply set down what they said, but remember the undercurrent: Stewart had struggled to make motor racing safer, Senna was the product of a generation for whom it was thought to be safe.

INTRODUCER: Hardly a season goes by in Formula 1 without at least one major row but never has a controversy split expert opinion so squarely as the one surrounding that first corner collision involving Senna and Prost at Suzuka two weeks ago. For example, our good friend Jackie here believes that Senna's driving has been highly questionable all season. What's more he doesn't mind saying so, even to Senna. In this interview a former World Champion and the new World Champion meet for a frank exchange of views.

[FILM OF THE CRASH IS PLAYED]

SENNA: He knew I was right with him, I was not far behind, I was right with him and when I was right behind him he moved to the inside line going towards the first corner, I just chased him then and he opened the gap. And knowing me like he does know, he must realise if there was a gap I was going to try and overtake him. Under those circumstances, he should never have opened a gap in the first corner and then come back again – because, by doing so, he opened the gap, gives the gap and then closes it. In those circumstances there was no way to avoid an incident.

STEWART: Right. But that only happened, Ayrton, because you saw the gap – and I accept that, you're a racer – but a mature racer has to also think if he closes the door again we're going to have an accident. And in fact there was a high-speed entrance so there could have been a very serious accident.

SENNA: Absolutely.

STEWART: So would it not have been more prudent under those circumstances to at least have seen if the gap was potentially going to close?

SENNA: Not at all. He was in a position where he could never – under no circumstances – put his car anywhere near mine in a difficult position, because if we happened just to touch – just to touch – and have a wing damaged or a flat tyre, he had everything to lose. And under those circumstances my understanding was that he would never move against me in the first corner. I was very surprised when I found myself with him moving the car over mine [WAVING FINGER].

STEWART: So in that case you were calculating that he would give way, that he would let you through?

SENNA: Of course. He would not close the way he did from the moment he made the initial room [STILL WAVING FINGER] he would not come back and close the door again.

STEWART: A calculated risk?

SENNA: Of course. [SHRUGS SHOULDERS]

STEWART: OK, let me ask you another difficult question. If I were to count back all the World Champions – and, after all, this is the 500th grand prix – if you totalled up all of those great champions [SENNA SMILES LANGUIDLY] and the number of times they had made contact with other drivers, you in the last 36 months or 48 months have been in contact with more other cars and drivers than they might have done in total.

SENNA: I find it amazing for you to make such a question, Stewart, because you are very experienced and you know a lot about racing and you should know that by being a racing driver you are under risks all the time. Being a racing driver means you are racing with other people and if you no longer go for a gap that exists you are no longer a racing driver – because we are competing, we are competing to win and the main motivation to all of us is to compete for a victory. It's not to come third, fourth, fifth or sixth. Right?

STEWART: But hasn't that always been the case?

SENNA: Sorry?

STEWART: But hasn't that always been the case with all the great champions?

SENNA: Absolutely. [FILM OF THE CRASH IS PLAYED AGAIN] And if you go back …

[TALKING TOGETHER]

STEWART: But it didn't happen …

SENNA: But if you go back in history and talk about the incidents and so on, then you'll find that I've been myself leading most of the races and finding back-markers in front of me and I was never involved in leading races with other people. [FILM OF A CRASH WITH BERGER IN BRAZIL, THEN THE CRASH WITH PROST AT THE CHICANE, SUZUKA 1989, IS BEING PLAYED] There were three, four events only when I was leading a race at the first corner and like many other people I've been involved.

STEWART: I have to believe though, Ayrton, there must be some fault and I respect totally your ability, you're the fastest grand prix driver in the world but I have to speculate that it can't all be right that you have this many collisions, if you like [SENNA STONE FACED] whether it be with back-markers or whether it be with lead changes, it just happens too often. Don't you question yourself if …

SENNA: But I think it's all irrelevant, all what you are saying Jackie is really irrelevant because I am a driver [VOICE RISING A LITTLE] that won more races than anybody over the past three years, I am a driver that's been on pole position more than anybody in history and I am a driver that won two titles in the past three years. I cannot comprehend how you can try to [RAISES LEFT HAND, PLACES TWO FINGERS HORIZONTALLY AND TWISTS THEM IN A CORKSCREW MOTION] turn things around to say that I have been involved in more accidents than anybody – because that is not true as well. I don't really understand the point.

STEWART: I'm sorry, I don't agree with that because …

SENNA: Then you should go back [POINTS FINGER AT STEWART THREE TIMES], you should go back ten years from the date of today and [WAGS FINGER] look not only at the leaders, you should look at the middle [HAND WAVING] the middle field drivers and the back field drivers …

STEWART: I speak of the champions …

SENNA: … and find, find by yourself that what you say is not quite right [FLICKER OF A SMILE].

STEWART: Well, I would be happy to go back with you and go through the Fangios and the Clarks and the …

SENNA: No, you only have to go back ten years, you only have to go back ten years, the modern Formula 1, that's what we are talking about [THIN SMILE].

STEWART: So you feel totally comfortable that the technique of driving that you use has not in any way developed into a situation where the gap opens up and it's taken spontaneously – because you do go for gaps, and we have all done it in our careers …

SENNA: When there is a gap [RAISES HAND], when there is a gap it is designed for being in a competition at a very high level [meaning the gap happens in a very high level of competition] with cars going so close as they go today, with the same horsepower, with the same level of grip, with the same low aerodynamics, you all know with the different circuits where it is very difficult for overtaking – because the circuits are designed not in an appropriate manner for overtaking manoeuvres – you either commit yourself as a professional racing driver that is designed to win races [WAVING HAND] or you come second, or you come third, or you come fifth and I am not designed to come third, fourth, or fifth. I race to win as long as I feel it is possible. Sometimes you get it wrong, sure, it is impossible to get it right all the time but I race designed to win [WAVING LEFT HAND] and as long as I feel I am doing it right some people agree, some don't. In the end I am the one who is doing it, I am the one who is driving and I can only do what speaks for my mind [meaning what I think].

The contrast between Spa 1966 and Imola 1994 could hardly be more complete, and this was a direct consequence of the Masta kink. In the years between, Stewart – and many others – had changed everything.

Now Professor Watkins and two other doctors sat in their fast car, positioned near the pits, ready to respond to any emergency. Watkins had already toured the circuit before the race began making sure that the "medical intervention cars" were in place, the doctors were at their ambulances and the track's impeccable medical centre was ready. All this was quite normal, quite routine in 1994 and happened at each race.

When the flags were hoisted, stopping the race, Watkins's car "took off" under the expertise of the driver, Mario Casoni. I don't think anyone has ever offered a precise timing of how long Casoni took to reach Tamburello but it could be measured in seconds, not minutes, *and* by then the doctor from the first intervention car was already there holding Senna's head. They all did what they could. A medical helicopter, packed with sophisticated equipment, was summoned to take him to the Maggiore Hospital in Bologna. It took off from the track at 2.34 – just 16 minutes after the accident.

And here is the image of Ayrton Senna being carried on a stretcher towards the helicopter. There were at least eight official vehicles at the site of the crash; at least 35 officials in their various uniforms – some red, some white, some orange – standing or milling uncertainly because there was nothing further they could do; at least eight men carrying the stretcher while a ninth holds the helicopter door open ready. Watkins, in red, hair nestling out from under his cap, is forever fixed at that instant because a photographer caught it: he is turned towards the stretcher, perhaps five feet away. His arms are by his side, his gaze is upon Senna and there is, somehow, subdued grief in the dignity of his bearing.

It was farewell.

The imperative to re-examine safety after Tamburello was not to be resisted and a great deal happened very quickly. It was understandable and also, because of the pressured haste, slightly disconcerting: it might lead to mistakes, especially with no time to think things through, experiment, test consequences. This resulted in the creation of a bizarre chicane for the Spanish Grand Prix, the second race after Imola. It was a white tyre wall on the right-hand side of the track and a blue tyre wall on the left with just enough space between the walls for cars to wiggle through.

Reportedly, Schumacher met the Spanish organisers at Monaco, the race after Imola, and on the drivers' behalf requested a chicane but when they arrived at Barcelona they found one hadn't been built and threatened to strike. Hence the instant tyre walls – and initially the space even for wiggling was too small and needed to be opened up.

More subtly, grand prix racing was reaching for an impossibly delicate balance between the *frisson* you get with danger versus the political correctness of an age obsessed with safety in everything, even soya beans and chickens' eggs. There was an unstated further dimension, that of the sponsors and television companies. Danger was good for the ratings – but death?

It's very easy to be cynical, and very easy to be callous, but grand prix racing could not survive repeated fatalities. The sponsors wouldn't be around any more, the television companies wouldn't either, and governments would be forced to banish the sport altogether. The spirit of the age would demand nothing less. Imola was a precise illustration of aspects of this, and here is the television nightmare expressed by those who had to cope with it.

A word of explanation first. FOCA's on-board camera coverage was only part of the universal feed provided by the host broadcaster, *RAI*. The system was the same at every race: the host fed the world. Everybody plugged in and took what *RAI* transmitted, meaning that if you were in Brisbane or Baltimore, Bologna or Bali you got exactly the same picture. Each company, of course, made its own arrangements about commentary.

By a haunting paradox among so many this anguished Imola weekend, the British Broadcasting Corporation – who'd covered grand prix racing since the 1950s – did have their own camera crew in the pit lane. It gave them what nobody else had: an option to switch from *RAI*.

Mark Wilkin was the producer. Wilkin nursed an affection for Senna because before the Brazilian Grand Prix, which opened the season, Senna gave the BBC "virtually a whole day" of access to him. "We did a feature piece for *Grand Prix* [the BBC programme] and he was marvellous. He showed us round his offices in the skyscraper in Sao Paulo. We'd been due to go to his farmhouse but the arrangements went awry for various reasons. He showed us his magazine – *Senninha* – which he'd just started then."

Now Imola. "Something we discussed, and we do discuss, as producers is what do you do *if* – and we had seen from the day before, when poor old Roland got into trouble and subsequently died, what *RAI* would do in those circumstances. I don't know if you remember the Ratzenberger pictures but they were even more graphic than Ayrton's. And *RAI* did nothing but show over and over again the replay of Ratzenberger hitting the wall and coming to rest – and the picture when he came to rest was a close-up of his helmet which by then was covered in blood. That was thoroughly unpleasant.

"We were not covering the qualifying live but we spent some time that evening discussing what we would do in similar circumstances if we were live. The rules are perfectly clear. It's common sense and common decency that you don't want to see people dying on the screen. Sport is not supposed to be about death: if you're doing a horse race and the horse and rider fall, you go to wide shots or you cut away from it. At the BBC we had some incredibly unpleasant scenes from over the years on tape" – but not broadcast and never going to be.

"It was clear from what we had seen on the Saturday that *RAI* would spare nobody's feelings and there would be close-ups where there could be close-ups and they would show things which we would not want to show to the British public. When Senna crashed it was pretty clear straight away that it was serious so I cut to our pit-lane camera. That maintained continuity and I could see both." In the pit lane stood the experienced Steve Rider who, as the nightmare was suddenly handed to him, reacted with calm, sensitivity and professionalism.

Wilkin also used the words which Murray Walker was speaking to the *RAI* pictures as a radio commentary over the pictures from the pit lane. "Murray and Jonathan Palmer had one of their finest hours in tragic circumstances. They hit the right tone, they knew exactly the right things to say. This was all by chance – because it was our first-ever time live with our own camera at a race. In other words, it was our first chance to do this. If you remember, in 1989 when Berger crashed at Tamburello [in a fireball], we had had no alternative because at that stage we thought he had killed himself. We had to cut back to the studio and go to some snooker or whatever. Now we were able to show our pit-lane camera whilst recording all the feed from *RAI*. I could replay their pictures a minute or so later, so maybe we'd have 50 or 60 seconds of the ambulance coming round the track or the helicopter landing: anything that wasn't too graphic and wasn't too close up. I remember those *RAI* pictures which were graphic and I am still grateful that my little boy, who was four at the time, was spared seeing things like that."

On the strength of Wilkin's words and their implications alone, grand prix racing could not survive repeated fatalities.

Now consider the nightmare which came to John Watson, who'd raced Senna once in 1984 and once in 1985, and was now with the television channel *Eurosport*. Watson had established himself as a thoughtful interpreter of grand prix racing and happened to be speaking before and during the accident – and *Eurosport* were simply taking the *RAI* feed with no alternative.

As Senna and Schumacher flicked through the left–right to begin the lap Watson was saying "well, Schumacher trying to keep in contact as much as possible and it is on this part of the circuit that Benetton feel his advantage lies. It's now here onto the start of the straight where Senna's got the advantage, he's got more horsepower. [SENNA IS AT THE FIRST DARK STRIP OF TARMAC] He's going to use it, he's going to try and get away through Tamburello. This is the long, long flat-out left-hand corner, 190 miles an hour. [THE WILLIAMS DARTS TO THE RIGHT] Oh, Senna's in trouble, Senna's gone off on the outside. [WATSON'S VOICE HEIGHTENS, THE DESTROYED CAR IS THRASHING BACK FROM THE WALL] Something went dramatically wrong for Senna. The car suddenly turned to the right three-quarters of the way through the corner.

"You see bits and pieces of his Williams-Renault are all over the race track, yellow flags being waved and something dramatic [THE FIRST FIREFIGHTER APPROACHES THE CAR; OTHERS SPRINT TOWARDS IT] … went wrong with Senna on the second flying lap of this grand prix. And once again drama at this San Marino Grand Prix. That was a very heavy shunt. We're saying 190 miles an hour. That was the speed at which Senna's car would have gone off the track, hit the concrete wall on the outside and this again a very, very serious situation [BY NOW A RED OFFICIAL CAR HAS ARRIVED]."

Allard Kalff, co-commentating with Watson, says: "So Ayrton Senna still in his car and we are waiting for Sid Watkins to arrive, Professor Watkins, to arrive on the scene of the accident and this race will be stopped."

Even with hindsight, which revealed the full consequences, this piece of commentary still stands as responsible and accurate but, because *Eurosport* were a prisoner of *RAI*, the nightmare was only just beginning for Watson and Kalff. Within the next few moments there would be no escape from the graphic images.

John Watson must be heard verbatim as he reflects. "One of the things I remember about that specific accident was literally seconds prior to Senna going off we were on board with Schumacher and I was describing how what Schumacher was doing was like a hyena hunting down an animal. I know that emotion, that feeling and it is amazing to have it – to know that you have your quarry in sight and you are going to take him. That's animalistic, but that's how it feels. Conversely, at the same time I had a balancing emotion of feeling what Senna must have been feeling – going into Tamburello he had this youngster on his tail closing, closing, closing all the time. Senna, who was maybe the proudest of men you'll ever meet in motor racing, knew he was under extreme pressure from Schumacher and he was totally committed to keeping the lead of the race.

"So I was pumped up watching this scenario because for me this is part of the real joy of motor racing, it's that ability to assert your superiority over another competitor. I also felt the discomfort of Senna. Then suddenly the camera shot changed from on-board Schumacher's car entering Tamburello to the shot on the exit of Tamburello and it was just unbelievable, inexplicable that Senna had gone off. But he had – and what the hell's happened? How did it happen? There was nothing obvious that I could see looking from Schumacher's car to Senna's car but something had clearly happened in that 'cut' from the on-board to the [*RAI* fixed-position] camera looking at Tamburello. At that moment those thoughts were somewhat secondary to Senna's condition.

"It had been a terrible weekend because first we'd had Barrichello, then we'd had Ratzenberger. I was staying at the same hotel as Sid Watkins, the Novotel in Bologna, and after dinner on the Saturday I went and sat down with Sid, partly because I wanted to understand more about Ratzenberger's accident and why it happened, having been broadcasting when it did happen. It was a discussion which lasted an hour, an hour and a half, and it was very helpful. I know that in our conversation, which wasn't a private conversation, how upset I was because Sid had told me about Ratzenberger's death. We talked about lots of things little knowing that within 18 hours we were going to be having to face the same thing once again.

"Then on the Sunday we had the crash at the start of the race. Finally the race gets under way again and of course because it was Senna who crashed it took on a totally different perspective. When the car came to a stop his body was motionless. Then – I don't know whether it was a second or a minute afterwards – there was a discernible movement of his head and neck and I said *oh look, he's moved, he's OK*. Movement is what you look for: you're expecting him to unstrap himself and step out of the car. Whilst it was a heavy impact, we've seen survivable accidents which have been much worse than that.

"Allard and I were both very unhappy because we were taking the world feed and that zoomed in pretty close up and Allard in particular was saying, during a commercial break or whatever, *let's go to something else*. Eurosport refused to do anything differently than take that feed and we said *we'll not commentate*. They said *if you don't commentate we'll put the stand-by crew on from Paris*. So we had to commentate.

"After Barrichello, Ratzenberger and the shunt at the start, Allard and I were shell-shocked. How the hell can you keep coming up with positive comments when you've had these serious accidents?

"I can go into a motor racing mentality which is detached emotionally – because that's how you drive, how you are when you're racing. You have to be unemotional about what is happening around you, particularly to friends and colleagues, so you move into something like a war reporter frame of broadcasting where you are in the presence of tragedy but you are still detached and logical and pragmatic.

"However, as the whole scenario unfolded, it became more and more evident that this was not just a bad accident and not just potentially a catastrophic accident. Arguably the greatest driver ever, and certainly of our generation, was dying in our living rooms. That I think is one of the most powerful images ever, ever seen in people's homes. Here was a man who was as famous as the Pope dying in your living room. That's appalling. You have witnessed a man getting killed. *Really* killed."

When you'd finished the broadcast what did you feel?

"Well, there was this uncertainty over whether he was alive or dead, whether he was going to make it or not. My signal that nothing could be done was a very simple signal: it was when Sid Watkins finally walked away from Senna as he was being taken to the helicopter. At that point my instincts said that Senna was dead.

"From a personal point of view I had to deal with it as a friend of Senna. I'd had the opportunity on a number of occasions to know the guy away from a race track and I knew it was a privilege because he was very selective about who he opened up to in his personal life. He never did it with people he didn't trust. You had to be one of the people he was comfortable to share things with.

"So I was sitting commentating and it was a confused sort of message I was getting. *Is he alive or is he dead? What's happening?* Of course we, as broadcasters, had to talk but at the same time not suggest that the guy is dead. I remember somebody wrote a letter to *Autosport* saying all I talked about was the technology of the modern car and how well it does in helping the driver – but what the hell are you going to talk about? Very, very difficult. And the BBC had the benefit of being able to cut away and go to the pits and talk to people in the pits.

"We weren't giving people the choice. We were saying *either you watch Eurosport or you turn off.* The BBC did give a choice, and it's a strange balance that a producer has to make because on the one hand here is the biggest news story in the world on the day – which is cynical, but it was – and, on the other, what do you do, turn that off?

"I had this discussion with my family and I said I thought it was unnecessary to be so obtrusive but they didn't agree with that because if it had been me – I had a couple of accidents which were televised – it was only through television that they knew that I was healthy and well. In a similar sense, for Senna's family not to know how grave or how injured he may have been – and somebody be making phone calls to them – is worse.

"When Martin Donnelly had his accident in Jerez [in 1990 during first qualifying – which was not shown on British television] I instantly rang my family and said *look, Martin's had a bad, bad accident. It could be fatal. Get somebody to ring Martin's family and alert them to the fact that he has had a serious accident rather than having, if you like, the drip-feed coming through from a media person ringing up or somebody showing up on the doorstep.* It didn't make it easier for his family but at least they couldn't have heard any quicker and they were prepared for what was coming. At Imola with Senna, while it is distasteful, that is the one mitigation."

Immediately after Imola there was a scramble for safety and we are still in the aftermath of that.

"Well, as I said earlier, what we saw was the greatest racing driver of our time killed in our living rooms and that, when you are selling a product called Formula 1, was the unacceptable face of it. As far as Formula 1 was concerned, at the promoters' and governing body's level, if it happens again it could only happen despite their very best efforts – and you cannot ask more of them than that. The changes in safety came following Senna's accident – almost exclusively as a result of Senna's accident, not Barrichello's, not Ratzenberger's. You have to face the fact that it was Senna's death which triggered the safety.

"We did it at Silverstone, we changed our circuit at Silverstone partly as a result of Senna's accident. So people reacted. They made changes to cars, they tried to slow them down. Overall, the level of safety in grand prix racing today is enormously higher than it was in 1994. And that applies to circuits as well as the cars.

"Part of the reason we are now getting these rather boring race tracks is because of that. The contrast, if you like, was the Goodwood speed event about a month ago. [The circuit in the south of England was re-opened in 1998 after three decades of closure and 75,000 watched historic racing.] You went back into a time warp. Take Silverstone, the safest circuit in the UK: that has been made so because of the responsibility and the reaction to Senna's accident by the governing body."

Part of the appeal of motor racing is the danger. Is it possible to strike the balance between the danger and the safety?

"One might say that that's the balance we've got right now. We're never going to go back to the days when there were trees and so on at the side of the racetrack. The other thing is that this business has grown and expanded – and, talking about the sums of money involved and the kind of investment coming in to Formula 1 today, it is unacceptable to have fatal accidents. There will always be the implied danger, there is always going to be the potential for another Senna or another Ratzenberger because you cannot truly make it safe. The miracle was in Belgium [1998, a multiple crash which looked potentially catastrophic for a moment] where, at the start of the race, the cars were coming down from *La Source*. How there were not injuries I'll never know. That to me was the greatest testament to the safety checks that have been implemented. In a maelstrom of suspension, wheels, whatever, going all over the place nobody was injured.

"I believe it is possible to make these cars significantly safer again. I am speaking purely as a layman and not as an engineer, but the level of safety for example in the North American CART series is greater than that in Formula 1, partly because there is a much more strict regulation about the construction of cars. You are told the materials you must use and how they must be applied. Let's say Formula 1 wanted to make the cars stronger. There would be great resistance from the teams to being told how they've got to make their cars. Suppose it was decided to increase the weight of the car. It's now 600 kilograms with the driver on board, so say they put it up to 650 – there's 50 kilograms more material that could be used to increase the strength of the car. What they'd do is put it at the bottom of the car, because that's the best place to put it – the lower the weight, the better the centre of gravity. People in Formula 1 will always seek performance but if you turn round and say *you can't do it that way, you've got to build the car like this, this, this and this* you would have them howling from the rooftops. So you have this sense of conflict …"

Unending conflict, perhaps.

Max Mosley, President of the FIA, charts the background to what happened after Senna's death.

Was there too much pressure for change immediately after Imola? Was it hard to keep a sense of proportion?

"Yes, but we all knew this was an emotional reaction. However, it did present an opportunity for bringing in changes which at the time, in my opinion, were long overdue."

Did Karl Wendlinger's serious accident at Monaco make the pressure worse – or rather, how much worse?

"Yes, because it began to worry the major manufacturers who supply engines. There were five very serious incidents at Imola (including Senna) and this was a further one, two weeks later. People were beginning to draw wholly irrational conclusions – for example, it was suggested that all these disasters were due to banning electronics on the cars. Interestingly, I have a Christmas card from Senna from December 1992 with a long hand-written plea to eliminate electronic driving aids."

Of the safety measures put in place, how do you evaluate them?

"Fortunately, the number of accidents in Formula 1 which result in injury is so low it is difficult to evaluate any particular measure, but the biggest single factor is probably the recognition that at a certain level of performance on given circuits quite a small increase in speed can result in a disproportionate increase in danger."

Is there a risk of sanitising F1 or is it possible to hold the balance between danger and safety?

"I don't think so. You can never race small, light cars at speeds of up to 340kmh on a narrow track completely safely. Our task is to minimise the danger to everyone concerned (the public, the track personnel and the drivers). We will never completely eliminate the risks."

A postscript from Ken Tyrrell. "The reaction of the international controlling body was because it was Senna. If it had been somebody else, it would all have been just one of those things, and the fact that somebody as good as

Senna could have an accident tells us that, in spite of the tremendous strides that have been made, motor racing is still dangerous."

When Jackie started the safety campaign in 1966 ...

"... it was about circuits, not about cars. At the Nurburgring there was a 100-foot drop ..."

Jackie took some abuse over it.

"Oh he did, yes he did, but what he did was right – and we all know now he was right – and he didn't hesitate to do it, didn't hesitate to make himself unpopular."

Is it possible to have an acceptable level of danger and retain the core of the sport?

"I think that's what we've got now."

Chapter 11

A case
of do or die

AYRTON SENNA'S CAREER grew as Formula 1 itself grew. They fed hugely off each other, and at moments of stress they needed each other. It is an interdependence rarely discussed.

When Senna began with Toleman in 1984, grand prix racing was a leading minor sport. When he left it a decade later it had become, in media coverage and general interest, a giant to stand comparison with the Olympics and the soccer World Cup. That placed unrelenting strain on any leading player, most of all on the drivers. They became a hunted species. The media (including me), a pack of ever increasing scale and appetite, were in constant pursuit – most of all in pursuit of Senna.

The driver was also confronting the price of money. His wages rose towards the multi-million dollars, but the sponsors paid that and they wanted value for money. Amid the hunt, the driver was becoming a marketable commodity, and that's another interdependence rarely discussed.

In 1984, Formula 1 remained homely. It did not really distort any of the people within it, and if you saw Senna striding along in his white livery he'd stop for a chat, likely as not. By 1994, when the circle between the kart track at Interlagos and the cemetery at Morumbi was about to close, drivers loomed at you as godheads shaped and honed by endless media exposure – every satellite up there humming with the imagery of it. In 1994 you couldn't see him at all in his blue Williams livery because the jostling pack – 50, 60, 70 strong – constantly closed on him for a word, a picture, a view, a touch, *anything*.

Did Senna accommodate all of this without changing the essentials of who he was or how he behaved? Did he succumb (as some insist) to believing himself a godhead? Did the decade – when he moved from homesick young foreigner to global presence – distort him? And what was it he had as a driver?

The search for these answers, the ultimate answers, reaches in many directions.

Dennis Rushen puts it perceptively: "He was not the same man later on that we saw in 1982. Well, underneath it all he was, but he wasn't *allowed* to be the same man because of the pressure and the media and all the rest of it. He had so much more he had to concentrate on. A very good example is when he was famous in Formula 1 and I went over to Interlagos to see a couple of drivers who wanted to drive for my team. I went to the circuit and chatted with Chico Serra, who I used to run in 1977. It was wonderful to see him and Chico phoned Harry and told him I was there. So Harry came over.

"He'd hardly got off the helicopter when he was surrounded by the media. This was his free day – he'd just popped along – and people kept poking him. They kept chanting *Senna-Senna-Senna, I want you to sign this* or *Senna-Senna-Senna, I want you to do that*. He looked at me and he had that haunted expression in his eyes. In the end, he and I managed to get up to the top of the control tower and we were able to sit and talk. And we did sit and talk, about the old days, about circuits like Castle Combe where they didn't have any pits ..."

Everyone noticed the world closing on Senna – they could hardly avoid seeing it. Rory Byrne says: "I think as Ayrton's fame grew he found it more difficult to handle the media, but as a person I don't think he changed. I remember having a chat to him at a test at Silverstone in 1993, and talking to him personally he hadn't changed. He came up and had a laugh. We weren't talking about racing – he and Michael [Schumacher] were having a hell of a battle virtually every race at that point in the season. He said *where's the surfboard and the tee-shirt?* I used to go to work in a tee-shirt in the early Toleman days, whereas I'd pitched up at Silverstone not in the team uniform [he was then with Benetton] but I'd a collar and tie on. We had a good five or ten minute chat and he was the same bloke I'd known in 1983 and 1984."

Celebrity crowds drivers, chokes them.

"Recently I went to a restaurant in Modena" [where Ferrari are], Byrne says. "There was myself, Ross Brawn, Jean Todt and Michael – and you can't even have a meal in peace. When the word spreads that Michael's there it is genuinely unbelievable. So if I put myself in Michael's position he seems to have no privacy. I'm sure he's fairly short sometimes with people who are, or who are trying to, invade his privacy. You think of going to the shops to buy something and it becomes a public ordeal."

Dan Partel of EFDA turns this into another direction. "The last time we met was in October 1993 in Estoril during tyre testing after the grand prix. The McLaren wasn't doing very well and Ayrton was leaning against the armco. I walked up and we had quite a long chat, about 45 minutes, and one of his feelings was *you know, I really need some of these other drivers to progress. The amount of press attention I am getting is ridiculous. The press needs to spend time with the other Formula 1 drivers rather than all heading towards me.*

"Then up came Mika Hakkinen and I said something like *how are you doing?* Then I said *Mika, I really want to thank you for welcoming Jos Verstappen into Formula 1, I really appreciate that. It's the kind of thing you guys should do with new people coming in rather than just give them the cold shoulder.* Mika said *well, Ayrton is the one who welcomed me in* and I said *that was kind of an EFDA thing actually.* Then I said to Ayrton *if you remember I had Emerson Fittipaldi present you with the trophy at Hockenheim.*

"All through our relationship I never would bother Ayrton when he was busy, we didn't really have to say a lot of words and I didn't like to have a conversation with him which was just *hello, how you doing?* We'd had heavy conversations in the past so it was a waste of time to just have little superficial ones. Either we sat down and had a serious chat or we didn't do anything except make eye contact.

"When I talk about heavy conversations, I mean I'd speak to him on topics like *you know, Ayrton, you could do a lot for your country as a Secretary of State or things like this when you retire. What do you think about afterward?* We weren't so much talking about racing, we were talking about people."

Interesting that Partel thought it quite natural Senna could become a Secretary of State. How many sportspersons can you say that about? Not many, although another Formula 1 driver has become a major political figure: Carlos Reutemann of Argentina.

Whether Senna was shy or not has been endlessly debated. Peter Warr, three years at Lotus, was an insider watching Senna cross from Toleman to McLaren. "No, I don't think he *was* shy. He built a protective wall around himself so he didn't get hassled by people he didn't know. He was always very open, friendly and, in fact, a bloody good laugh with the people he did know. But he got so pestered in the later stages that I think he built the wall and said *no, I don't want to do this or that, I'm going to walk through this lot looking straight ahead, not getting any eye-contact because it might draw me into something.*"

It's natural to assume that famous people forget where they have come from. The present is so perfectly succulent and who cares about yesterday? Some do forget, or pretend they have. Senna remembered. If you had known him from the early days – even just a little – he remembered and showed respect for the shared experience. He'd been there, you'd been there.

Partel hammers this out. To my statement that *through your hands must have passed most of the leading drivers* he responded: "I think it's 36 of them into Formula 1 and there's ten of them in CART right now."

Who was the best you had, not in terms of what they subsequently achieved, but at the time?

"Well, I would still have to say Ayrton. The only question mark I have is how competitive that series of 1982 was compared to some of the other series we did do." Partel explains that years later, and despite a certain pressure not to bother, Senna was prepared to give an interview about Formula Ford 2000 because "he felt he could help other people out. Ayrton never, *never,* forgot. Now there's one thing that gives him character over everybody else I know – which is unique – and it is: he *never* forgot the people he passed on the way up and he *never* forgot people who helped him. *Never, ever* forgot."

A pertinent, amusing example is provided by Frank Bradley. "The last time I met him was 1986 at Hockenheim and I was *still* racing 2000. I was on the rostrum, I'd come third and he was now with Lotus, he was a star and he presented the prizes. He looked at me.

Senna: "You're still here!"

Bradley: "Yes. I like it here, Ayrton."

Senna: "Yes, but *why* are you still here?"

Bradley: "I love racing."

Senna: "Yes, but *why* not move upwards?"

Bradley: "I'm too old and I love Formula 2000."

Senna: "Well, good luck" – and he handed Bradley the prize.

It's pertinent because Senna could not conceive of a static career, a career without crossroads, without progress, and the driver not only content with that but relishing it.

Brian Jones, the suave commentator at Brands Hatch who'd watched in 1981, met Senna when he had become a giant. "Senna could always be surprising, not least after he reached Formula 3 and then disappeared into Formula 1, but when he came back he still recognised you. As a commentator you can be quite influential when their careers are beginning and when they become grand prix superstars they still hark back to their early days and they are prepared to have a chat.

"I remember going to a 'do' at the Grosvenor House Hotel in London held by Jackie Stewart. I was standing at the back of the room and there was a flight of stairs coming down to the entrance of this room. I turned – it was about half way through the evening – and saw this vision of Ayrton flying down these stairs, taking them two or three at a time. He was wearing a pair of what I imagine were very expensive grey jeans and an open-necked white shirt. He bounced into the room and came up and shook hands and was beaming all over his face. He was more relaxed than I had ever seen him in his life before.

"Now this was something of a revelation because it occurred to me that I'd only ever seen him in racing overalls before. Away from the track he was a lot of fun but once he got to the track he became very focused: taciturn is a word that almost comes to mind, nearly morose. It was fascinating to have had glimpses of two of the characters he was, but the fact is that the contrast between the two shocked me. In a way it was a great delight to see somebody who had switched off and was enjoying himself totally in the normal way. I contrast that with the Formula Ford 1600 days when the fact was he didn't try to be sociable. It seemed to me that he was focused in a way that was nearly frightening in the intensity of his concentration.

"To see him at the Grosvenor House in this relaxed, bouncy frame of mind – he was chatting to everybody, and we were going back over the old days – was a great joy to me. He signed an autograph to my daughter Charlotte, which she has proudly in her bedroom now, and he was in particularly good form. That was the last time I saw him in person."

Barry Griffin worked for Goodyear from 1980 to 1995 and had a good working relationship with Senna. "I thought he was an absolutely first class person, a very compassionate person, a very nice person, a dignified man – but having said all that he didn't suffer fools gladly. He didn't want you to waste his time. If there was something to be said then he'd always got time for you. I'm not quite sure that he always made it easy to have time with him but that's the nature of a superstar, isn't it?

"He got the most out of his tyres, he didn't abuse them, he knew how to use them to their ultimate. He understood that fully but he understood *every* aspect of motor racing. He was a very complete man. We had a lot of respect for Ayrton and I think my interest in Formula 1 almost died with him. The most devastating thing about Imola was the impact it had on people after that race: grown men with tears in their eyes. I suppose it was all the more hard because did anybody expect him to die in a racing car? I've only met one person who could come to terms with that.

"It was a life-enriching experience to have known the man. You'd be in Ayrton's presence and the hairs on the back of your neck would stand up on end and you weren't quite sure why – but they did. I listened to him in a Press Conference in Japan, I don't know what year it was, and even now when I think of it my hair goes up on end. He was somebody very special, that man. Probably the last Christmas he was alive, a personally written Christmas card came *To Barry and wife – Ayrton.* I just couldn't believe that would happen because we were not close. It wasn't a printed signature, it was hand-written. On the card was an accelerator pedal and it said something like *Keep Your Foot Down!*

"The years he was World Champion, at the end of the season he would give me a little interview on the tape recorder so I could do a press release to send out within Goodyear. He would say nice things about Goodyear in it. We'd do the interview down at Adelaide usually, ten, fifteen minutes or whatever. He was brilliant, you didn't have to prompt him at all. Once I said *perhaps you'd say this* and he replied *Barry, I know what I am going to say!* I thought *you've put your foot in there, trying to tell him.* And he was superb. Great bloke."

To try to fix Ayrton Senna's place in the history of grand prix racing is easier now because in the five years since Imola there has been time for a calm to settle. The tumult of the career has subsided into memory. The scalding laps in qualifying, all 65 of them for an absolute record of pole positions, have lost their passion: they linger as somehow intellectually satisfying. They don't burn any more, like they did when he was constructing them – a gaggle of team-members waiting, breathless, on the pit lane wall for the missile to approach and pass, or crouching round a television monitor in the darkened pit. Silverstone burned one time in qualifying because he lost control of his McLaren and it rotated in a great thrash of motion full through 360 degrees until it was facing the way it had been, directly ahead; and during the thrashing the speed of the McLaren seemed unabated. Instantaneously as it was facing ahead he catapulted it back into the lap he'd been doing.

While the world was spinning, the tyres shrieking and the engine wailing in his ears, he knew precisely where the car was in relation to the track and what he would do the instant it stopped. The whole thing was rigid and fluid, wild and tamed, alarming and calming: a glimpse of immortality. And he was gone, full bore to complete the lap and begin another; gone into memory.

Who shall we compare him with in order to find his place in history? Dare we pit him against Tazio Nuvolari and Bernd Rosemeyer of the 1930s and their brutal, brutish cars? Might we reach to the 1950s and match him against Juan-Manuel Fangio and Stirling Moss? Is it fair to look at the sleek-nosed Lotuses which Jim Clark stroked so elegantly round the circuits of the world and wonder aloud *could Senna have done that?* Might we not at least scan the records of Piquet, Mansell and Prost, and draw him up against them? OK, simple statistics:

	Races	Poles	Wins	Championships
Piquet	204	24	23	3
Mansell	187	32	31	1
Prost	199	33	51	4
Senna	161	65	41	3

You can haggle over these things for ever, so some more simple statistics: Piquet's average was a win every 8.8 races, Mansell one in 6.0, Prost one in 3.9, Senna – one in 3.9. Over a career, that seems a pretty reasonable yardstick. Nor can Prost and Senna really be compared (except in results) because, although each was the other's main rival, their approach to virtually everything was so different. Prost hated the wet and sometimes refused to drive in it. Senna saw the wet as giving him an advantage to exploit. Prost once felled a driver called Francois Goldstein in the teenage karting days but never, so far as I am aware, even jostled with a driver again. Senna was involved in push-and-shove in a Formula 3 race (where he got Mansilla by the throat), then with Mansell, then with Irvine, then with Schumacher. Prost brought precision to his driving and was so smooth, so natural that he could appear deceptively slow even on pole laps. Senna radiated the thrill of the chase for a pole position, which was what all those people down the pit lane were doing hypnotised by the TV monitors. Prost kept his emotions largely to himself and never shed a tear in public. Senna cried often and when he was in the mood gave his emotions full play. Prost abhorred unnecessary risk. Senna spent years living on risk. Prost created controversy quietly. Senna let the planet know.

It's easy to succumb to eulogy when you're discussing Senna, difficult to raise the uglier questions – like was he the driver who pushed everything so far that dangerous driving became acceptable? Was he the first driver who'd prefer a crash to losing? The argument runs that the drivers of the 1950s, 1960s, 1970s and early 1980s (maybe) did not behave in such a way because their cars were intrinsically dangerous anyway and a crash was a very nasty thing – or worse. By the late 1980s drivers were regularly trotting back from major crashes to get into the spare car. Brian Hart has several definitions of what constitutes a great driver, and one of them is that they are mentally unaffected by just such a major crash.

"I remember Hockenheim one year when Senna somersaulted in testing near where Jim [Clark] was killed. A puncture, I think. You always know something's happened because everything goes quiet and you see the ambulance heading out there. Anyway, he'd been end-over-end or whatever at real speed. They took him to hospital and a day or two afterwards I was speaking to him. He discussed it quite calmly …"

John Watson judges that Senna wielded his reputation for being dangerous as a weapon. Because other drivers knew of it they kept out of his way. Tactically, Watson feels it was shrewd thinking by Senna.

This is confused territory. Senna did of course know that motor racing was dangerous. But to win he was prepared to push *all* limits further than anyone else and occasionally he pushed too far. Suzuka 1990 was the definitive example of it. The fact that the cars were so strong and the general safety precautions better than they had ever been before *permitted* the limits to be pushed. We must never forget that Ayrton Senna, whom many have tried to deify, was a very, *very* hard man indeed when he wanted to be.

There is a comparison which is intriguing. If you accept Senna as the greatest driver of his era, you must accept the man who succeeded him, Michael Schumacher, as the greatest of the next era. The comparison is valid because, while Prost and Senna were separated by those differences of approach, Senna and Schumacher were much closer in philosophy. By exploring the comparison we shall learn – via Schumacher, as it were – a lot more about why and how Senna was what he was.

Here we will call several witnesses, each of whom worked with one or both of them.

The first is Eddie Jordan because he was the first man to put Senna into a Formula 3 car (in 1982) and to put Schumacher into a Formula 1 car (in 1992). He tried to sign Senna for a season of Formula 3 and couldn't, ran Schumacher for one race before losing him to Benetton and when we spoke, in 1998, he was running Damon Hill and Ralf Schumacher in Formula 1. Jordan immediately points out that he was also the first to put Hill in a Formula 3 car: "three World Champions."

Trevor Foster says that the thing these guys have is that you take them up a formula and it makes no difference. They're straight in.

"Yes."

What is it they've got that I haven't ...

"... or any other human being hasn't: a special thing you find with out-and-out sportsmen, the people at the very top of their game, and you find it very quickly. They have total confidence, they know they can do it. The situation is not *can I or can't I?* and they're not there hanging about all night wondering if they can. They take it in their stride. They have an inner knowledge, an inner belief – and interestingly it may not transfer into the rest of life because you can see that they make mistakes in all sorts of other things, but in terms of driving the car they are outstanding, I repeat outstanding.

"They just know what's going on, they just know what's required and they also have a sixth sense – they find the right team because they are able to position themselves better than anyone else. Historically, the best driver winds up in the best car and it's a merit system which is self-controlling and self-policing. There's no-one there to pre-design this, it just happens. I don't know why but it just does. You don't have the best driver in the world signing for the worst team."

Do you regret not having managed to sign Senna for Formula 3?

"No. I suppose it all helps with the CV. The thing about life is that it's very important not to be either spiteful or vindictive. I'm fortunate. Part of the history of the Jordan group – when it finally blows the candle light out – will say it gave his first chance in F3 to Hill and Senna, it gave his first F1 drive to Michael Schumacher, and then there are countless others."

If things had fallen the other way, you could have been running a Formula 1 team with two drivers whose names began with S.

"But that would probably never have happened because you would never keep the two brothers. My opinion is that Ralf would probably have been off."

No, no, you could have had Senna and Michael Schumacher.

"... and Ralf as the test driver! Well, that's a thought. One of the great things about Jordan is that, unknown to itself, it seems to create excitement in a driver, seems to create action. I don't think about that. People ask if I'm bitter because if I had kept Michael Schumacher the team could perhaps have been much further up the tree much quicker. The other extreme is that if I hadn't got baled out by someone else I could have been bankrupt the same year so it really is six of one and half a dozen of the other."

If I held a gun at your head and said: identical cars, Senna or Schumacher to win to save your life, which would you choose?

"Different circumstances, different thoughts. If it was wet it would be an awesome duel because they were both genuinely fantastic. One of the most exciting things I've ever seen was Senna passing two and three cars on the outside at Stowe when everyone else was lifting off to go around the inside. He could see that there was more grip on the outside and he used to fly by them. *That* was awesome but then, having said that, you'd have to add that Schumacher is equally as awesome so that would have been a battle like you can't imagine. To be honest, no-one at the moment can hold a candle to

Michael Schumacher in the wet – except Senna would have been able to.

"Senna, for all his greatness, made mistakes. Michael doesn't seem to – or rather makes less. I say that on the back of Spa [1998, running into the back of Coulthard in the spray] although I don't think that was a mistake, I think he just didn't see him. But that's life. He didn't need to be going at that pace ..."

Let's move through this in chronological order, as we've done – with detours – through so much of this book. In 1982 Senna drove Jordan's F3 car and, on the short circuit at Silverstone, broke the lap record. In 1983 he was invited by the Williams team to try their Formula 1 car at Donington. On the short circuit he was *one full second* quicker than the team's test driver, Palmer, but then, as Frank Williams said many years later, Senna thought the engine was going to blow – actually because he'd frightened himself and wanted a reason to stop. (Gugelmin, who's recounted the tale of the Williams team giving Senna more fuel to slow him down, may be quite wrong about that.) Then in the autumn he drove the Toleman fast and a week later drove the Brabham fast. Then he went to unknown Macau and, jet-lagged, took pole and won.

Schumacher came to it the other way, via Mercedes and the Sportscar World Championship. Eddie Jordan decided to give him a chance at the Belgian Grand Prix and this is what happened next. Trevor Foster is the narrator.

"Well, we did the deal for Michael to drive the car in Spa and hopefully for the rest of the season. He came here to the Jordan factory one afternoon the week before Spa because it was the only chance we had to do a seat fitting – remember we'd had very limited resources in those days, a very limited number of engines. If we burst one before a race that was it, we were an engine down for the next race. We couldn't go to Cosworth and say well *here's another £30,000, can we have a fresh engine* because we didn't have it.

"We made the seat and we said we'd give him 25, 30 laps on the South Circuit just to acclimatise himself to a Formula 1 car because he'd never been in one before. So we put him in there, I went through it all and he was very cool, very calm. I said *look, this is not the spare, it's your race car and as of this afternoon, when we finish bedding it all in and making sure the seat fits and everything else, it's going in the truck for Spa."*

Schumacher: "Yeah, yeah, yeah, no problem."

"So he got in the car and he had the pressure of never having been in one before, the pressure of the race coming very quickly – it was the Tuesday – and the additional pressure of *don't damage it.* In those days we had a mechanical gear change. It was very easy to over-rev the engine on the downshift or you missed a gear and if you did, the engine would have to come out. It wasn't a question of *OK, we'll risk it.* Cosworth monitored all that and if it happened it came out. End of story.

"Now obviously here was a young boy in the car, very easy for him to mis-shift first time. He did an installation lap, we checked it all out and I said to him *right, off you go, do a four or five lap run* and all the time we were repeating *this is the car and this is the engine you've got to use on Friday at Spa, take your time because if we don't use this engine we haven't got one!* He went out and within three laps the brakes were glowing into the chicane, he was flicking it through and I remember to this day turning to his manager Willi Weber and saying *we've got to call him in, slow him down by getting him out of the car!* He'd been immediately on the pace, immediately, like bomp-bomp-bomp. Three laps, there he was. No question of *I'll feel the brakes in because they're carbon brakes and I've never driven with them before.* No, just bomp-bomp-bomp.

"Willi talked to him and came back and said *Michael doesn't understand what the problem is. He's in control.* Anyway, we did another three or four runs of five laps and it was a toy, it was just a toy, there was late braking, he was flicking it through – effortless, that's the word you would have to use: effortless. Yet the car looked loose, loose but in control. When he did overstep the mark it was an almost immediate correction – and not a single over-rev.

"We went to Spa and our other driver, Andrea de Cesaris, was a bit of a Spa specialist and knew the circuit well. Michael hadn't ever driven it. I asked Andrea to give Michael a couple of laps in a road car but Andrea was negotiating with Eddie for the next year's contract. Michael said *no problem. I have a bike in the boot of my Mercedes, a fold-up bike which I've brought with me. I'll go round on my bike.* He'd had the foresight to take a fold-up bike in the boot of his car to be able to go round the circuit. Didn't come and say to the team *have you got a bike I can use? Can I borrow a scooter? Can I use somebody else's hire car?* He'd thought coldly: what will I need when I get there?

"At the end of the first day we de-briefed and Andrea was going on about a couple of bumps on the very fast section into the Bus Stop – *ah, it's very difficult, the car's very nervous there.* Michael didn't say much, just sat there. Eventually I asked him *did you have the same problem, Michael?* He said *well, I did for a couple of laps but if you lift off, the car becomes nervous* – it was one of those places which was marginal flat – *but then what I did was, I'd go through the first bump in fifth, then I hit sixth in the middle and I just left-foot braked. That calms it all down for the next corner.* And Andrea didn't know that at all. Michael hadn't even mentioned it because for him it was totally natural."

What do the Sennas and Schumachers have?

"Every day they wake up and they have to prove they are the best. That has to come from inside. It doesn't matter how strong the team is on the outside, they have to want it more than anybody else and they have to prove that they are the best. It's difficult really to compare them – but both see opportunities where they have to dig deep to win races. Look at Senna at Donington in 1993. He'd got a Ford engine, realised that in the dry he wasn't going to live with the Williams-Renaults, qualified fifth or sixth – obviously pulled a lap from nowhere to do that – and it was raining at the start of the race. He knew that to win he had to be in the lead by the end of the first lap. Right? That meant going round the outside of people, inside people – wherever he saw the opportunity. And that's what he did.

"You look at these drivers, the special ones like Senna and Michael, and you see essentially the same thing. You look at Michael two or three years ago in the Benetton when he was at Spa, when he'd qualified sixteenth. Where was he by the end of the first lap? Eleventh. Where was he by the end of the race? First. Anything can play into their hands, the pace car, wet, dry, whatever, and they will exploit the situation. I remember one time when Ayrton actually got it wrong at Spa. It was raining and he stayed on slicks far too long – he didn't often make a mistake like that – but even then he was braking later at La Source hairpin *on slicks* than other people were on wets. You think to yourself *how can that be? That cannot be possible* – but he knew what he had to do.

"Drivers like Michael and Ayrton have a belief in themselves and I saw it time and time again. You go to a grand prix and when you look back you think *that was a stunning drive by him, I won't remember a better drive,* and two or three races down the road he does something else again and you think *that was a stunning drive by him, I won't remember a better drive,* and two or three races …"

Which of them would you place your money on?

"Very difficult, but I'd have to put Michael ahead because you can only judge it by the people or the competition around at that moment in time. In my opinion, when I reckon it back, there is a bigger gap now between Michael and the rest than there was between Ayrton and the rest." [Foster said this before Hakkinen won the 1998 World Championship.]

But a cynic might say that Senna had to contend with Piquet, Prost and Mansell – tougher than the competition for Schumacher.

"Well, I don't know. You look at it this way: how fast is Mika Hakkinen? Don't forget he came to Portugal [in 1993] and he outqualified Ayrton. OK, come the race Ayrton was physically and mentally much stronger and much faster, but Mika hadn't driven a race for a long time. So it's always a hard call and you're always going to have your favourites because of your personal situation. The thing that I feel about Michael is that Ayrton did all these things and when he stood on the winners' rostrum he looked like he'd done them whereas Michael doesn't.

"You saw the race at the weekend [Hungary, 1998]: he took his balaclava off, he's fine, no problem. Probably driven the best race of the season so far, knew he had to win the race, k-n-e-w if he didn't win it – and Mika did – the championship was almost over. He had to go for it and he still looked fresh at the end. That doesn't mean to say he hadn't given it everything, it means he has got the driving ability – it's so natural, if you like – that he's not using any of his mental capacity to drive the car. He's working on strategies and where he should be.

"I just feel that Michael has the edge but it's always very difficult when they are generations apart. People ask, was Senna better than Moss, was

Senna better than Fangio, or whatever? Very, very difficult. You can't have reincarnation so that these people return and drive directly against each other – but I feel that Michael is head and shoulders above the opposition now whereas at the time Ayrton was the class of the field but he wasn't always head and shoulders above it. I think for a little while the jury was out, but to perform the way Michael does, well, he comes to every race believing that he can win it, *really* believing: not walking into the paddock thinking *oh, it'd be nice if I won this race* or thinking *well, if I was in a McLaren I would win this race.* No. His total focus is on *this is what I have, I've got to make the most of it to win this race and I have to come away from this race with a win.* I don't think Michael ever looks around and thinks *I wish I was driving this car* or *I wish I was driving that car.* Perhaps if Ayrton did have a fault it was his temperament – just a little bit Latin – while Michael is cool. He's not a cold person but he thinks coldly."

Dick Bennetts ran Hakkinen in Formula 3.

It's a reasonable assumption that these guys – Senna and Schumacher – are at a level above the others.

"I think I'd have to add Mika in there. I can only relate to Schumacher through Mika and when they drove against each other in 1990. We went to Schumacher's home territory – Hockenheim where we had never been as a Formula 3 team before – and took pole, fastest lap, first. I think every now and then exceptional talent comes through. Mika I regard as very talented. I've never worked with Schumacher but from what I understand he's got a computer in his head. And Ayrton was like that. Mika drives by the seat of his pants – or used to."

If I ask you to choose between Senna and Schumacher …

"I couldn't really give an honest answer because I've never run Schumacher. My only real comparison is that in 1990 we went to Italy with Mika and beat 42 Italians, we went to Hockenheim and beat however many were on the grid, and they wouldn't let us in the paddock in France. Then we went to Macau and beat Schumacher again.

"These people, the driving flows naturally to them and they don't seem tired when they get out. Schumacher always looks amazingly composed after a race, but I've learnt that some people do naturally sweat more than others. I'd always say *how come so-and-so looks knackered,* but he isn't. It can be how your body functions."

Rory Byrne worked with Senna at Toleman, of course, and with Schumacher at Benetton and Ferrari.

"It's very difficult to compare them because their careers are almost a decade apart and Formula 1 itself has changed so much over that decade. However, Michael displays exactly the same characteristics as Ayrton: attention to detail, total commitment, expects total commitment from the people around him, the team and so on: *precisely* the same and, to put it another way, fundamentally the same."

Tell me about tactics because it seems to me these people have this strange ability to go to a race meeting to win it and they seek out little advantages even when everything seems to be going against them. They still think: I can win here, and they work out how they can win.

"The classic with Michael was in Spa '95 and he was sixteenth on the grid – he had had a bad qualifying, he wasn't out at the right time for whatever reason – and he won the race. I'm sure that on the grid he still believed he could win the race and he worked at it."

Do these people see things in a different way from us?

"Well, I don't know but they have obviously got tremendous self-confidence and they approach the thing with the attitude that whatever happens they can win, so they work out how to do it."

If I asked you to choose …

"No, I'm not going to answer that. You can't compare drivers a decade apart. All you can look back on is the races they were in together. They had a pretty ding-dong season in 1993 and they were headed for a pretty ding-dong season in 1994. In 1993 Senna got the better of Michael and, in 1994 until Imola, Michael had got the better of Senna. Really that's all you can do. A direct comparison is impossible. In terms of their characteristics – well, I worked for a short while with Nelson Piquet and they all do have the same characteristics. The characteristic that stands out for me is that while they are able to drive so quickly they still seem to have some brain capacity left to deal with all the various other things they need to think about, like race tactics and all that. I just cannot imagine myself 100 per cent committed to driving on the limit round a corner and still being able to think about the next pit stop or whatever else: the weather, which tyres are going off, where my opponents are. It just staggers me that they can do this. To me, looking at the World Champions I've worked with, that's where they are different."

Here's another difficult question. Senna just missed skirts but he faced the whole shooting match after that: turbos, normally aspirated, qualifying boost, qualifying tyres. Now with Schumacher you've what you might call the telemetry era. Which era would be more difficult for a driver?

"I think the degree of difficulty has not changed but the way you go about things has, massively. Now you have a car from your Saturday practice to qualifying to the race and it doesn't change much but, because it doesn't change much, everyone can really optimise their set-up. It makes the racing very competitive and the grids are very close. You just have to look at a grid ten years ago at the height of the turbo era – or just over ten years ago – and a grid today to see the difference. So now it's extremely difficult because the driver has to get the very best out of everything.

"Before, in the turbo era and the qualifying tyres, a driver would be setting up his car. He probably did a couple of runs on qualifying tyres, a bit of increased boost and suddenly he had a serious increase in power and a difference in engine response and he had one lap per set of tyres to get the best out of it. It required quite considerable adaptation to his driving skills – but if you just look at the grid spacing, it was obviously tremendously elusive in terms of getting everything perfect. Probably no-one ever did, or very seldom ever did. However, if you got 80 per cent right you were still in the first three or four. Today you get 80 per cent right and you're fifteenth. There is more pressure on the driver now than there was then, yes, sure."

Here is the comparison:

Hockenheim 1987. Pole, Nigel Mansell (Williams-Honda turbo) 1m 42.616s. Last man on the grid, Alex Caffi (Osella-Alfa Romeo turbo) 2m 07.752s – a difference of 25.136 seconds. That's a slightly unfair comparison because Caffi's car was, for whatever reason, so slow. Next up, and more representative, was Pascal Fabre (AGS-Cosworth) on 1m 54.997s, still a difference of 12.381s.

Hockenheim 1998. Pole, Mika Hakkinen (McLaren-Mercedes) 1m 41.838s. Last man on the grid, Esteban Tuero (Minardi-Ford), 1m 47.265s, a difference of 5.427s.

In the months before Senna's death, Antonio Monteiro, the school contemporary, met him again – Monteiro's legal firm have had Milton Senna as a client for many years.

There had been inadvertent contact already, Senna ringing Monteiro's office to talk to Milton, who was there. "The first time I talked with him by phone was when I was already a lawyer, acting for his father," Monteiro says. "At the beginning of the conversation I tried to say to Ayrton that I had studied with him at *Rio Branco* several years ago but he didn't permit discussion about that. He was very nervous, very anxious to speak with his father and he said *OK, OK, thank you. Can you put my father on the phone please?* The contacts we had when we were older were very cold, very professional. The sensation I had was that he was a very difficult person in terms of relationships. Very distant. But then we had this party and because of this party – because we sat very close to each other at the party, watching a show of country music – we established a conversation, a very friendly conversation."

This is the brief story of that.

"I was invited with a lot of other people to a big party at the kart track at his father's farm. I went there, we stayed a little bit together, we talked. Then he told me *look, I just remembered your nickname from Rio Branco.* I asked him what it was and he said *Portuguese* and I said *yes, that's correct!* It was Portuguese – because my father was Portuguese and my name is Portuguese. A very Portuguese name. At this party I told Ayrton that I had two boys who were crazy to meet Ayrton Senna. I think that one month later or two weeks later – I cannot remember exactly – Ayrton invited me to visit him with the children. We stayed an entire afternoon. It was the last time I saw him. I was so sad: I think that because we work as his father's lawyers, and so I had ways to meet him, in the future I would have met him more frequently."

Ayrton Senna was a devout Catholic. He believed, full stop, and that was it. He'd discuss his religion with care and a certain sensitivity because it was so personal and so easy to mis-represent in a largely Godless age where orthodox science – the maker of every racing car that he drove – was so destructive to beliefs which could offer no evidence, just faith. This is Senna in 1989:

"I am very religious. It had become more and more important for me to learn – to learn about God, to understand God's power, to learn about faith. But I am only at the start of my search. It will take a long time."

Sportswriters (and most other writers, too) like public figures to be one-dimensional because it makes describing them and interpreting what they do so much easier. But each human being is many-dimensional of course, and some of the dimensions seem to contradict each other. Prost has mused aloud about how Senna was "extremely religious" and when he joined McLaren he'd talk and talk about it. Prost was puzzled about how that could be reconciled with some of Senna's actions on the race track and concluded Senna "really didn't know he was sometimes in the wrong." That's the charitable view, anyway.

My own feeling is that Senna was different people in different situations, with a central, unchanging, private Senna holding it all together. For instance, it is not really a contradiction that he savoured pitting his command of practical jokes against those of Gerhard Berger, a master of that dark art. This was quite a different Senna from the implacable, stony, obsessive gatherer of pole positions, quite different again from the person who was in Sid Watkins' phrase a "dignified gentleman."

Nor is it a contradiction that Senna learnt a lot about life beyond the racing car from Berger, and Berger learnt an awful lot about life in the racing car from Senna. More than that, they could build a friendship because Berger of the intuitive speed was no match for Senna in the car, and consequently no threat. If he had been, the naked ladies would have been distinctly unfunny.

I was a comparative stranger to Senna and he was a comparative stranger to me. I observed him from the no-man's land, from near and far, in good times and bad. I saw somehow a spoilt-child who never quite grew up and all in the same moment a warm, infinitely polite human being who could light up a room with his smile, and all in the same moment a tortured big man who'd grown into the gigantesque.

Emerson Fittipaldi is also a believer. "I always make this comparison: I lost friends outside of racing, in aeroplane crashes, road crashes, motorcycle crashes, and I think everyone has a destiny and I always have a lot of faith. Yes, Christian faith, and that helps me a lot. I went through a very tough period in my career – the 1970s. A lot of people died on the track. I was talking the other day with Carlos Reutemann in Argentina. We were saying we were both very lucky to survive a very tough period of racing. So Ayrton's death was such a big, big shock – for me, for racing, for Brazil – because we weren't used to people dying on a racetrack any more. Ayrton … that hurt me very bad. It was devastating to me and for Brazil, all the people in my country.

"I had followed him since he was testing karts at Interlagos. He would come and talk to me with his father. I remember 1991 or 1992, Ayrton came by my house in Miami Beach. We had dinner together and then he was talking to Frank Williams. We called Frank from my house and I said *Frank, you're going to need a big cheque. Get ready because I'm going to pass the phone to someone who wants to drive for you – but get your chequebook ready!* And I passed the phone to Ayrton, and it never happened then, but it did happen for the 1994 season. Terrible.

"You know, I'm here at Hockenheim [in 1997] to drive one of Fangio's cars – a Mercedes. I'm really going to enjoy driving Fangio's championship car. My father was a motor racing journalist, and Fangio was one of my idols when I was a little boy. My father used to take me to races and Fangio was always the one. Then in 1973 I am at Interlagos, and a young boy is brought to see me by his father, and it is Ayrton ..."

I asked Mauricio Gugelmin what he felt now, winter 1998, when he looked back on Senna's career. "I just think it's such a pity that when he really became like perfect it was cut short. I'm pretty sure that he was still going to drive for a few more years and he was going to pass all the records. Over the years he'd changed as a driver and as a man, and that's why I say perfect – he was very close to being perfect. In the early days, if he fell out with you you were as good as dead, but later in life he got together with people he admired – and hadn't been able to before because they were competitors – like Prost. Those guys were competitors and he wouldn't share anything. By the time he got together with them they were no longer competitors."

Gugelmin expands on this by broadening it into a theme: the place which Senna came to occupy in Brazil's national life and consciousness. "He was really proud of being Brazilian, really proud. The hardest thing for him wasn't racing and all that, it was how much he missed Brazil. Any break that he had, he used to go back to Brazil. He missed his family, missed his friends, the food, the weather. All that was definitely a very important thing for him. Even when he was very successful he went back to his house because that's how he recharged his batteries. Italy he liked and Portugal too, but Portugal was second best. Brazil was the place to be. He made it common knowledge that he was proud to be Brazilian."

And winning, when he'd do the slowing down lap with the Brazilian flag and the whole nation was fluttering through the flag with him?

"For him those were very proud moments. He thought: *I came out from Brazil and in other people's eyes we're supposed to be peasants or whatever, I go over there and I beat the best in the world.*"

A delightful 65-year-old called Lula May Reed was born in Sao Paulo, has lived there all her life and broadens the context of what was Senna's parish. "In my lifetime it has grown from a small, pleasant town where people felt a certain security and a certain comfort to now, literally, a jungle." She lives in what she describes as an oasis: a mini-estate of manicured gardens and swimming pools hidden in one of the endless, cramped suburbs but you "have to come in through the big walls and the electric gate and everything else to get here – because you have to try to keep the rest of the city out. When I was a child here there were no paved streets, no street lights, no telephones. This was out in the country, rolling hills, pastures, woods, and I had cows, horses and chickens.

"Now we are talking about the third largest city on the planet, with all that goes with that. It's the increase of population, pollution, crowded conditions, overloading of all the infrastructure. It's difficult to get a dial tone on the telephone. So, if you can, you protect yourself by getting all these things: the cellular phone, the electric gate. Otherwise you can't live here.

"Each year another 350,000 come, and they come because there is a possibility of living better here than wherever they were. They might, by a stroke of good fortune, be able to find food, some sort of shelter – even if it's sleeping under a bridge – which they don't have at home. There is no answer to this, no answer. If you don't get the city to function, what about the 15 million who are here to start with? It's 15 million counted and all the others in the shanty towns who have not been counted. How many people live in the shanty towns? We have no idea, but a lot, a hell of a lot. It's an immensity, and the city keeps on growing outwards. It's a very ugly city because there's no green belt, it just goes on and on. It's sprawling and totally uncontrolled."

How violent is it?

"Very violent. I've just bought myself some tear gas spray with pepper in it. I walk a lot and everybody thinks I'm mad, because as soon as I walk out of the gate here I'm vulnerable. There are kidnappings, with various degrees of violence, there is a lot of crack, a lot of people who are on cocaine and you can't reason with them."

Overall, is there a special feeling that Paulistas have about Sao Paulo?

"Oh yes. Of course. Sao Paulo is the locomotive of the country. This is where the business is done, this is where the money is made, this is where most of the industry is. This is where the tax money is generated for the whole country. Rio is a wonderful city, it's a fun city, it's the beach mentality. People take it easy. It's the holiday place. Brasilia is the capital but you don't want to go to Brasilia."

Senna was extremely proud of being from Sao Paulo.

"Well, of course. Sao Paulo is … is … is such a complex mess most of the time that it's very hard to define what keeps people here. I could go and live anywhere but I live here because this is my home, this is where my roots are. Same with Senna. *If the city is a mess I have to try to do something about it.* Many of the people who live in Sao Paulo feel that. I am sure that Ayrton Senna felt that. This is home and he wanted to do something about it. Anything else was running away, and it's not going to solve the problem if you just go and live somewhere else."

He had, inevitably, broadened the scope of his life so that he had an apartment in Monte Carlo, the house in Faro – southern Portugal – a farm in Tatui which is some 70 miles from Sao Paulo. He had the custom-built estate at Angra dos Reis. That's not the real point. The real point is that he had his offices in a skyscraper right in the middle of Sao Paulo – what they call the *centro*. You can see this skyscraper as a very visible and public statement.

I have not run away.

Antonio Monteiro broadens the context. "Ayrton represented a Brazilian who tried to prove that if you work hard, with some kind of determination, you can win. This is his legacy for Brazilian people. The interesting thing is that it's very common to have people like footballers who are very proud to be Brazilian and very proud to show the flag, but at that time – at the beginning of Ayrton's career – you didn't have an upper middle class guy so anxious to show that he was Brazilian. He'd want to be British or American or something else – the high middle class in Brazil had received strong influences from there and from Italy, from Germany. We live in a very poor country but we learned with Ayrton to give some value to our own country and to our people. We proved with Ayrton that we can win, that we can be at the same level – at least in sport – as the very developed countries."

This was possible through football, but not possible through politics, the economy, or the law – and possible through him and motor racing.

"Yes, yes, because motor racing is another kind of sport for which Brazil has some special talents: Emerson Fittipaldi, Carlos Pace, Piquet and then Ayrton, but the thing which was so important when Emerson Fittipaldi was World Champion, he was not so worried to show that he was Brazilian as Ayrton was. Ayrton was a big idol but to the common people he appeared to be a common man, appeared to be just another guy proud to be Brazilian."

Excuse my impertinence, but do you think that is important in the whole history of your country?

"Yes. Ayrton gave to the people in general a little bit more self-confidence. He was the proof that we can do these things if we work hard. On Sunday mornings I'd watch the races with my two boys and we were very, very happy because it was common for Ayrton to win. *TV Globo* used to put very beautiful music at the instant Ayrton crossed the line holding the Brazilian flag [on the slowing-down lap]. We were happy and *we* were proud to see this, especially my sons. We heard every day, especially five years ago, that we were an under-developed country, that we were poor, that we had a lot of crime, a lot of children dying with no food to eat, the slums and everything. To see something positive in terms of the name of your country, to see that this kind of society can produce someone who is a winner was very important for ordinary people.

"Sometimes when you are abroad you are very ashamed about Brazil. You see on TV that if there is an airport shooting the only person doing it is Brazilian; if a store is robbed a Brazilian did it and so we are very – well, I don't know if sometimes you feel that you have to tell people you are from England, we Brazilians had the necessity to say that we were not Brazilian.

But then, when you have this kind of example – like Ayrton – you learn that it is not always this way. You could say *look, I am Brazilian too, I am from the same country as Ayrton Senna.* This was especially important for the poor people. Someone living in the slums and they'd seen him winning a race in England or in Germany or in Australia – well, he made his victories our victories because he shouted to everybody, including us: *I am Brazilian also."*

Senna must have known all this in exquisite, unremitting, inescapable detail. He must have sensed the full panorama of what he really meant to 160 million strangers – many, many of these living desperate, devastated lives in conditions where genuine achievement was staying alive until tomorrow. He must have known the weight he carried and I'm sitting here trying to think of any human being in a similar context who carried quite so much, carried it quite so alone and did this week after week, year after year for a full decade. He was unelected, held no public office, worked to no political manifesto, was no Pope or prelate, and had absolutely no authority over any other human being: he just drove expensive cars round and round until he got back to where he'd started from an hour and a half before.

And one other thought, before we leave it.

The burden did not crush him.

November 1998 and in the mixed-up Sao Paulo sprawl you see banks of advertising hoardings beside the choked roads. You know the kind, tall and broad and with a way of catching your eye in spite of yourself. The blonde girl in the blue Lycra bikini would catch your eye anyway.

Adriane looks sensuous.

She's making money and who can blame her? You couldn't expect her, from her early 20s, to act like a widow for the rest of her life and, glimpsing the bikini hoarding, she certainly isn't. Lycra bikinis are not, let us say, widow's weeds. (She also appeared in *Playboy* magazine in 1995, although evidently the photographs had been taken in 1992 – before she met Senna.)

Adriane has married. The bridegroom, Roberto Justus, owns an advertising agency which had sales of $120 million in 1998. She reportedly insisted on a pre-marriage contract stipulating a total division of assets – she doesn't get his $120 million, and he doesn't get the $3 million she is said to have earned. Her wedding present was a Mercedes coupe which she garages next to the Fiat Uno Senna gave her. None of Senna's family was invited to the wedding.

The feelings in Sao Paulo about Adriane are, I suspect, confused and imprecise. Nobody I met blamed her for exploiting her moment of fame, however much the moment was purely the reflection of someone else. For a large tract of the 160 million, the mechanisms of survival are understood and if you have a chance at prosperity, well, the alternative is too terrible to contemplate.

So she's up there, not shameless but certainly sexy.

She looms at you, real and unreal, an image of a person, close and far away, almost like Senna himself. Each time I pass a hoarding I think: *of all of them – the karting charioteers, the trusted boyhood friends, the immense number of advisers, admirers and foes in car racing – were you the one, the only one from the whole living panorama of it to unlock him? Were you already unlocking him? Was he finally finding himself in those arms which are now draped across the hoarding?*

There's a curious footnote too. After the funeral, according to Adriane, Senna's mother offered a cheque of "5,000 or 10,000 dollars" to help her make a life for herself. She refused.

The kart track at Interlagos is called the *Kartodromo Municipale Ayrton Senna*. The long grass grows across the infield, grows through the red-and-white tyres which form a barrier to keep anyone from hitting the wall behind them. There's a large painting of Senna on the white wall beside the grandstand. It's kitsch but that doesn't matter. Somehow he's here and he's overseeing the half dozen kids working and churning their karts through the contorted corners. The engines make a howling, ripping noise, the little hands are pump-pumping the steering wheels, the helmeted heads bob and batter, the karts grip into the corners and emerge from them *whaaaang*. This day in 1998 four men sit beneath a parasol behind the wall, two on garden chairs, two on upturned tyres. They're taking times. So is a mother under the pits with their corrugated roofing. She holds a stop-watch and when her son has brought his kart to a halt and dismounted he strides to her, careless of his mortality, and they lock on to the times together, he nearly on tip-toe.

The opening of another circle?

The simple humanity of Ayrton Senna was often obscured because it happened in private. Kindnesses do not often make headlines.

So far we've had Senna's career with all its storms and eddies, we've watched a slender, homesick teenager mature into manhood, we've had a whole vista of aspects of that man – from God to Berger and, I hope, all the necessary points in between. We've paused at the crossroads with him. With the public Senna. Then there were the small kindnesses which, coming from a giant, felt very large to ordinary people. *Here* he gives everything and gains nothing except, perhaps, the knowledge that he has behaved like a human being.

The person who recounts the tale is a 45-year-old mother called Sue McAleese. She lives near London but that doesn't matter at all. She could have lived anywhere. The tale is rather like Senna's life and times: it doesn't need embellishment.

"When my son James was born he was named after James Hunt – my hero. James was the biggest trouble you can imagine and he drove me nuts. He wouldn't sleep, he screamed and screamed. I remember this particular time he was three months old, it was 3 o'clock in the morning and he was screaming the place down. The 1989 Formula 1 season had just begun with the Brazilian Grand Prix and I'd recorded it. I stuck a video on. It was just something to do but James stopped screaming. He sat there glued to the TV screen watching Nigel Mansell win in a Ferrari. So from near his birth he's been a Formula 1 fan.

"He loved Ayrton Senna and Mansell and he kept on and on about going to a grand prix but I said *no, no, no, you're too young*. I did however take him to tyre testing at Silverstone in 1992 – you paid your £5 which went to charity. James was now three and a half and he talked his way into the pit lane. Don't ask me how because I don't know! I went in with him. He met Mansell and was then taken to the McLaren garage.

"The security guard who'd taken us into the pit lane went and spoke to a McLaren mechanic and then left us. I thought *what am I doing here, what am I doing here?* The mechanic came over and said to James *are you an Ayrton Senna fan?* and James said *yes!* The mechanic asked *would you like to meet him?* And James said *oh yes please*. The mechanic took him into the garage and sitting in the corner was Ayrton Senna talking to a Honda engineer. The mechanic said *this is James and he's a big fan of yours*. Ayrton was laughing but at the time I couldn't understand why. Afterwards I realised that James was wearing a tee-shirt with a picture of Nigel Mansell on it …

"I was totally speechless. I was more in awe of the man than James was – probably he was too young to be. Anyway, he sat with him for about 15 minutes and Ayrton talked to him and gave him a signed photograph and bits and pieces. Then we left.

"I'd taken some photographs and they didn't come out. I got in touch with McLaren and asked if it would be possible to have a photo of Ayrton. I had no reply. A few weeks later we bumped into James Hunt in Watford – he was doing a presentation or something and we just happened to be there shopping. We got chatting to him and asked if he could get a photo of Ayrton. Just after the German Grand Prix a letter arrived from Hunt with a signed photo of Ayrton Senna to James.

"I'd written this letter to McLaren, got no reply and been really cheesed off. I thought *well if James Hunt can organise a photograph at a Formula 1 meeting, why can't McLaren?* What I didn't know was that my letter had actually been passed to Ayrton and he'd been hanging on to it. I'd been to the European Grand Prix at Donington and James had gone nuts because I wouldn't take him. He went on and on and on: *Can I go to the British Grand Prix?* I couldn't decide whether or not to take him. Then about a week before the grand prix I had a phone call from Fiona McWhirter [who worked for Julian Jakobi, who looked after Senna] inviting James and myself to Silverstone to meet Ayrton. I thought it was a wind-up – one of my friends winding me up! So I rang her back a couple of days later just to check it was all legal, above board, legit and everything.

"We arranged that on the Friday at Silverstone at about 2.15 we would meet Ayrton. Friday morning was like Donington, very wet. It took us ages to get to the circuit because the traffic was horrendous and by the time we arrived we had missed most of the morning practice session. At this stage I still hadn't told James he was going to meet Ayrton Senna. I had butterflies.

"We got to the McLaren motorhome and I decided it was still better not to tell James until Ayrton arrived. We sat at one end and I drank coffee and the wait seemed endless. I was very glad James didn't know what was going to happen because he would have driven *everyone* crazy. Whilst we were waiting, Jonathan Palmer came and sat with us and we also saw Michael Andretti and Ron Dennis.

"At last Ayrton arrived, followed across the paddock by photographers, television cameras, journalists and a lot of other people. My intention had been to take James's photograph the moment he spotted Ayrton but he was too quick for me. He was running across the motorhome before I could stop him, launched himself at Ayrton and gave him a huge hug. I missed the photo because I couldn't focus in time.

"There were two camera crews at the far end waiting to speak to him and they both called to him as he walked through the door but he said he had other things to do first! He then came over and sat at our table, apologising for being so late. He explained that this was due to the session being delayed and he'd had a problem with his car. He'd had to stay and discuss this with his mechanics.

"I felt guilty about being there because I felt I was increasing the pressure the man was under. He was brilliant with James, who was totally speechless. James just kept looking at him in wonder. He couldn't answer any of Ayrton's questions, he just kept nodding his head. Ayrton gave James a large colour photo which he signed for him."

How did you find Senna? It was a fairly daunting experience for you.

"It was. The thing is, I remembered watching him way, way back in 1982 when he was still driving a Van Diemen in the lesser formulae. I'd met him very briefly then and thought he was an absolutely brilliant driver but didn't actually follow his career. Being a Brummie, and being the same age as Nigel Mansell I was a huge fan of his. My cousin used to race karts against him when he was eight, nine years old so I had seen Nigel race at that very young age. I've met Nigel four or five times and chatted to him no problem, but I couldn't talk to Ayrton Senna. I was very in awe of him.

"You've probably heard of a company called Epson. They sponsored Lotus, I used to work for them and I was involved in all that sponsorship. I met Senna several times and didn't like him – absolutely detested the man, and I couldn't tell you why. It wasn't until the tyre testing in 1992 when I met him again in the garage with James that I realised he was human and he was extremely nice. He was brilliant with James.

"I sent my photos to Fiona to say thank you for arranging for us to meet him. She sent them back and asked *would it be all right if Ayrton had a copy?* So I had an enlargement – an 8 x 10 – which I sent to him and he wrote me back a little two-liner thanking me for the photograph and saying *it's one of the best I've ever seen.*

"I'd been able to appreciate the constant pressure he was under. That day at Silverstone they put a rope across the door of the motorhome and he was still signing champagne bottles and hats and so on behind it. I see a lot of the way Michael Schumacher behaves, he's adopted it from Ayrton and I think it's the only way they can keep their sanity. Ayrton was getting changed in the motorhome and all these people from Japan were looking through the window watching – they had to shut the curtains.

"The thing was, he was so good with children because they expected nothing from him whereas adults, he always thought, wanted something. All the time we were at the motorhome, well I won't say he ignored me but I was only there because James couldn't go on his own and he knew that. In the photograph James has that smug look on his face saying *he's got his arm round me, not round you.*

"The night Ayrton died James couldn't sleep. He'd watched the accident on television and asked me why he didn't get out of the car and I just had this feeling that he was never ever going to get out of the car, that he was dead.

"In 1995 I took a trip to Italy to go to Monza. It was a week-long holiday, I didn't take James and on the Monday after the race we went to Imola. At Tamburello, we found a hole in the fencing and crawled through – which we shouldn't have done, really – but we did and we all went and stood at the spot. I felt – I don't know what the words are – I felt quite close to him. It helped me to get over his death by going and standing there. We signed our names on the wall and laid some flowers and then we got thrown out.

"When I came back and I showed the photographs I'd taken to James he said *now I've seen where he died and I know he's in Heaven, I know he's going to watch over us.* I think the photographs helped James to believe that Ayrton had died because before that I'm not sure he believed it.

"We went to the grand prix at Silverstone in 1994 and I was sitting in the grandstand on the Saturday, twenty past one, and a man sitting next to me – never seen him in my life before – turned and said *Senna will be out in a minute* and then he realised what he said and he added *oh, no, no he won't.* He and I and James burst into tears and we just sat there crying, the three of us, and I don't think we saw the rest of the session. I still don't know this man's name, I still have no idea who he was – but this was the effect that Senna had on people: the three of us holding hands and crying."

Then and now

The interview with Eddie Jordan took place at the Hilton Hotel, Heathrow, just before an FIA meeting in October 1998. I asked at the reception if a Mr. Jordan was booked in. He wasn't, so had he arrived? The receptionist said no, Mr. Jordan hadn't. I wondered how, in a place of so many people and such transience, he could conceivably know that. "The FIA use the hotel regularly but anyway how can you forget a man like that?"

Jean Todt arrives first and has breakfast while talking into a mobile phone; Tom Walkinshaw is next and joins Todt; then Jackie Stewart, crisp and immaculate in a suit; then Jordan, and he heads straight to the message desk. There's a message for him and he scans it, says he's expecting more. The all-day all-year urgency of Formula 1 holds him.

We sit and he switches his mind from all its other preoccupations to my questions. It is so with motorsport people: they teem with pressured ideas but can isolate themselves at will. At the end of the interview I asked how much he paid for his first racing car. "£460 all in, everything. It was a Lotus 61." I know inflation bites but an executive room in the Hilton costs from £215 a night and it is this world which Jordan now inhabits. The comparison between £460 for a Lotus and £215 for a night's sleep remains stark, even though so much time has gone by. In between the two, Eddie Jordan has prospered, and entirely on merit.

Lula May Reed lives, truly, in an oasis of calm behind an iron gate in Sao Paulo. We had a family lunch beside the pool and a South African businessman, Michael Henn, was a guest. He travels South America extensively and by chance happened to be at Sao Paulo airport when Senna's body was brought back. The scale and depth of the grief he witnessed pressed down on him "for several weeks." He reaches for words to capture the enormity and doesn't find them, shakes his head instead, falls silent for a long moment. He'd glimpsed eternity.

The images of that return to the lying-in-state remain alive: the outriders, the coffin and, as it passed, the crowd – a million strong, two million, three, four – moving and gathering and standing two deep, three deep, four; this crowd which had the strength of a mighty collective and had, all at the same moment, the isolation of each individual who made it up. The coffin was the reality and the reality broke them as it passed.

The faces in the crowd had a haunted, hollowed look of abandon, the battered emptiness of grief: Senna was taken towards his final resting place through the tears of children, and the tears of women, and the tears of men.

The cemetery at Morumbi could be an English meadow: perhaps Norfolk, where such a big part of the circle opened. As lush as that. It is a tranquil, quietened place guarding the dignity of those laid here. Even the workforce who tend the flowers and cut the grass move about unobtrusively, held by the silence of ultimate respect.

If it had to be, let it be here.

Statistics

The karting years

First race, Interlagos, 1973 (victory); 1974, Sao Paulo junior champion; 1976, Sao Paulo champion; 1977, South American champion; 1978, World Championship, Le Mans (6th); 1979, World Championship, Estoril (2nd); 1980, World Championship, Nivelles (2nd); 1981, World Championship, Parma (4th); 1982, World Championship, Kalmar, (14th).

The pre-Formula 1 years

1981 (Formula Ford 1600/Van Diemen): P&O Championship, 1 race, no wins; Townsend-Thoresen Championship, 13 races, 8 wins, champion; RAC Championship, 6 races, 4 wins, champion.

1982 (Formula Ford 2000/Rushen Green Racing): Pace British Championship, 19 races, 10 poles, 16 wins, champion; EFDA, 9 races, 8 poles, 6 wins, champion. Other races: Shell Super Sunbeam for celebrities, Oulton Park (victory); Formula 3 (West Surrey Racing), Thruxton, (pole, victory).

1983 (Formula 3/West Surrey Racing): Marlboro British Championship, 20 races, 14 poles, 12 wins, champion. Note: round 10, Silverstone, which Senna did not finish, was also a round of the European Championship. Other race: Macau Grand Prix (pole, victory).

The Formula 1 years

1984 (Toleman-Hart): 14 races, 0 poles, 0 wins, 13 points
World Championship 9th
Other races: Mercedes-Benz Cup, Nurburgring (victory)
World Sportscar Championship, Nurburgring (8th)

1985 (Lotus-Renault): 16 races, 7 poles, 2 wins, 38 points
World Championship 4th
1986 (Lotus-Renault): 16 races, 8 poles, 2 wins, 55 points
World Championship 4th
1987 (Lotus-Honda): 16 races, 1 pole, 2 wins, 57 points
World Championship 3rd
1988 (McLaren-Honda): 16 races, 13 poles, 8 wins, 93 points (90 counting)
World Champion
1989 (McLaren-Honda): 16 races, 13 poles, 6 wins, 60 points
World Championship 2nd.
1990 (McLaren-Honda): 16 races, 10 poles, 6 wins, 78 points
World Champion
1991 (McLaren-Honda): 16 races, 8 poles, 7 wins, 96 points
World Champion
1992 (McLaren-Honda): 16 races, 1 pole, 3 wins, 50 points
World Championship 4th
1993 (McLaren-Ford): 16 races, 1 pole, 5 wins, 73 points
World Championship 2nd
1994 (Williams-Renault): 3 races, 3 poles, 0 wins, 0 points.

Records (as at 1 May 1994)

Most points: Prost 798.5, Senna 614, Piquet 485.5
Most poles: Senna 65, Jim Clark 33, Prost 33
Most poles in a season: Mansell 14, Senna 13, Prost 13
Most successive poles: Senna 8, Senna 7, Prost 7
Most wins: Prost 51, Senna 41, Mansell 30
Most wins in a season: Mansell 9, Senna 8, Prost, Clark and Senna 7
Most fastest laps: Prost 41, Mansell 30, Clark 28
   (Senna seventh equal with Stirling Moss, 19).

Index